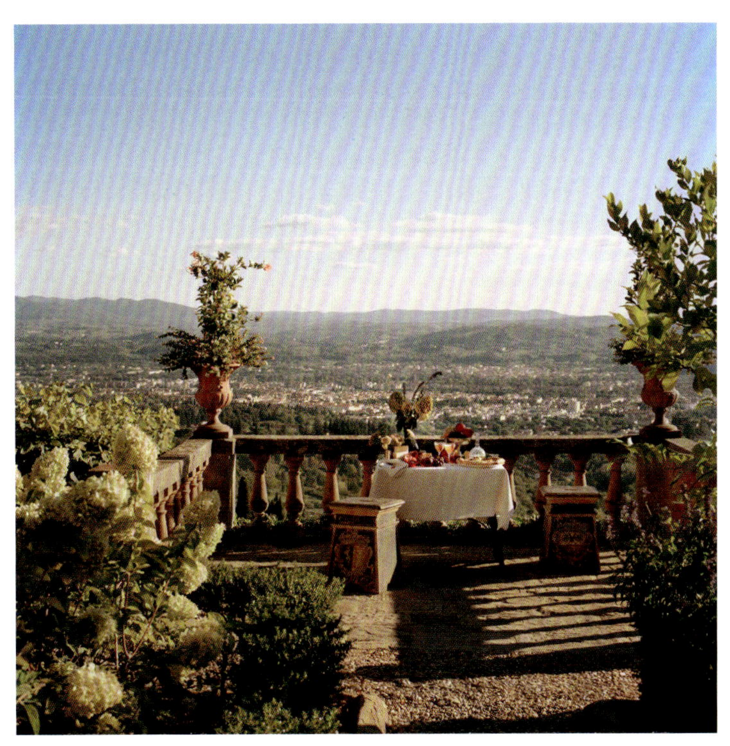

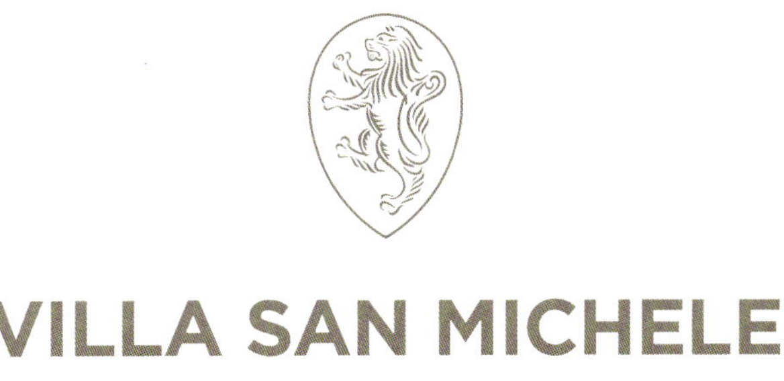

VILLA SAN MICHELE

A BELMOND HOTEL

FLORENCE

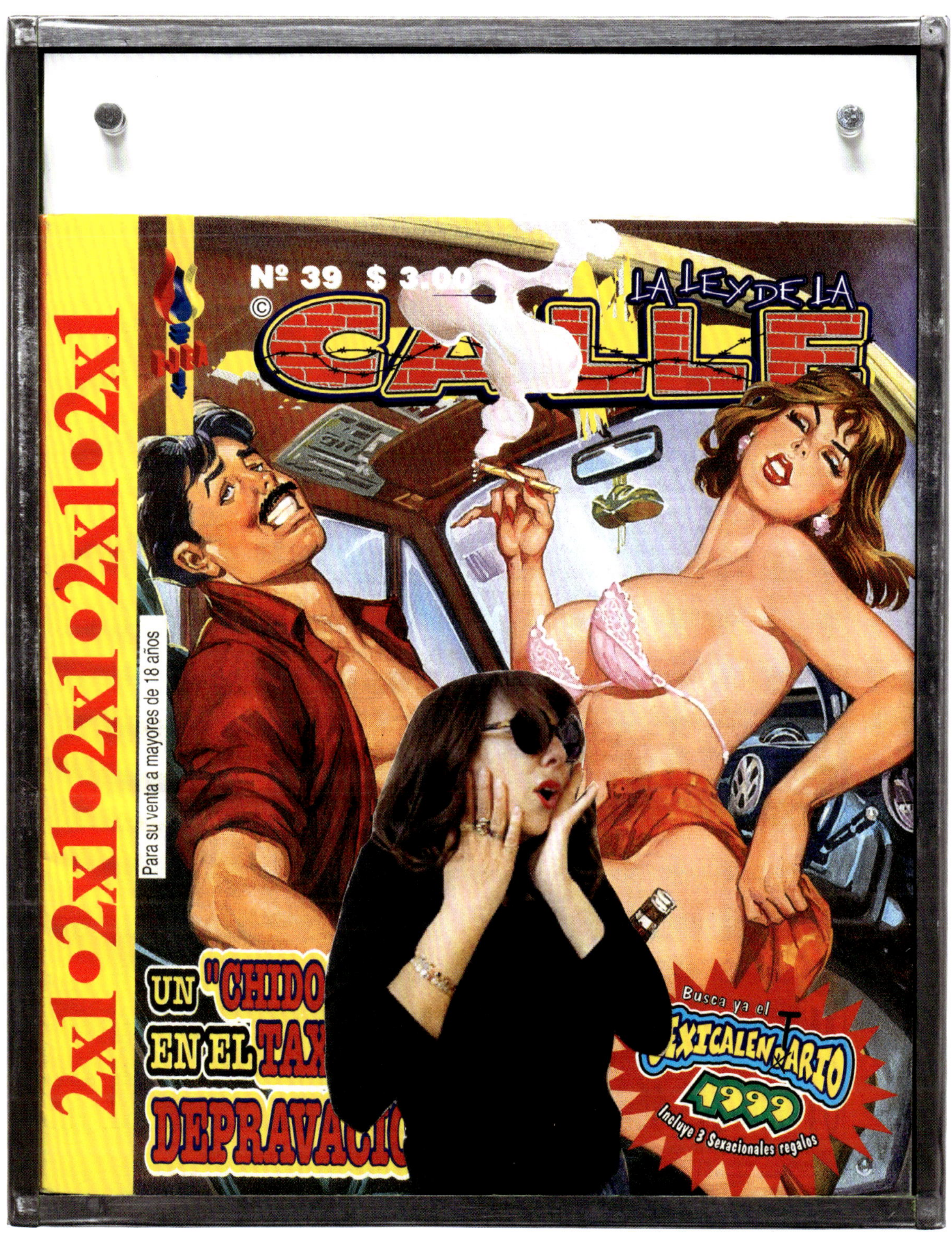

SOPHIE CALLE, *La Ley de la Calle (What's the point?)*, 2025 [detail]

Secrets
Summer 2026

Columns

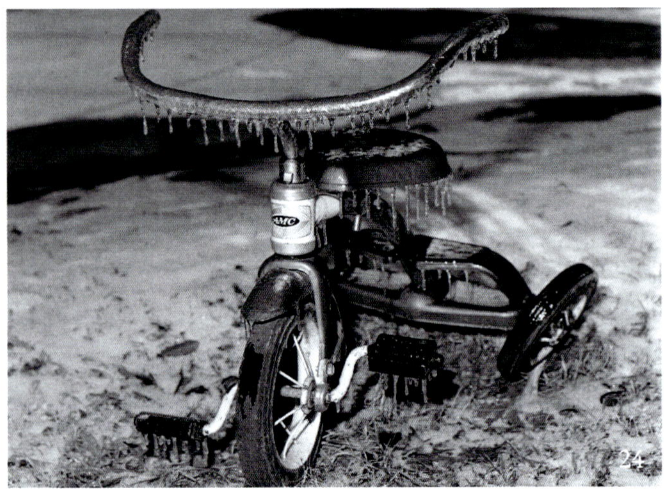

24

Features

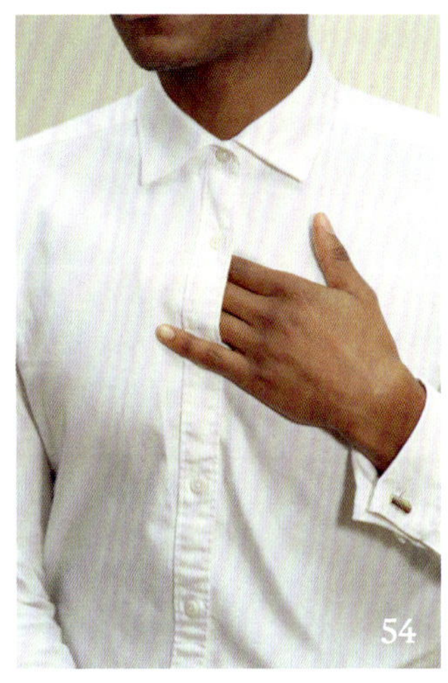

54

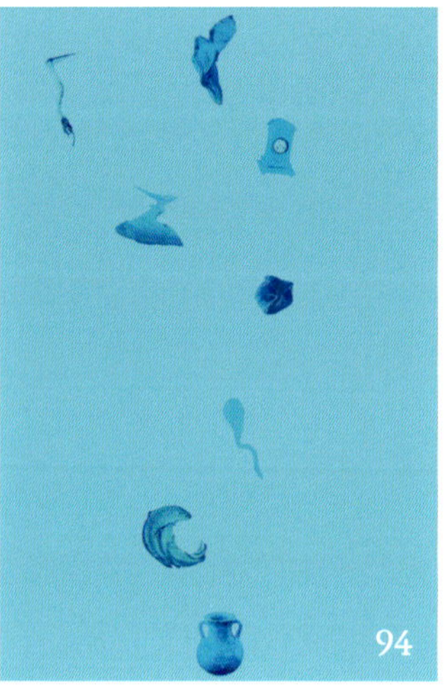

94

Features

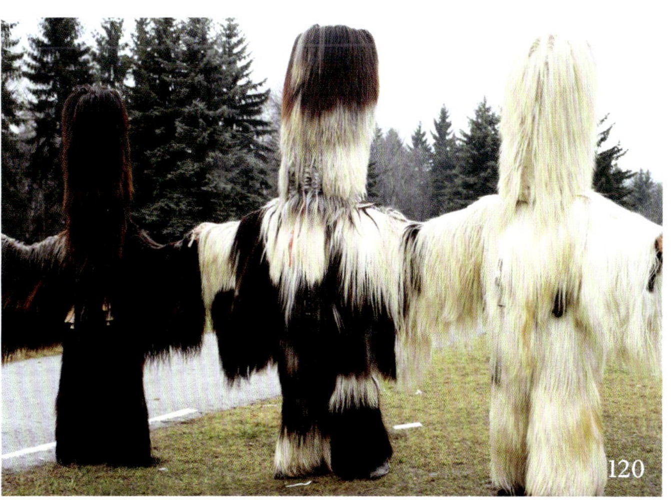
120

The PhotoBook Review

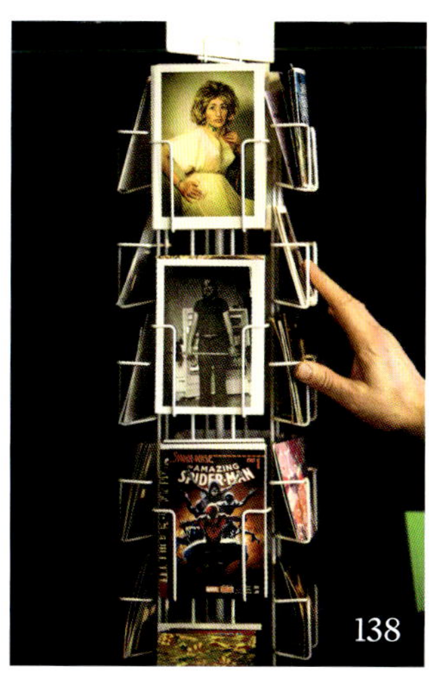
138

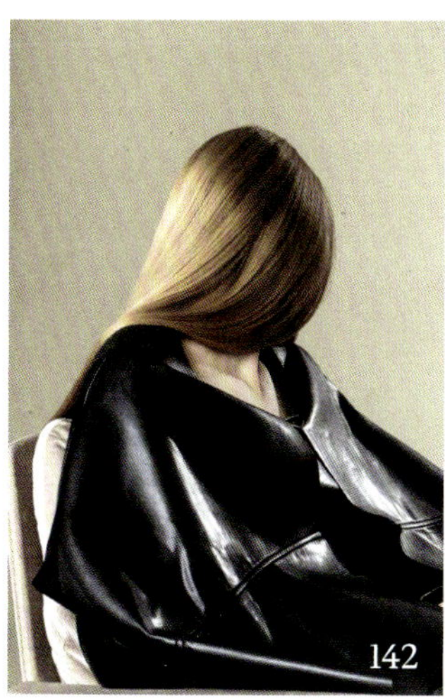
142

Front cover:
Polly Brown, *Stag Do*, from the series *Secret Gestures*, 2026
Airline stewardesses' secret signal for "bachelor party onboard"
(See page 54)

Subscribe to *Aperture* and read more at aperture.org.

aperture

The Magazine of Photography and Ideas

Editor in Chief
Michael Famighetti
Managing Editor
Zack Hatfield
Contributing Editors, The PhotoBook Review
Brendan Embser, Noa Lin
Copy Editors
Donna Ghelerter, Chris Peterson
Production Director
Minjee Cho
Production Manager
Andrea Chlad
Press Supervisor
Ali Taptık
Work Scholar
Gia Sidhu

Art Direction, Design & Typefaces
A2/SW/HK, London

Director of Business Development
Flynn Murray
fmurray@aperture.org

Marketing Assistant
Connor Von Brain

Advertising
Elizabeth Morina
emorina@aperture.org
Michel Manzo
mmanzo@manzomediagroup.com
Isabelle Friedrich McTwigan
imctwigan@aperture.org

Executive Director, Aperture
Sarah Hermanson Meister

Minor White, Editor (1952–1974)
Michael E. Hoffman, Publisher and Executive Director (1964–2001)
Melissa Harris, Editor in Chief (2002–2012)
Chris Boot, Executive Director (2011–2021)
Lesley A. Martin, Founder and Publisher, The PhotoBook Review (2011–2021)

aperture.org

Aperture is a nonprofit publisher dedicated to creating insight, community, and understanding through photography. Established in 1952 to advance "creative thinking, significantly expressed in words and photographs," Aperture champions photography's vital role in nurturing curiosity and encouraging a more just, tolerant society.

Aperture (ISSN 0003-6420) is published quarterly, in spring, summer, fall, and winter, at 548 West 28th Street, 4th Floor, New York, NY 10001. Subscriptions are $75/year. For delivery in Canada, add $20; for other countries, add $35. Single copies may be purchased for $24.95. To subscribe or buy single copies, visit aperture.org. Periodicals postage paid at New York and additional mailing offices. POSTMASTER: Send address changes to Aperture, PO Box 3000, Denville, NJ 07834. For customer service, please call 866-457-4603 (US and Canada) or email custsvc_aperture@fulcoinc.com. Newsstand distribution in the US is handled by CMG. For international distribution, contact Central Books, centralbooks.com. Other inquiries, email orders@aperture.org or call 212-505-5555.

Credits for "Curriculum," pp. 30–31: Richmond Hill: Nick Knight, ca. 2015, courtesy the artist; *Bird in Space*: Constantin Brancusi, 1927: © Succession Brancusi and ADAGP; *Fountainhead*: courtesy Photofest; *Third Wave*: Cover of Alvin Toffler, *The Third Wave*, 1980; McQueen: Erin O'Connor, McQueen Spring/Summer 2001 *Voss* collection, courtesy firstVIEW; Kettle's Yard: *Spiral of Stones*, courtesy Kettle's Yard, photograph by Paul Allitt.

Library of Congress Catalog Card No: 58-30845.

Support has been provided by members of Aperture's Magazine Council: Jon Stryker and Slobodan Randjelović, Susan and Thomas Dunn, Kate Cordsen and Denis O'Leary, and Michael W. Sonnenfeldt, MUUS Collection.

ISBN 978-1-59711-602-2

Printed in Turkey by Ofset Yapimevi

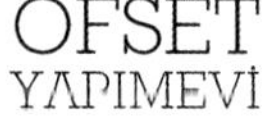

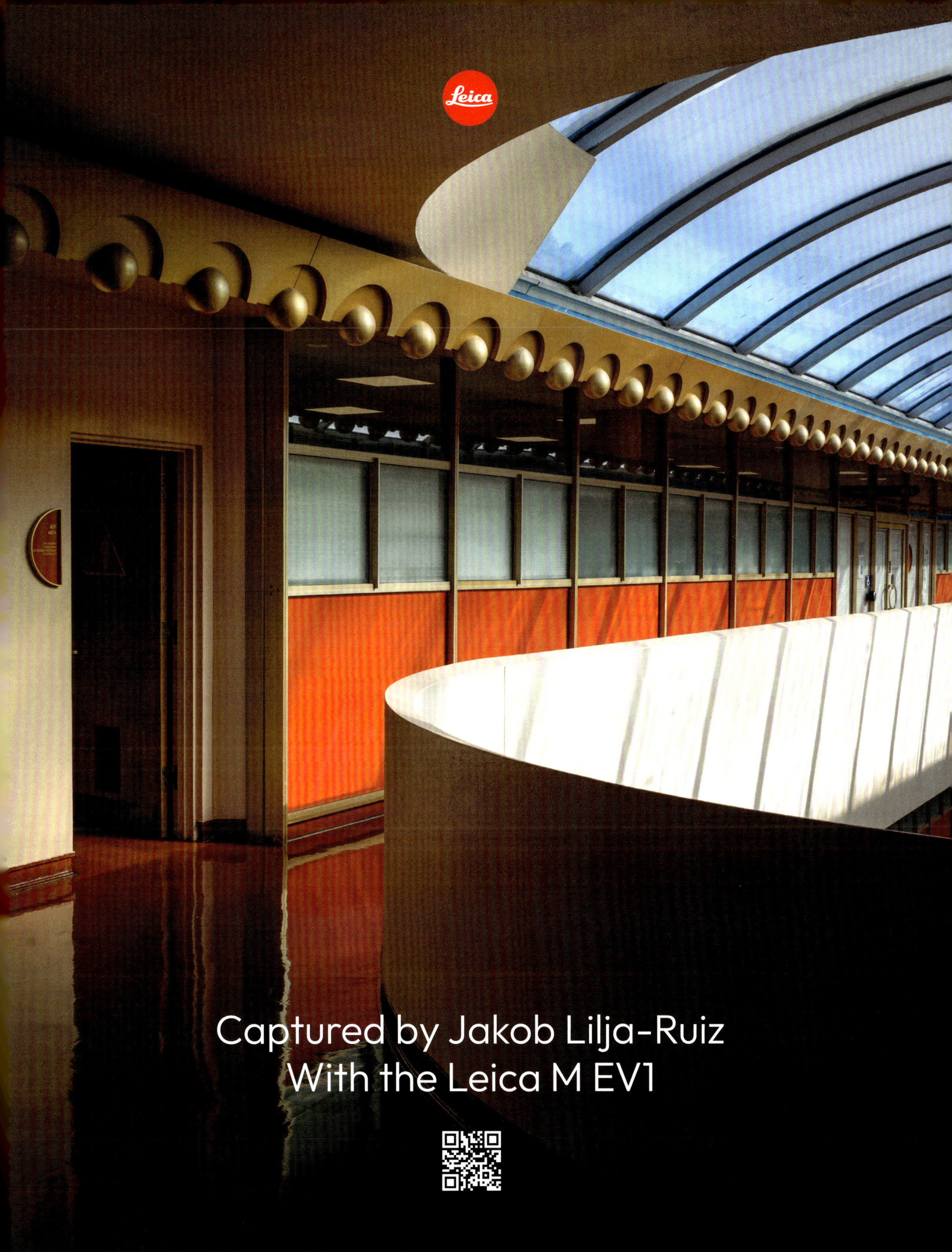
Leica
Captured by Jakob Lilja-Ruiz
With the Leica M EV1

Contributors

DAVID CAMPANY ("Private Eyes," page 112) is creative director of New York's International Center of Photography. His curatorial projects this year have included *Eugène Atget: The Making of a Reputation*; *Latitudes: François-Xavier Gbré and Nuits Balnéaires*; and *HARD COPY NEW YORK*, all at ICP; as well as *Walker Evans: Now and Then* at Fundación MAPFRE in Madrid. A longtime contributor to *Aperture*, in this issue he considers Dennis Wheatley's crime dossiers, enigmatic marvels of publishing that turned readers into would-be detectives.

DANIELLE JACKSON ("Viewfinder," page 15) is a writer and researcher living in New York. She is a cofounder and former codirector of the Bronx Documentary Center, a nonprofit gallery and educational center focused on documentary photography. Her criticism has appeared in *Artnet*, *New York Review of Architecture*, and *Cultured*, and she teaches courses in photography and visual culture at Stanford in New York and New York University. In this issue, Jackson takes a close look at Larry Clark's epochal photobook *Tulsa* (1971) against the backdrop of the city's misbegotten urban renewal policies.

EMILY LABARGE ("Perfect Strangers," page 78) is a London-based critic and the author of *Dog Days* (2026), a nonfiction book about trauma, narrative, and art. She is a regular contributor to the *London Review of Books*, *4Columns*, and *The New York Times*, and teaches writing at the Royal College of Art. For this issue, she reflects on photography's relationship to voyeurism and weighs the possibilities of the female gaze, anchoring her essay in Merry Alpern's controversial *Dirty Windows* series from the 1990s.

THESSALY LA FORCE ("Signs & Signals," page 54) is a writer and editor based in New York. Her writing has appeared in *The New Yorker*, *The New York Times*, *Vogue*, *The Paris Review*, and *T: The New York Times Style Magazine*, where she was previously the features director. She last contributed to *Aperture* for "The Design Issue" in Summer 2024, writing on the photographer and jeweler Coreen Simpson. Here, La Force introduces a new series by the British photographer Polly Brown exploring the secret hand gestures of airline stewardesses, waiters, Queen Elizabeth II, and others.

CHIARA BARDELLI NONINO ("Inside the Box," page 104) is the deputy editor in chief of features for *Harper's Bazaar Italia*. Previously, she served as the senior photo editor of *Vogue Italia* and as editor for the photography section of Vogue.it. In 2020, she curated *Paolo Roversi: Studio Luce*, the largest monographic exhibition of Paolo Roversi's work, held at MAR Museum in Ravenna, Italy. Nonino profiles the enigmatic Szilveszter Makó, a fast-rising Hungarian-born, Milan-based fashion photographer known for his absurdist sets and costumes.

DAN PIEPENBRING ("Redux," page 24) is a writer and editor living in New York. With Tom O'Neill, he cowrote *CHAOS: Charles Manson, the CIA, and the Secret History of the Sixties* (2019). With Prince, he cowrote *The Beautiful Ones* (2019), the musician's posthumously published memoir, a no. 1 *New York Times* bestseller. Piepenbring is currently the New Books columnist for *Harper's* and is working on a book about ketamine and dissociative anesthetics. In his *Aperture* debut, he writes about a recently rediscovered album of 1970s photographs made by Rosalind Fox Solomon in and around William Eggleston's home in Memphis, Tennessee.

LOU STOPPARD ("Dark Rooms," page 34) is a writer and curator based in London. Since beginning her career as an editor at Nick Knight's SHOWstudio, she has gone on to write for *The New York Times*, *The New Yorker*, and the *Financial Times*. Photobooks she has edited include *Shirley Baker* (2019) and *Exteriors: Annie Ernaux and Photography* (2024), which coincided with a show she curated at Maison Européenne de la Photographie, Paris. For *Aperture*, Stoppard has covered Cecil Beaton's bright young things, the heterodox interiors magazine *Nest*, and nightlife photography around the world. In these pages, she writes on the ethereal darkroom experiments of Alix Cléo Roubaud.

ANA KARINA ZATARAIN ("Barragán's Closets," page 46) is a writer based in Mexico City. Her work has appeared in *The New Yorker*, *The Paris Review*, *GQ*, and *New York Review of Architecture*. For her first piece for *Aperture*, she considers photo-conceptualist Iñaki Bonillas's clever intervention inside the home of renowned architect Luis Barragán. A collection of Zatarain's essays, titled *To and From*, is forthcoming from Knopf.

YECHEN ZHAO ("Witness," page 70) is the Karen Frank Assistant Curator of Photography and Media at the Art Institute of Chicago. A specialist in twentieth-century American and East Asian photography during the Cold War and its aftermath, he received his PhD in art history from Stanford University and completed a postdoctoral fellowship at the Yale University Art Gallery. Zhao last wrote for *Aperture*'s Fall 2025 edition, "The Seoul Issue," on the work of Doyeon Gwon. In these pages, he explores the work of Li Zhensheng, who documented the tumultuous years of the Chinese Cultural Revolution in thousands of secret photographs.

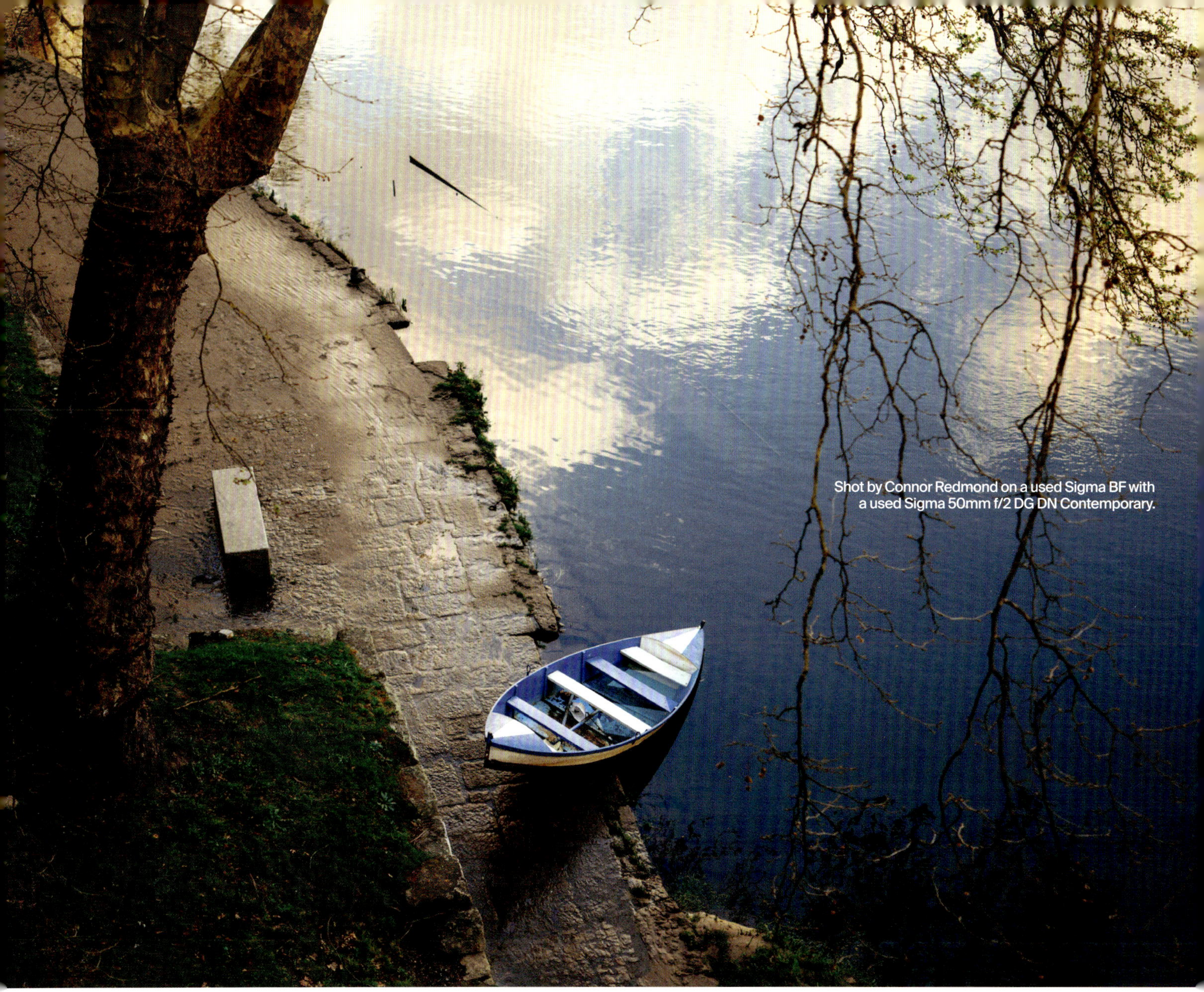

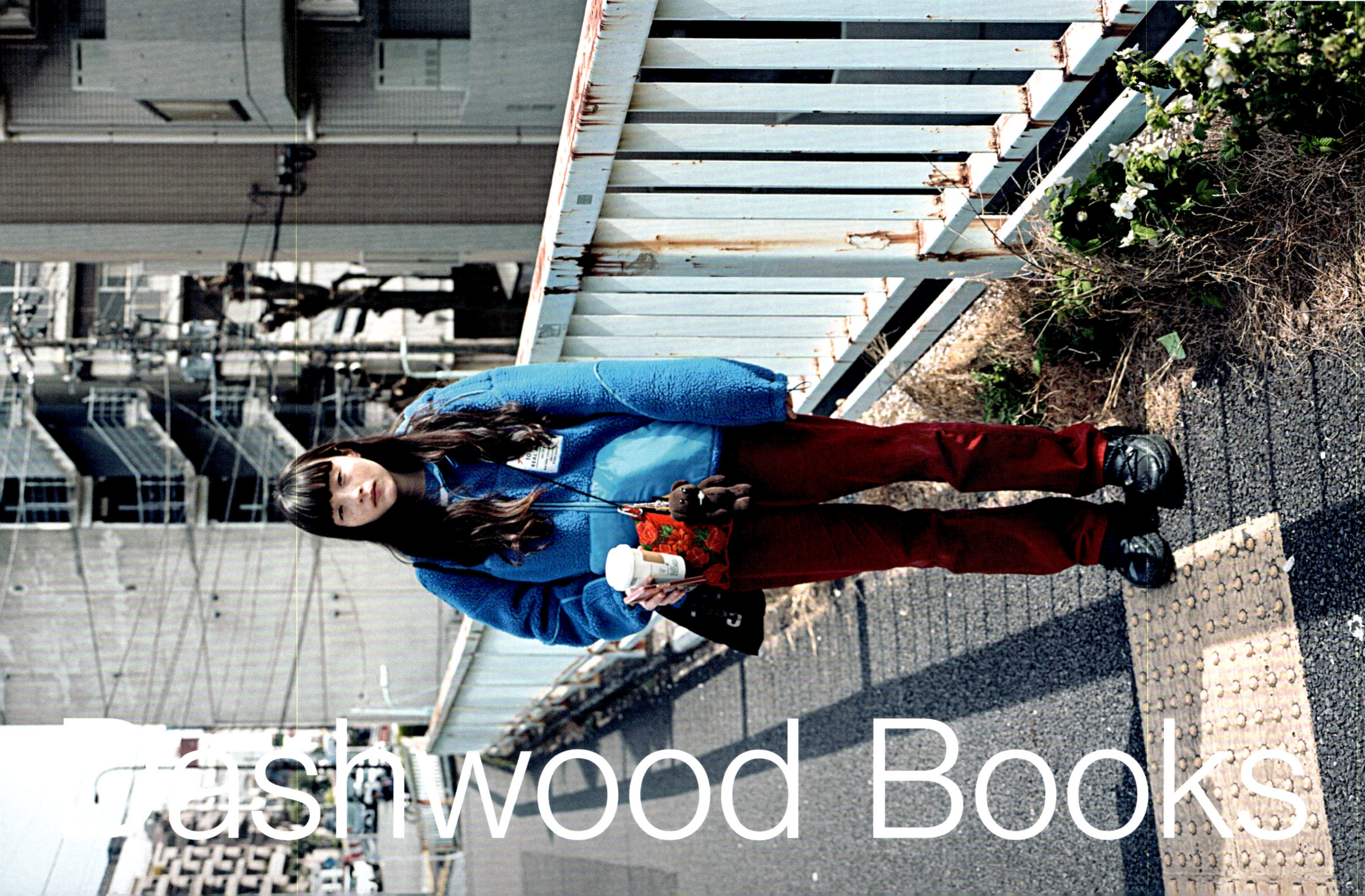
Dashwood Books

Agenda
Exhibitions to See

Triennial of Photography Hamburg

"To open our hearts more fully to love's power and grace we must dare to acknowledge how little we know of love in both theory and practice," wrote bell hooks, a lodestar of the ninth Triennial of Photography Hamburg. At a time of deeply fractured global politics, the artistic director Mark Sealy has convened a transnational group of photographers who offer a love letter to the medium that doubles as a blazing polemic. The citywide festival includes themed exhibitions, solo shows for young artists including Melike Kara, Abdulhamid Kircher, and Nina Porter, and an exhibition celebrating the centennial of the triennial's late founder, F. C. Gundlach, whose exuberant fashion pictures reflect the shifting tides of style and society.

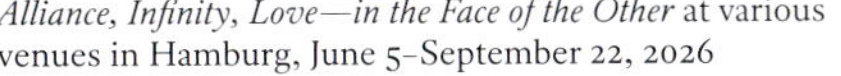

Alliance, Infinity, Love—in the Face of the Other at various venues in Hamburg, June 5–September 22, 2026

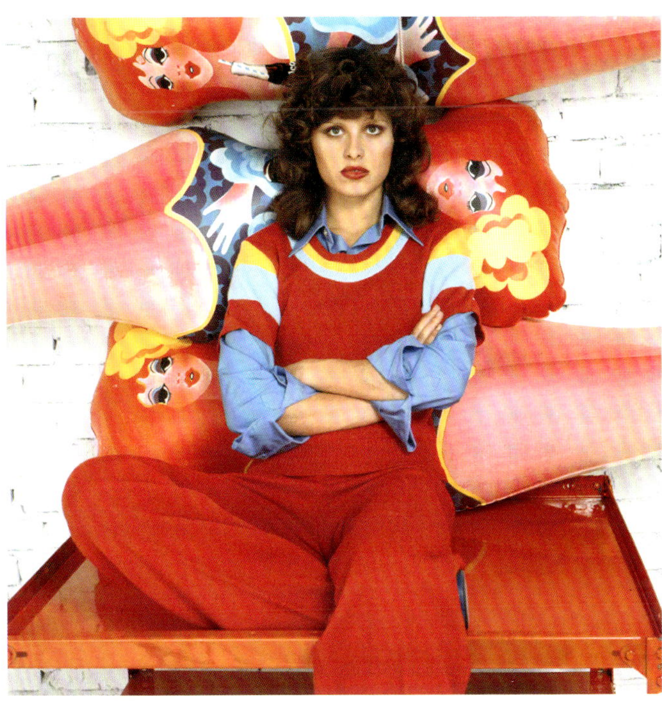

F. C. Gundlach, *Uschi Obermaier*, 1970
© Stiftung F. C. Gundlach

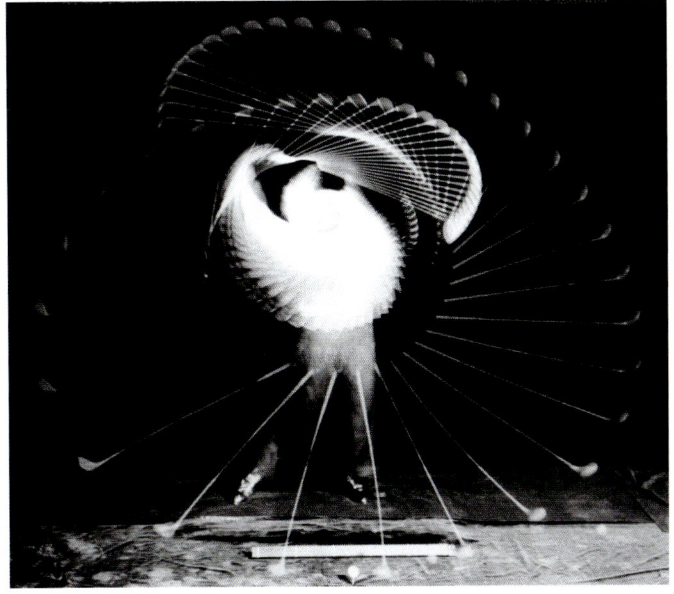

Harold Edgerton, *Bobby Jones' Driver*, 1938
© and courtesy MIT Museum

Harold Edgerton

A bullet piercing an apple, a drop of milk splashing onto a red pan, every phase of Bobby Jones's golf swing: When the engineer and researcher Harold "Doc" Edgerton first applied the stroboscopic flash to high-speed photography, it allowed him to reveal things previously invisible to the naked eye. A retrospective at the Massachusetts Institute of Technology, where Edgerton pioneered his technique in the 1930s, delights in such microsecond spectacles, exploring how his influence rippled beyond science and into the realms of art, war, and Hollywood.

Freezing Time: Edgerton and the Beauty of the Machine Age at the MIT Museum, through October 8, 2026

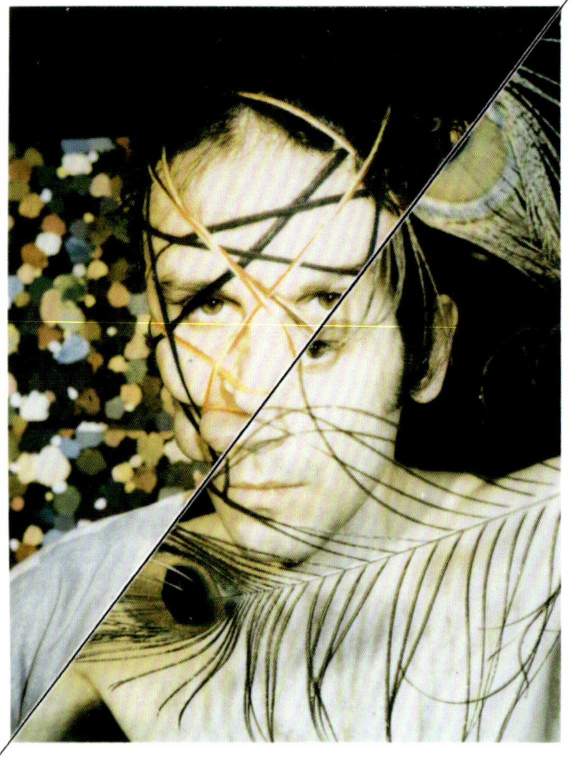

Lucas Samaras, *Split*, 1973

Lucas Samaras

Lucas Samaras's great subject was Lucas Samaras. Though a staple of New York's art scene beginning in the 1960s, the Greek-born artist never committed to a single school or style, instead forming a one-man movement—sprung from the confines of his apartment—that expanded the boundaries of self-depiction through paintings, installations, performances, and a dizzying array of other media. An exhibition in Chicago focuses on his photography, including the famous *Photo-Transformations* series (1973–76), in which he manipulated the wet emulsions of Polaroid film to create psychedelic selfies *avant la lettre*.

Lucas Samaras: Sitting, Standing, Walking, Looking at the Art Institute of Chicago, through July 20, 2026

Camille Vivier

For over two decades, Camille Vivier has shrouded the pages of *i-D*, *Dazed*, and *Purple* in an air of fantasy and myth, working in a loose tradition of surrealist fashion photography stretching back to Man Ray. Now, an exhibition in Paris brings her work to museum walls for the first time. Whether on assignment for Cartier, collaborating with female bodybuilders, or dabbling in equestrian portraiture, the French photographer imbues her subjects with an alien beauty and a dreamy eroticism that is bracingly bereft of convention.

Camille Vivier at Maison Européenne de la Photographie, Paris, June 10–September 26, 2026

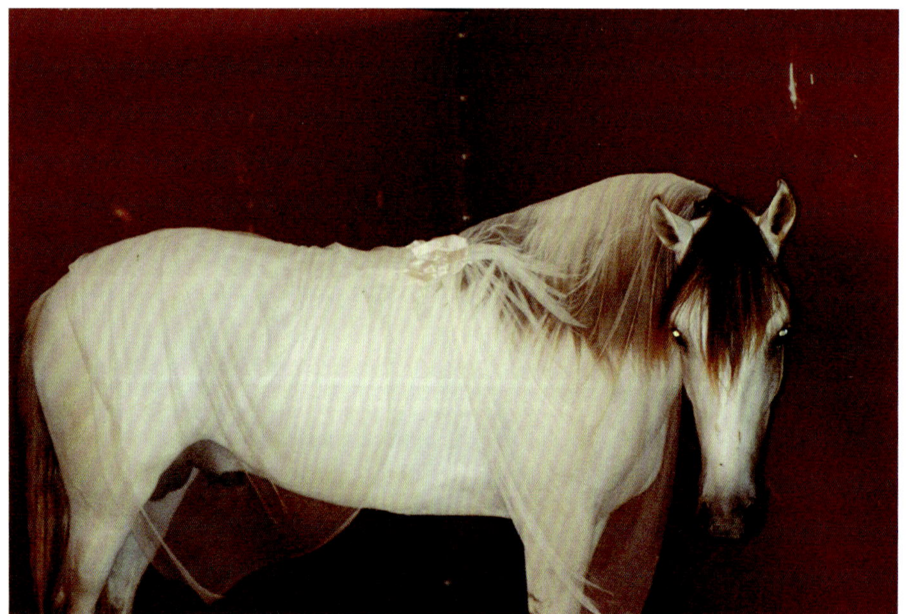

Camille Vivier, *Horse (I)*, 2002

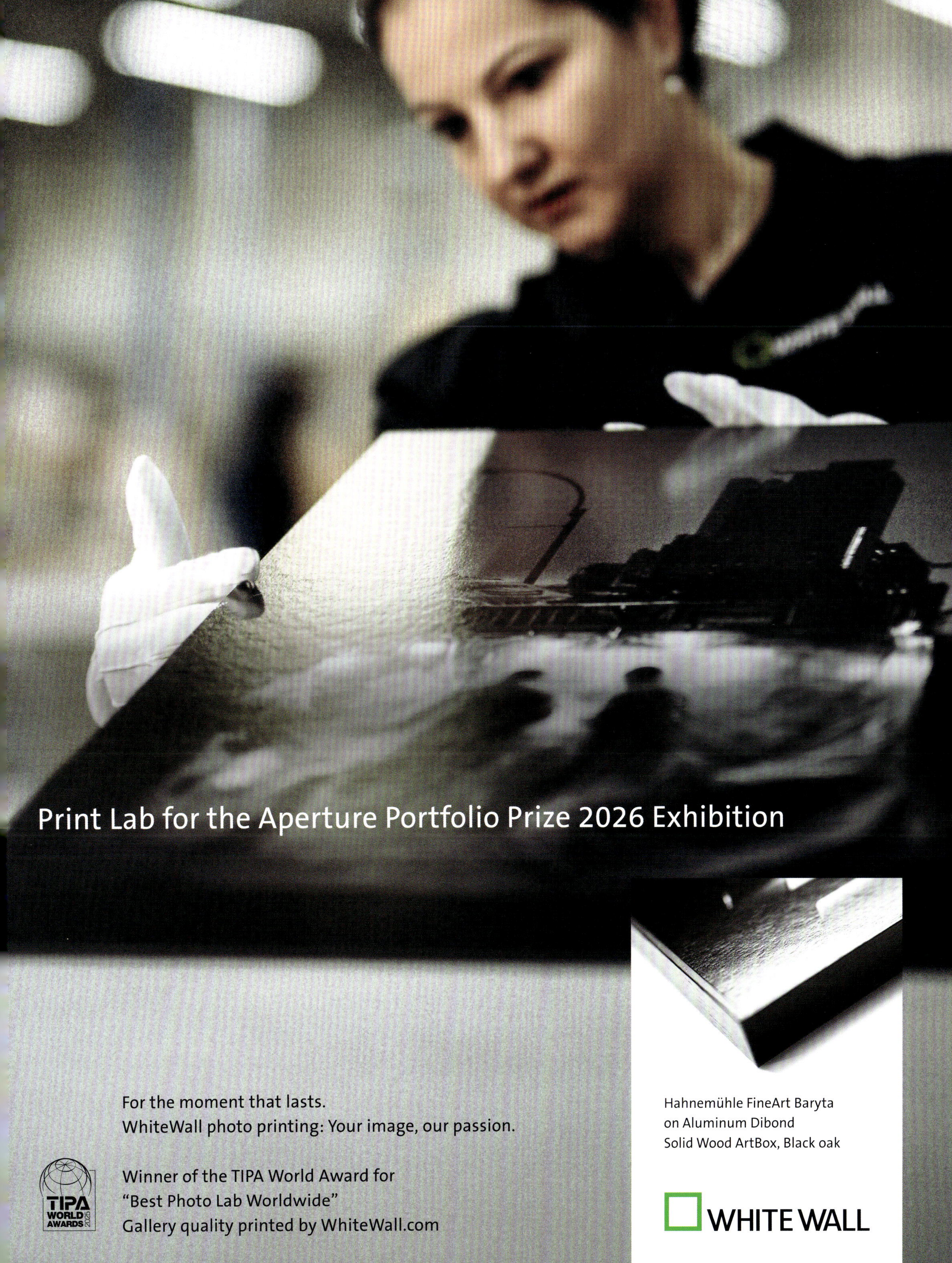

Viewfinder

As Larry Clark made his chronicle of young outcasts, Tulsa was being upended by an urban renewal scheme.

Danielle Jackson

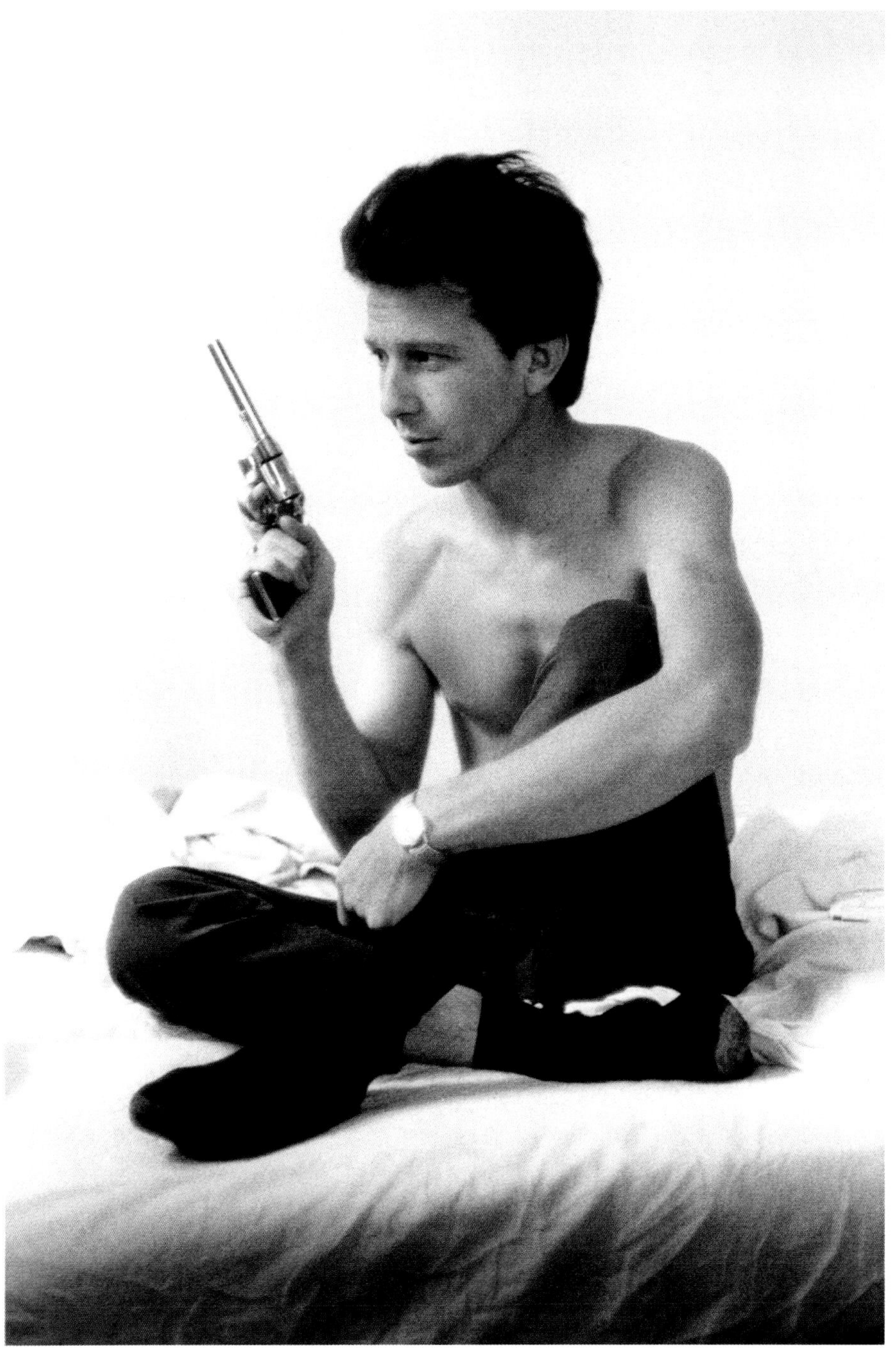

Among the most influential photobooks ever published, Larry Clark's *Tulsa* (1971) conveys little sense of place. In its near-ecclesiastic treatment of life and death, Clark's tight interiors of teenagers shooting up and acting out appear at once personal and broadly familiar, a commercially appealing vision of rebellion removed from the city that gives the book its name. Yet Clark's images, far from being universal, belong to a particular history that is still unfolding.

At the same time that Clark photographed *Tulsa*, between 1962 and 1971, his hometown was upended by a series of federal, state, and local policies, chief among them the construction of an interstate highway that segregated the neighborhoods of Clark's youth from the rest of the city. At the Greenwood Rising history center, in Tulsa, the construction of the Crosstown Expressway is considered the death blow to the city's historic Black neighborhood nearly fifty years after a horrific race massacre. However, a racial-justice lens tells only part of the story. *Tulsa* can help us understand how so-called renewal policies have failed residents on the wrong side of the city's economic divide.

Tulsa's four-lane highway brought long-simmering class divisions to a boil. After wildcat drilling on a Muscogee farm in 1905 uncovered what was then the largest known oil reserve in the world, the city's bankers, merchants, and real-estate speculators acquired federally designated lands from the Muscogee people to build lavish personal residences and profitable subdivisions. Meanwhile, a group of business leaders sought to establish worker housing for the "poorer classes" along the recently constructed railroad tracks and north into Cherokee territory. By the time of Clark's childhood, in the 1940s, much of Tulsa's oil, gas, and aviation industries had been sited on Cherokee lands. North Tulsa became a working-class enclave of factories and their employees; wealthy managers and executives continued to live on the former Muscogee lands on the city's south side.

Furthering the city's economic segregation, throughout the 1950s companies that had formed the basis of Tulsa's economy reorganized and decamped for Texas—a flight of capital decades before other parts of the country would experience the devastating effects of deindustrialization. At this time, Clark, a middle-schooler

Previous page:
Larry Clark, *Dead 1970*, 1968
© the artist and courtesy Luhring Augustine, New York

This page:
Detail from Tulsa Model Cities Program brochure, 1971

Clark's images, far from being universal, belong to a particular history that is still unfolding.

who had grown up in a relatively middle-class subdivision, started attending school in North Tulsa's blue-collar neighborhoods and met the children of boiler men and oil drillers who would later appear in his controversial photobook. "I got in a fight with a teacher. And then I had to go to a school across the tracks," he wrote in 1981. "I went into that school, which was a lower-class school, right? . . . And so that's when I started hanging out with [David] Roper and Billy Mann and all those guys."

Clark began injecting Valo, a cheap over-the-counter nasal inhaler containing amphetamines, during his parents' financial troubles. By the time Clark was in high school his father was an unemployed door-to-door bookseller and his mother sustained the family by hustling up business as a baby and pet photographer. Clark began to photograph his circle of "police characters" (as they were named in the local press) and their drug use during a break from art school in Wisconsin in 1962.

By this time, the city's plans for the highway were gathering force through a series of municipal bonds and federal matching grants. The new highway would span the entire length of the city to anticipate Oklahoma's new suburbanites' commute to the business district downtown. In 1965, when the state began acquiring through eminent domain the residences slated for demolition, the Clark home, situated in the center of the proposed roadway, was auctioned and sold for scrap. Clark's parents relocated—with Larry's early *Tulsa* negatives in tow—while he served in the Vietnam War.

When Clark returned to Tulsa, the city's transformation was well underway. Aerial photographs from the period show a gash of dirt spanning miles in the place where hundreds of houses once stood. Nested beside an article on Clark's arrest while working on the 1968 section of *Tulsa* is a small item about the state's purchase of even more North Tulsa land. Critics of the mid-century highway boom cite the federal government's role

Model Cities Target Area

There are seven divisions of the Model Neighborhood (A, B, C, D, E, F, and G). Over 35,000 people live in this area, 70% of which are black. The remaining are Indians, Mexican-Americans, and disadvantaged whites.

The Tulsa Model Cities Program is currently concentrating all planning efforts in this under-privileged area. It is anticipated that eventually this Program will turn its planning to approach all the problems of the Metropolitan area.

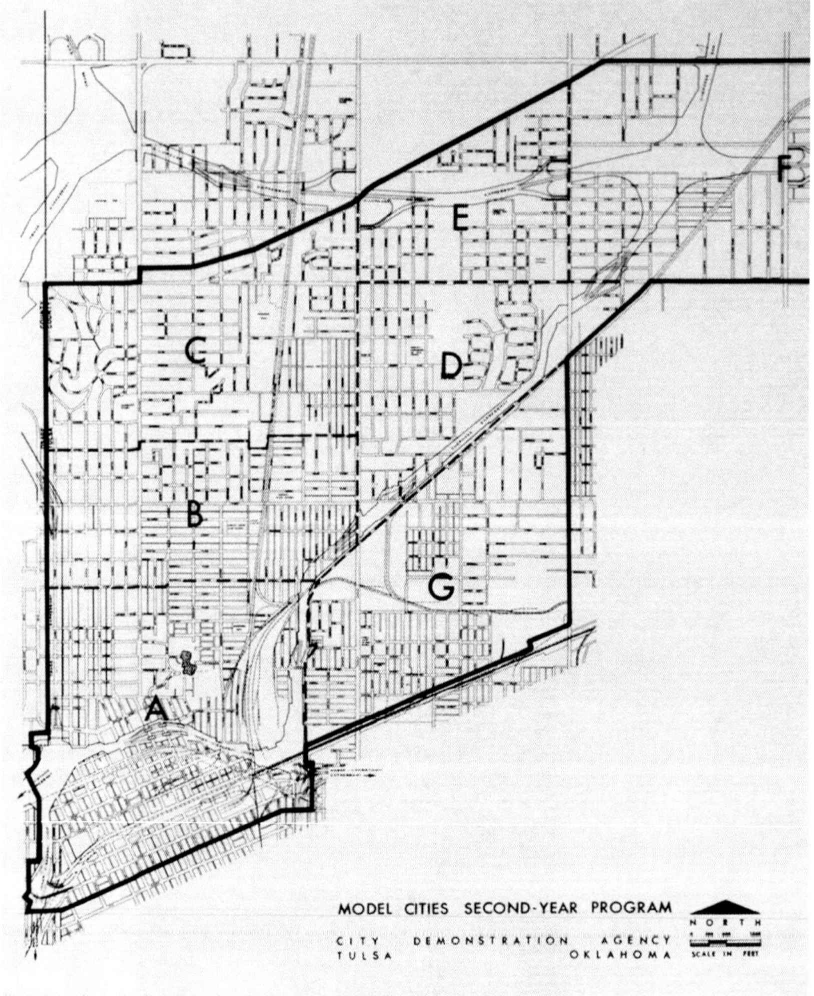

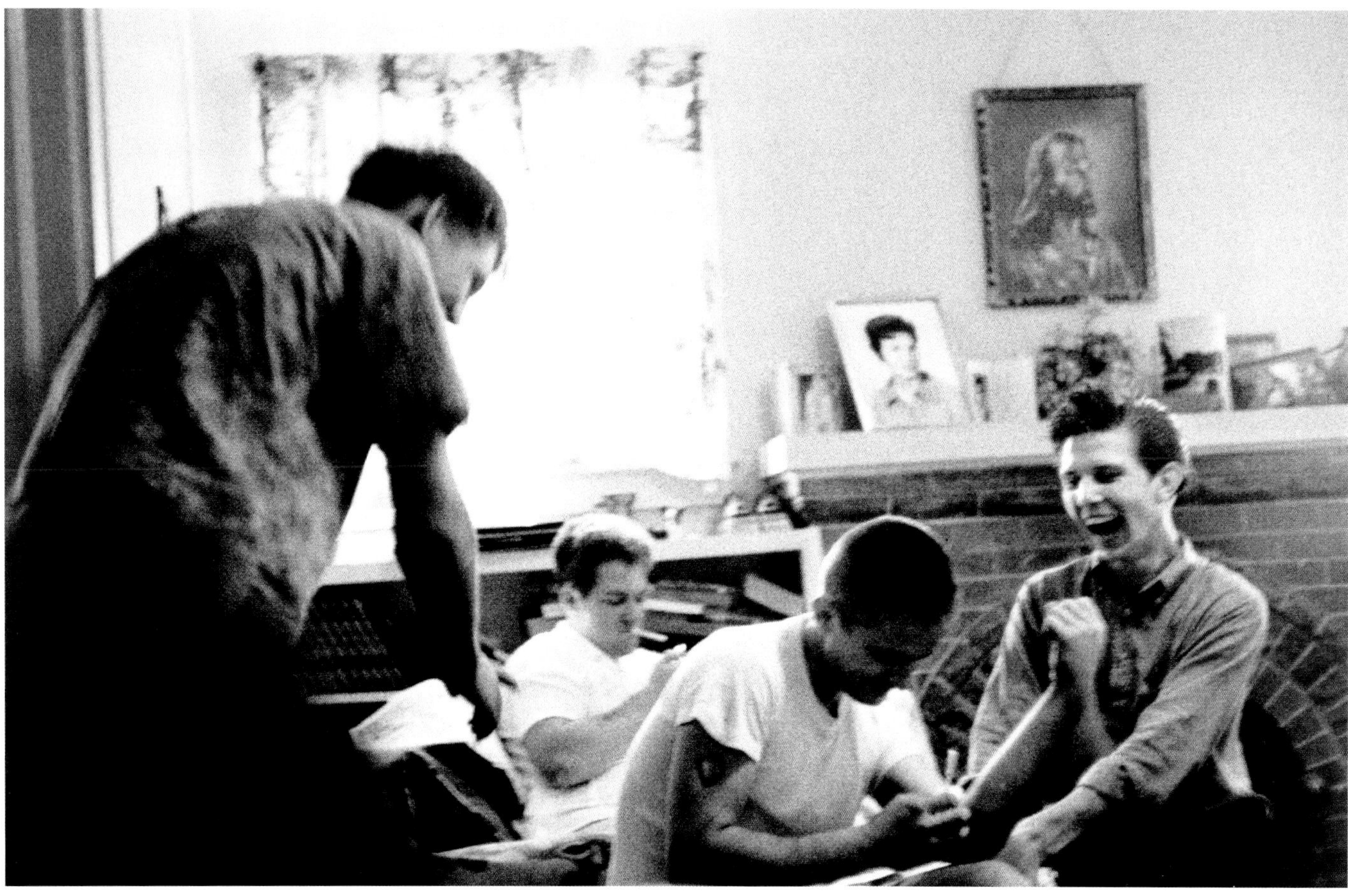

Larry Clark, *Untitled*, 1963

in demolishing healthy neighborhoods with vital community resources. A set of survey photographs from 1955 charting the future highway route shows the site of Clark's grandfather's long-standing used-car business, a neighboring beauty parlor, tidy bungalows. The demolitions continued apace as Clark came in and out of the city to photograph his dwindling circle of friends.

A year after *Tulsa*'s publication in 1971, the final section of the Crosstown Expressway was completed, leaving Tulsa's working-class neighborhoods in shambles. As Clark's friends fell deeper into lives of crime and addiction, the city was unable to address the urban problems it had exacerbated. Mere blocks from the homes of Clark's subjects, a massive federal program under Lyndon B. Johnson's War on Poverty was devised to target crime, unemployment, and juvenile delinquency in Tulsa's working-class neighborhoods; the bulk of the funds were used to relocate Black residents in the highway's path.

The results of these policy failures are yet to be undone. After the state failed to create exit ramps to the area's popular shopping centers, North Tulsa's businesses could no longer survive. Residential streets that flanked the new roadway became undesirable and were rezoned for other uses. David Roper's neighborhood eventually became a red-light district. Within two years of the publication of *Tulsa*, the oil shocks of 1973 led North Tulsa further down a path of corporate and municipal disinvestment. Habitat for Humanity now owns hundreds of abandoned lots in the neighborhoods Clark frequented.

After decades of advocacy, things may be changing for the better. In 2025, Tulsa's City Council and the Cherokee Nation both announced millions of dollars in investments to improve neighborhoods north of the highway. They share the hopes of civic groups, residents, and young artists in their vision to finally rebuild their communities.

Danielle Jackson is a critic and researcher based in New York.

Spotlight

Winner of the 2026 Aperture Portfolio Prize, Aaryan Sinha recasts familiar visual tropes of life in India.

Chris Wiley

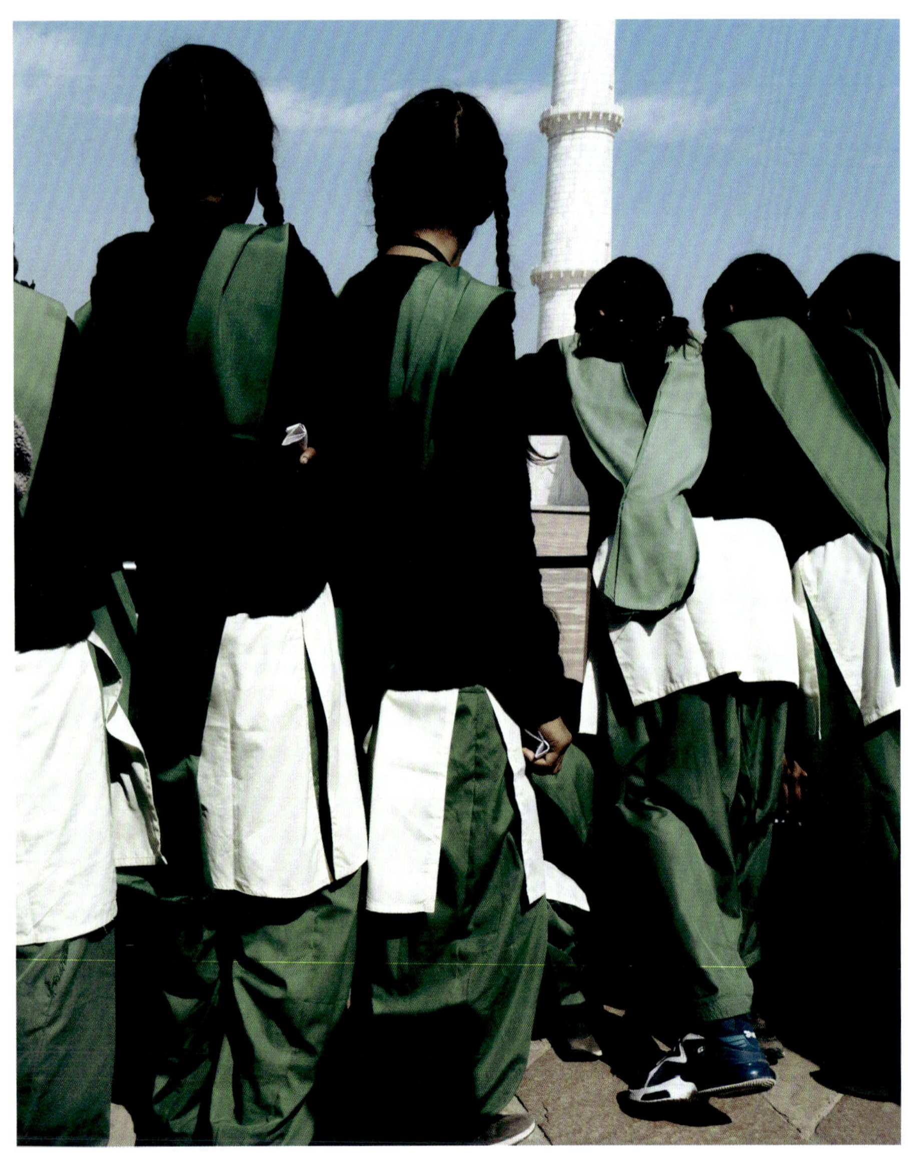

With a title like *Namaste or Whatever*, you would expect the work of Aaryan Sinha to be absolutely sodden with sardonic wit, aimed in the direction of his home country of India. You might imagine it to be flecked with visual barbs targeting, say, woo-woo Westerners gorging themselves in the country's well-stocked spiritual supermarket, or cargo-shorted adventurers jockeying for selfies at the Taj Mahal. Instead, the project's flippant title belies the thoughtful, ravishing nature of the photographs, which find Sinha wrestling with the legacy of the colonial imagination of his homeland and attempting to quarry authenticity out of the obdurate granite of cliché.

Sinha, who graduated from the Royal Academy of Art, The Hague, in 2023, has been working on this collection of pictures for the past few years. When I reached him over a video call in February, he was on a photoshoot in India's remote northern region of Ladakh and recalled that the title sprang from a real-life encounter. As he was sitting with a classmate on a stoop one evening, a friend's mother happened to walk by and stop for a chat. On her departure, the woman bid farewell to Sinha's friend in their native tongue (Norwegian) before turning to Sinha and, seemingly at a loss as to how to say goodbye, settled on "Namaste, or whatever."

As the only Indian student in his class at art college until his third year, Sinha was used to this kind of confusion about his culture, if not to the outright

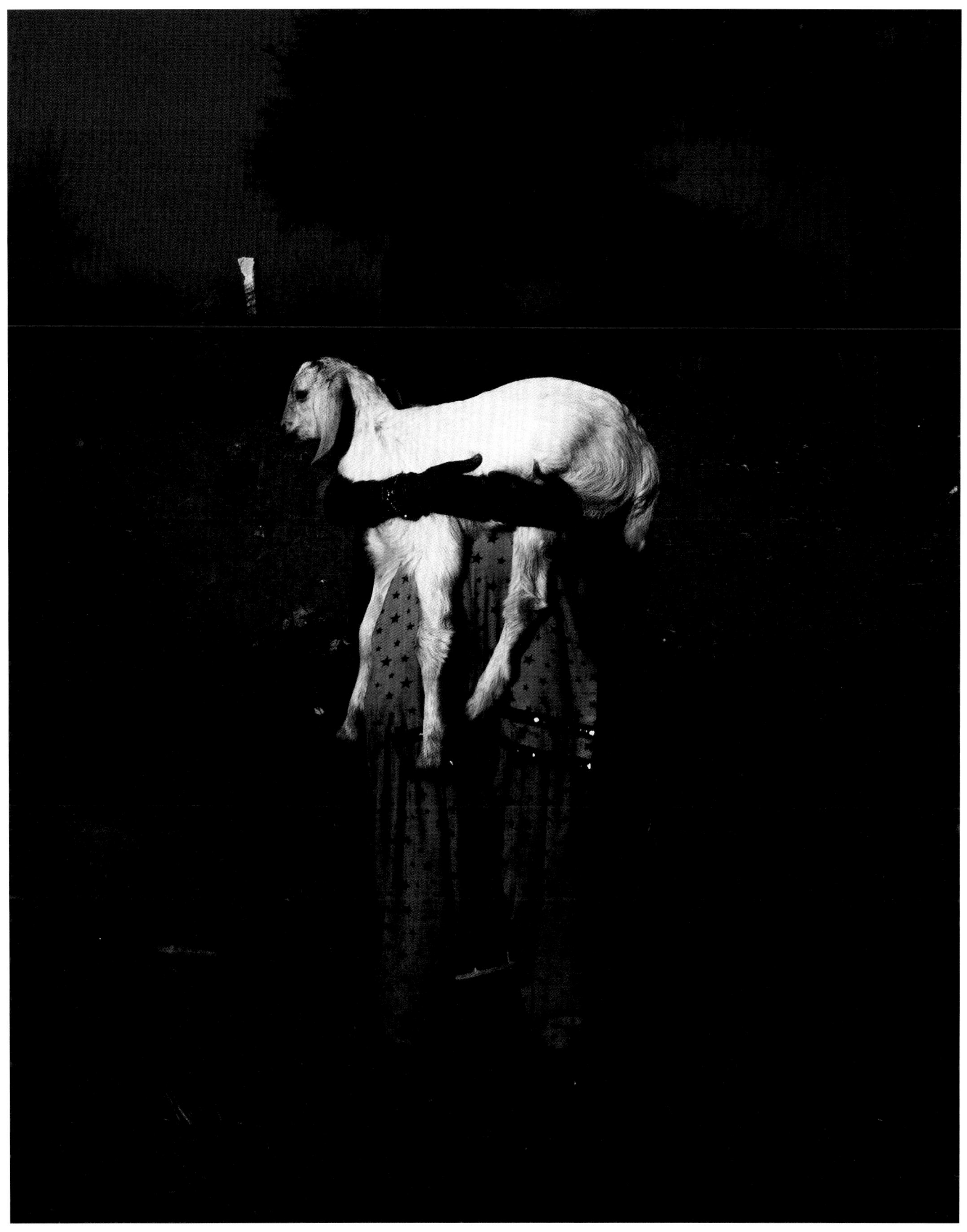

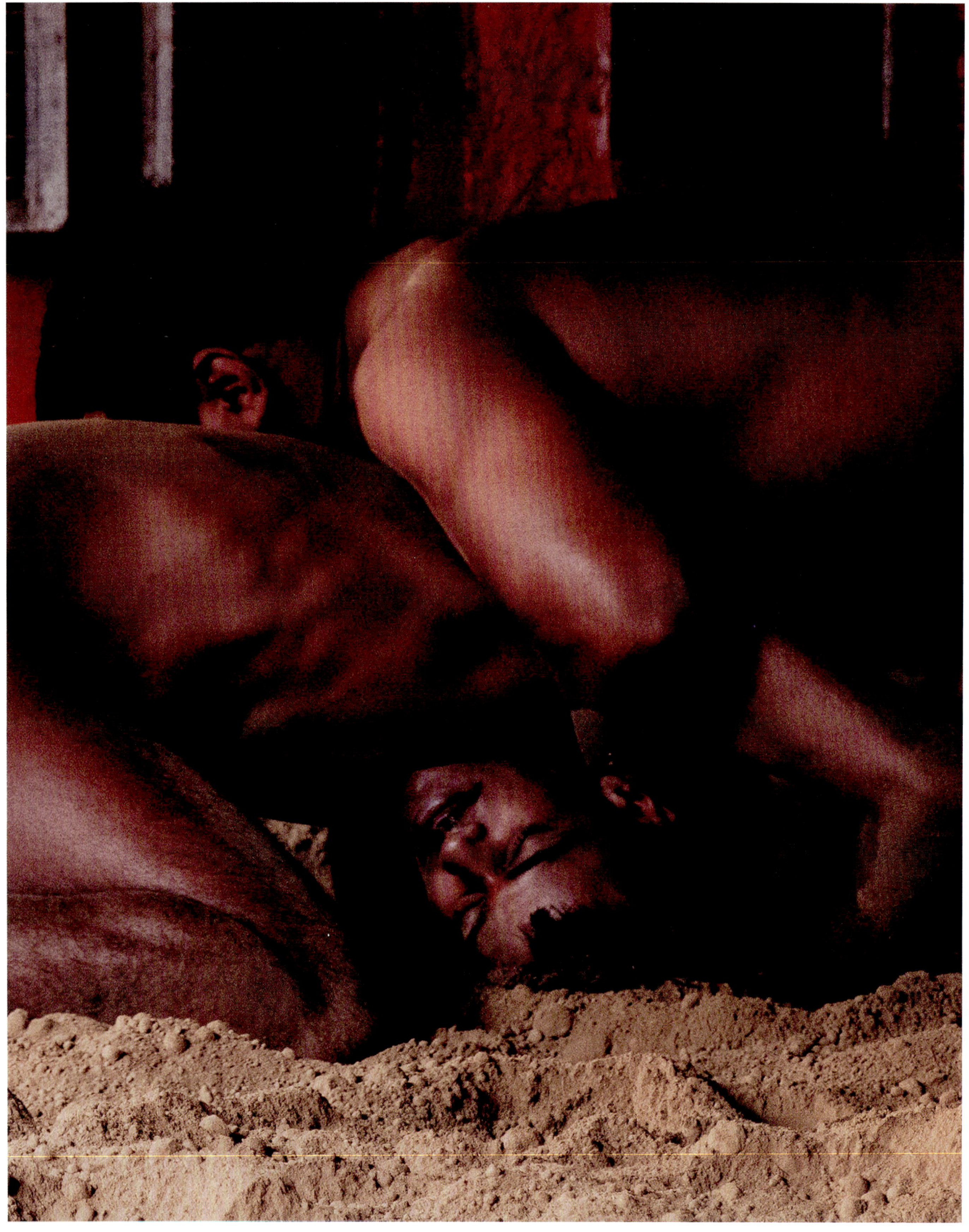

Page 18: *School Girls*, 2025; page 19: *Fragments of a Gaze*, 2023; opposite: *Grappling Histories*, 2024

This page, left: *Untitled*, 2024; right: *Anti-Photographer*, 2024

racism that often undergirded it. He could maybe even relate. "Through the media that I consumed, I was more connected to the West than to my own country," he told me. "And even though I was not born in the West, I felt like I belonged there, which led me to see India through the Western gaze."

When he was in his teens, first toting his camera around the streets of New Delhi, he sought out picturesque images of poverty, focusing on the city's street children. He learned to hunt these kinds of images down, he told me, by following the example set in the many photobooks by famous photographers, such as Steve McCurry, in his family home. A brief, life-changing critique by the Magnum photographer Rafal Milach, for whom Sinha interned, set him on his current path. His pictures, Milach warned him, merely skimmed across India's surface, rehashing stereotypical scenes that wide-eyed Westerners might snap on vacation. Chastised, Sinha swore to himself that he would become a more self-critical image maker.

In 2022, he began a body of work, still ongoing, titled *This Isn't Divide and Conquer* that documents the five Indian states that border Pakistan and Kashmir. Sinha was so mindful of his role as a

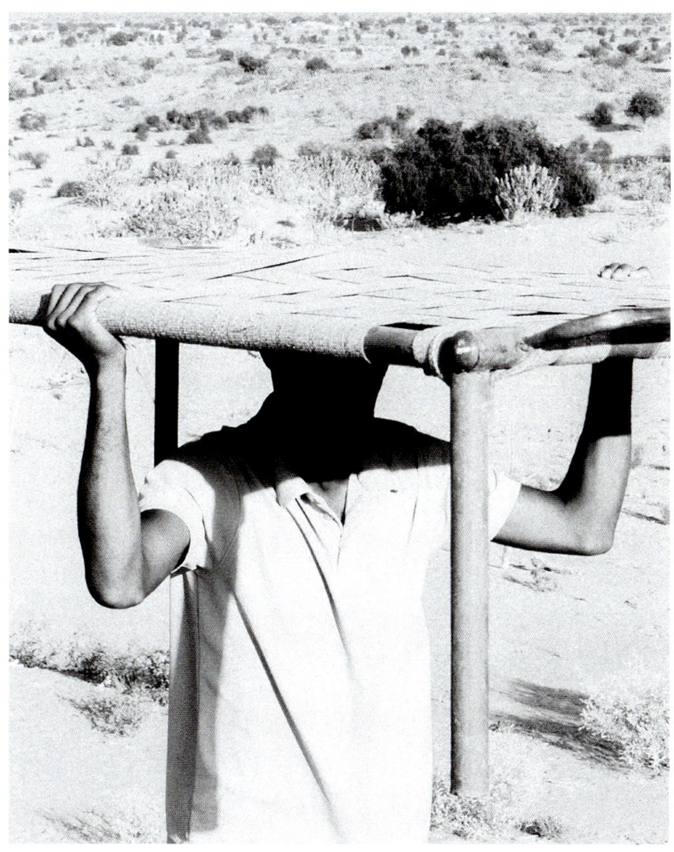

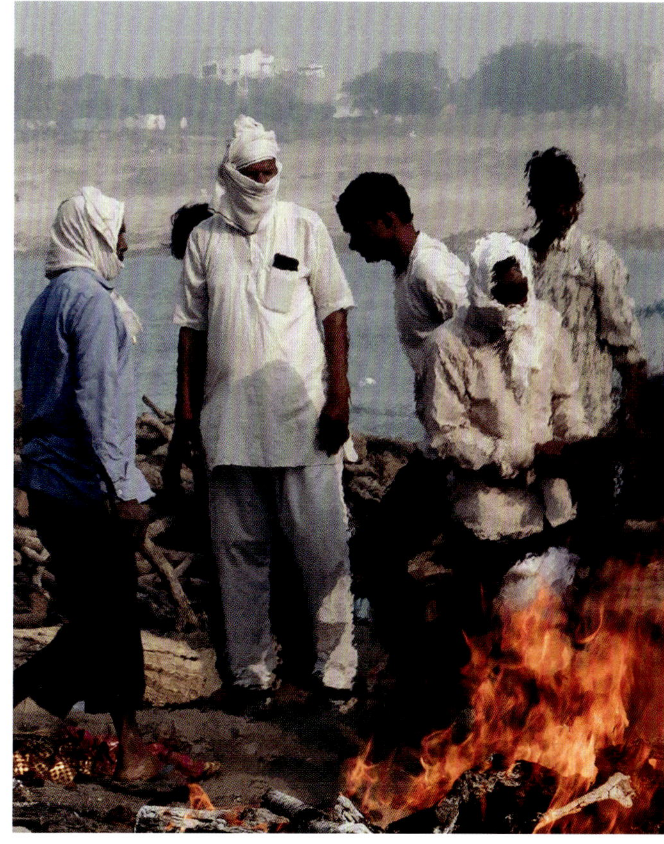

Left: *Closer to Gods*, 2021; right: *Snake Charmer*, 2024

photographic observer and the power relations implicit in it that he assiduously avoided including any of his subjects' faces, for fear of somehow exploiting them. Aesthetically, he also kept himself on a short leash: Anything with even a whiff of cliché was immediately chucked in the discard pile.

Soon, however, these self-imposed constraints began to look like opportunities. Might deeper truths be found within the tropes that cast India as a mystical land of stark contrasts? *Namaste or Whatever* began with Sinha's decision to revisit his abandoned pictures and endeavor to "do a complete one-eighty, and just focus on the clichés." Indeed, the series gives you much of what you'd expect: A snake charmer's cobra rears its head into the frame; men immolate a corpse on the banks of the Ganges; handprints in white paint left by pilgrims pile up on a ruddy temple wall. What distinguishes these pictures from the many like them is the sheer lushness of Sinha's seeing.

Namaste or Whatever began with Sinha's decision to "do a complete one-eighty, and just focus on the clichés."

But even when Sinha is trying to lean into what he considers his own worst tendencies, unexpected moments arise. His photograph of a pair of shirtless wrestlers twisted together in a strange embrace, for instance, is both erotically

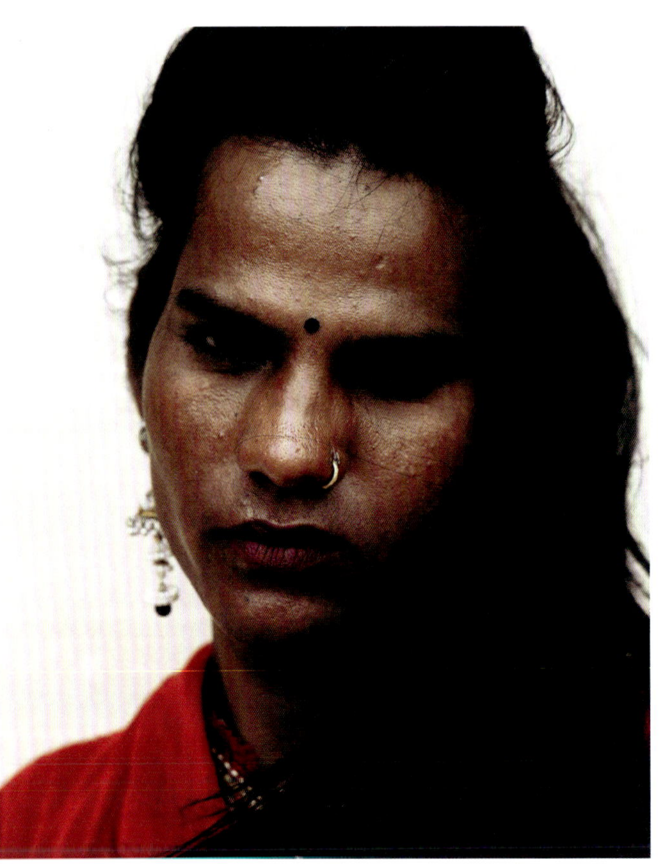

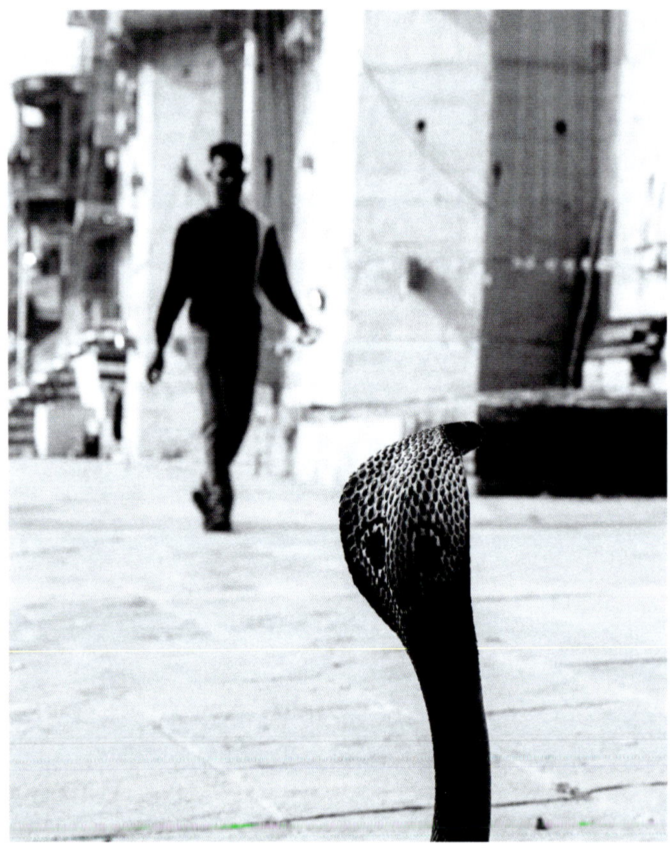

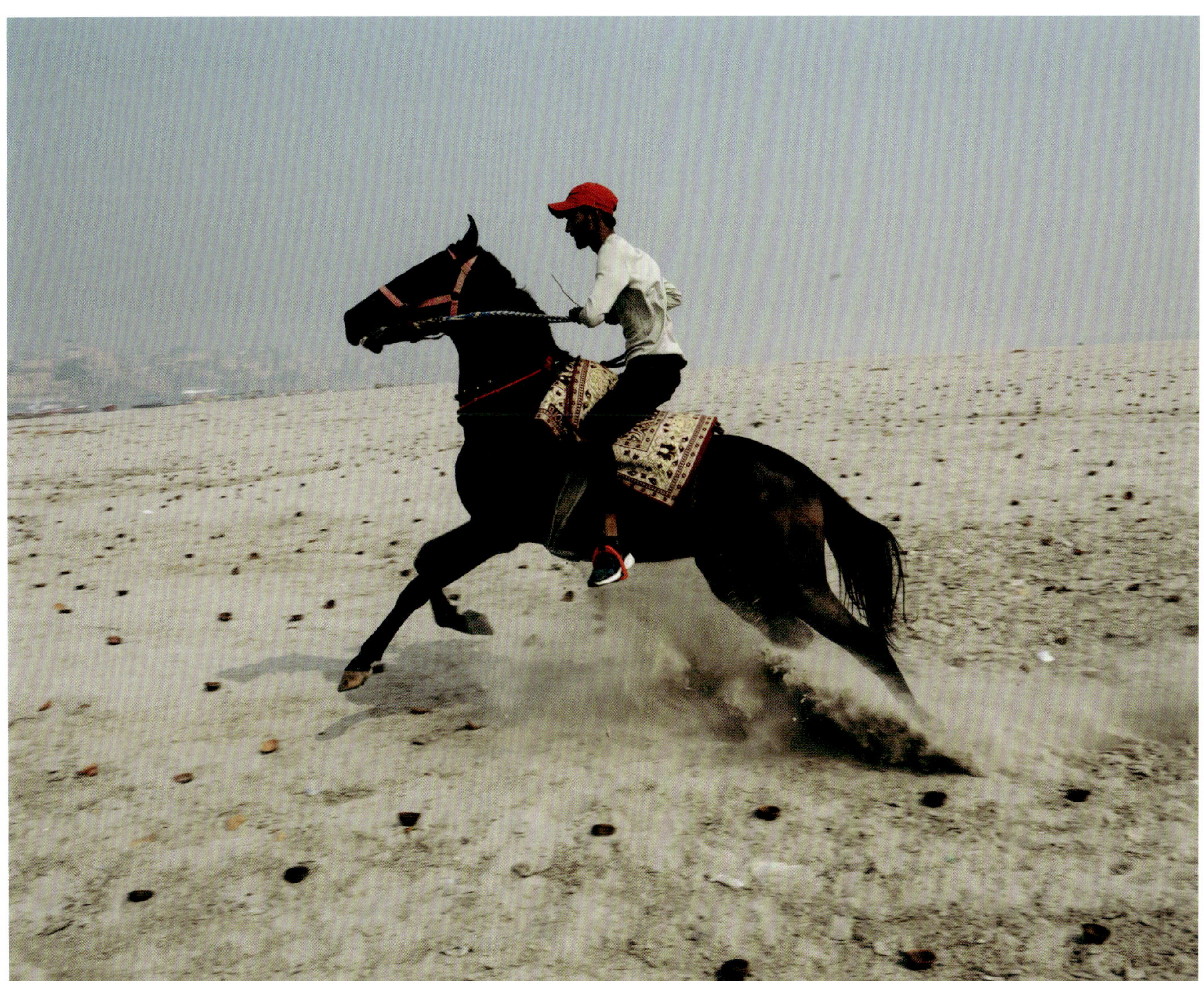

The Man and the Horse, 2024
All photographs © the artist

charged and physiologically flummoxing. A shot of a burned-out metal building in a misty mountain landscape, its siding distorted and picturesquely discolored, conjures both the hazy, baroque gardens of Jean-Honoré Fragonard and Morris Louis's *Veil* paintings.

Sinha is the first to admit that crawling out from under the blanket of stereotypes that have been thrown over the Indian subcontinent by generations of colonial interlopers and assorted photographic lookie-loos is no easy task. But you get the sense that, even in the face of possible failure, his effort is passionate and dogged. Where cliché flattens the world into a dull procession of the foreknown, Sinha's work intercedes, doing its part to revivify our vision.

Chris Wiley is an artist and writer based in the Catskills.

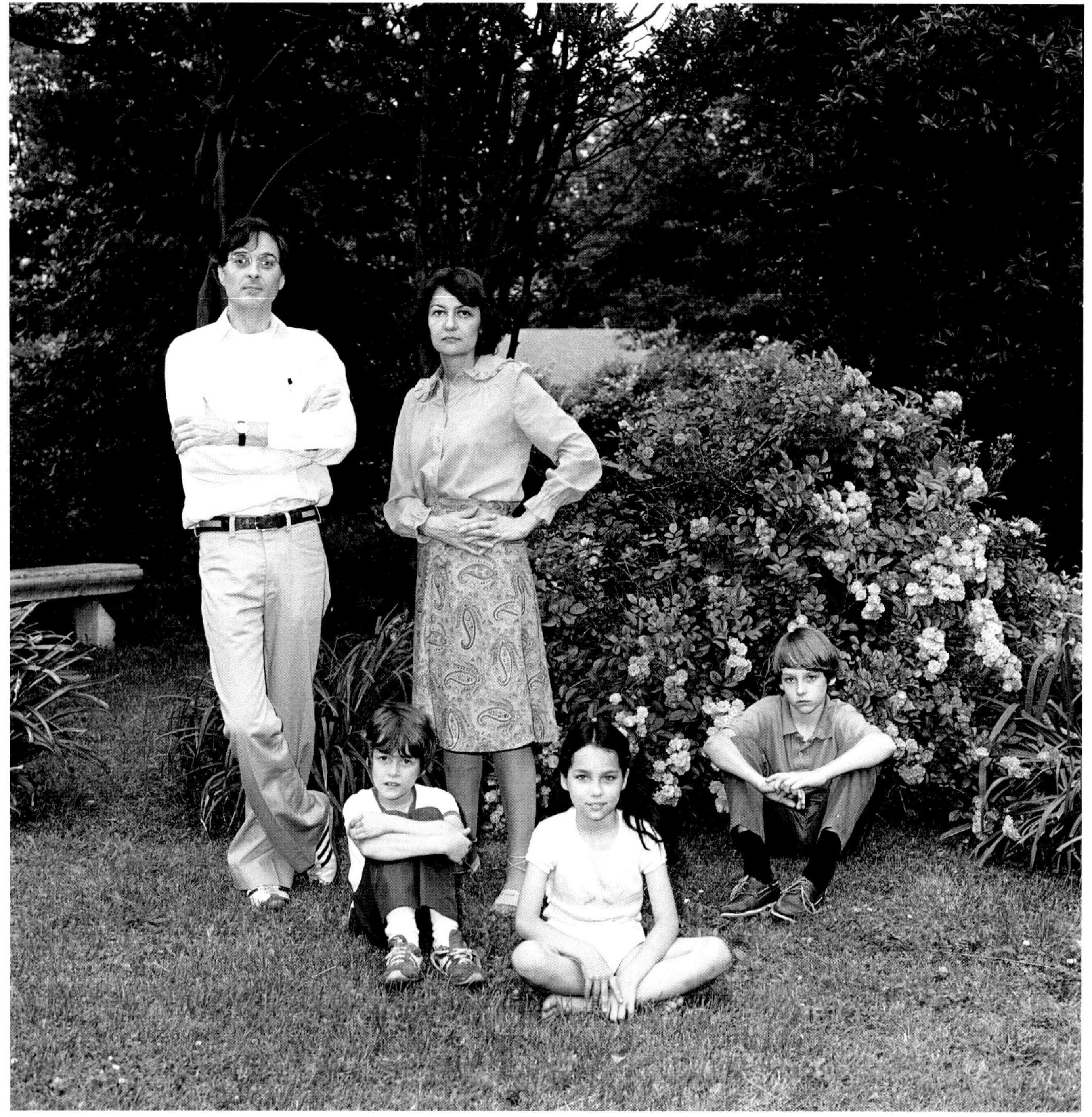

Redux

In the late 1970s, Rosalind Fox Solomon embedded with William Eggleston, his family, and a circle of Memphis eccentrics.

Dan Piepenbring

Opposite
William Eggleston and Family, Memphis, Tennessee, 1980

This page:
William Eggleston, Memphis, Tennessee, 1977

It was 1977, and Rosalind Fox Solomon did not want to move to Washington, DC. The new president, Jimmy Carter, had tapped her husband for a high-profile (albeit unglamorously named) position as administrator of the General Services Administration. That meant the Solomons had to leave Chattanooga, Tennessee, where they'd lived since the early 1950s and where Rosalind, then forty-seven, was finding her métier as a photographer. Her work coalesced around intimacy and infirmity. She took pictures of dolls, mannequins, and their eccentric collectors; patients young and old at the Baroness Erlanger Hospital; and Jimmy Carter himself, whom she photographed sweating and smiling through a breakneck campaign in the New South. In the future president and a scuffed, shopworn figurine Fox Solomon could isolate the same broken longing. She had begun to investigate the ways the New South met the old, and the multitude of forms in which segregation persisted—some subtle, some shockingly visible.

Her life in DC, she feared, would

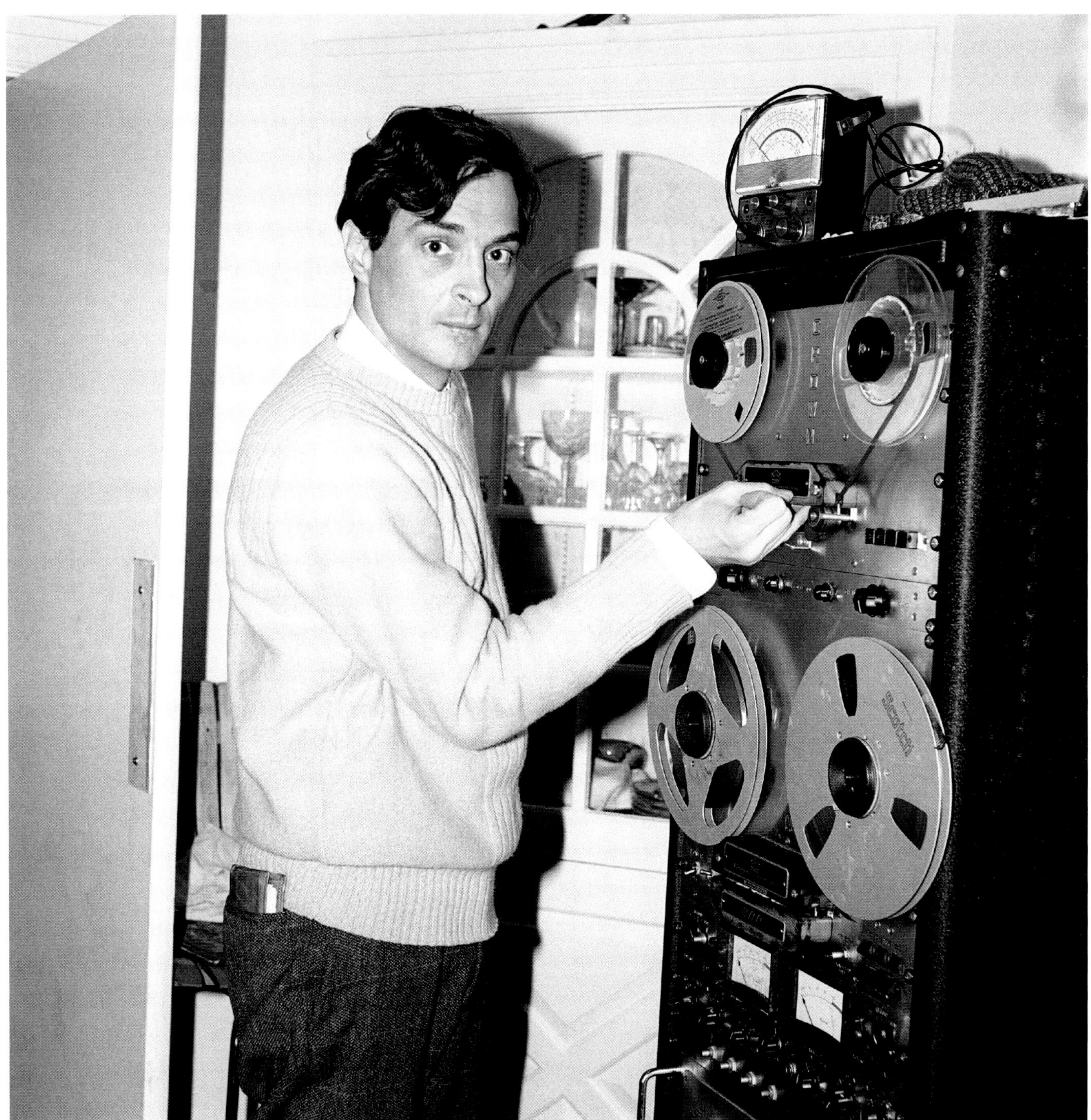

interrupt that work. Perhaps to forestall the possibility, Fox Solomon arranged to visit William Eggleston in Memphis. Eggleston, a decade her junior, was then less than a year removed from his landmark Museum of Modern Art exhibition, the museum's first-ever solo show of color photographs. When did he and Fox Solomon meet? How well did they know each other? The record is too scanty to say—but their time together, however it came to pass, deepened Fox Solomon's practice in astonishing ways.

For what became her *Eggleston Album*, she immersed herself in Egglestoniana, photographing him, his family, their home, and, eventually, their entire milieu. She interviewed his closest friends and took around 140 rolls of film, not just in Memphis but throughout Mississippi, where Eggleston had spent his formative years. Her pictures, vacillating between diary and documentary, observe a family and a region in a state of sublime, disquieting, sometimes ridiculous contradiction. At one point, alone on a Mississippi road,

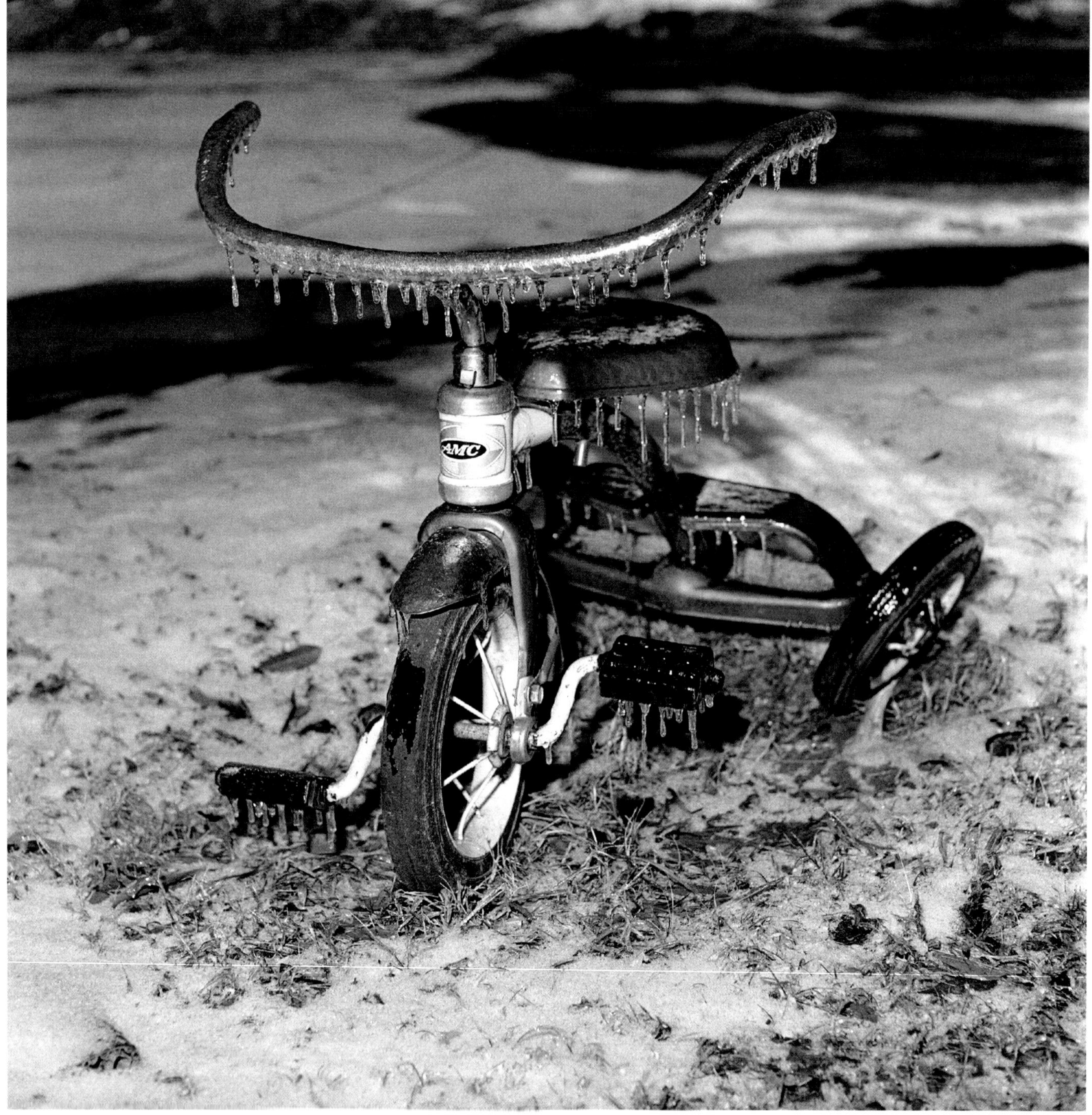

***Eggleston's Tricycle*, Memphis, Tennessee, 1977**

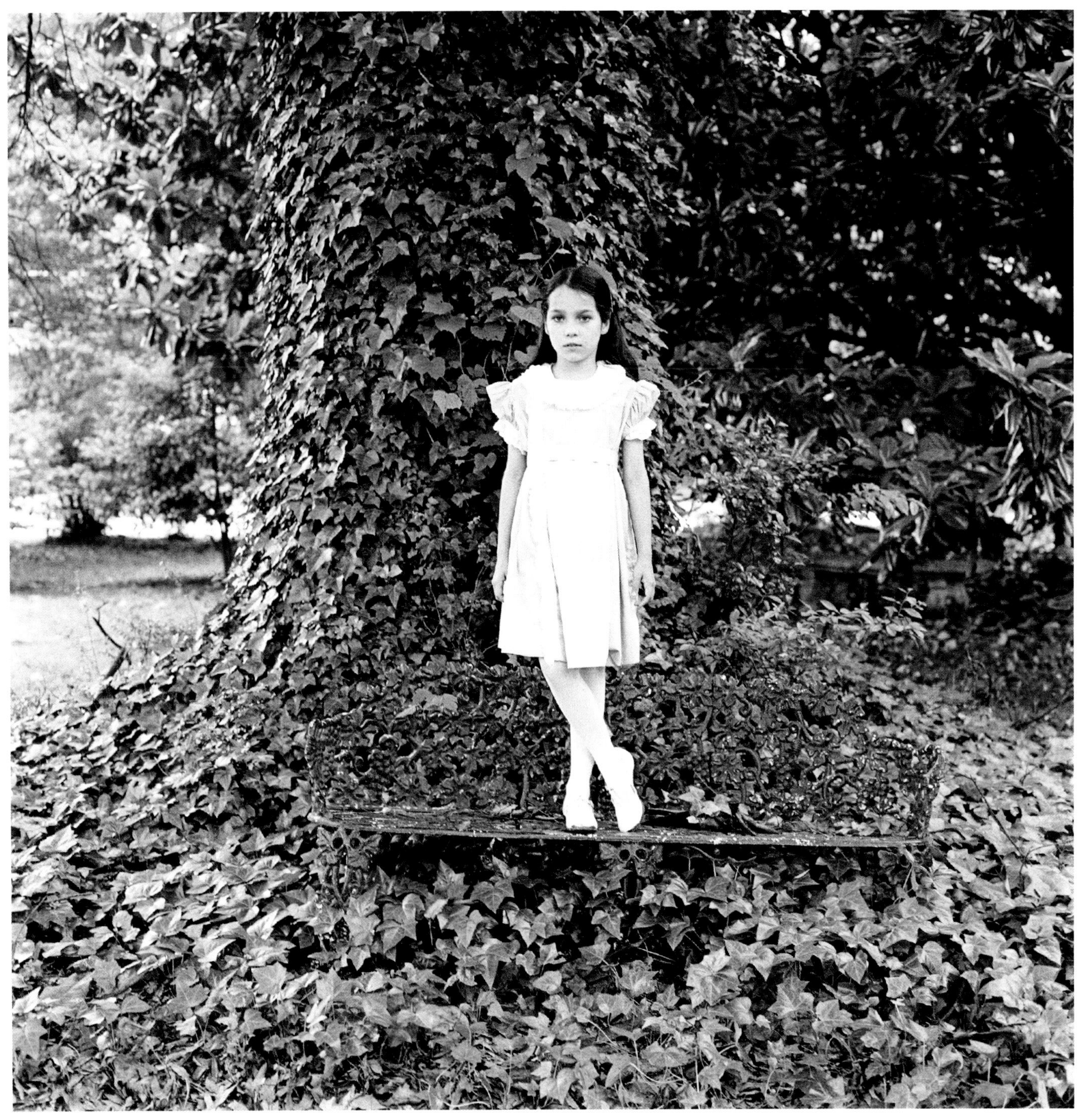

Bill's Daughter, Memphis, Tennessee, 1980

The *Eggleston Album* observes a family and a region in a state of sublime, sometimes ridiculous contradiction.

Fox Solomon spoke into her tape recorder: "It is very quiet and ever so private. . . . So private that I feel out of place. The ever-present mystery of the bayou carrying its secrets downstream."

Her photographs somehow slip into that privacy without disturbing it. She finds Eggleston's cousin sitting on a gently disheveled bedspread in a spare, unadorned room, a telephone dragged before her feet. Elsewhere, a child's tricycle stands in a snowy yard, forgotten for the winter, with one of its wheels out of joint and icicles dangling from its handlebars. (It looks to be the same tricycle that appeared in Eggleston's iconic photograph *Memphis*, ca. 1969, when it was already the worse for wear.) Eggleston's daughter, Andra, poses for a portrait in a frilled dress, tights, and dainty white shoes, seemingly disenchanted with the grand green tree swarming with leaves behind her. As for Eggleston himself, he appears most memorably in a large bathtub, joined by his friend Julien Jefferson Hohenberg, a loofah floating between them like an accusation; with their startled expressions, the pair resemble two boys caught washing up before tucking themselves in for a sleepover.

The interviews Fox Solomon conducted revealed Eggleston as a man of close confidences and unlikely friendships. He liked deranged people: He seemed to have cobbled together a community comprising every eccentric within a hundred-mile radius. Fox Solomon was especially fascinated by his bond with Tom C. Boring, a dentist and debauchee

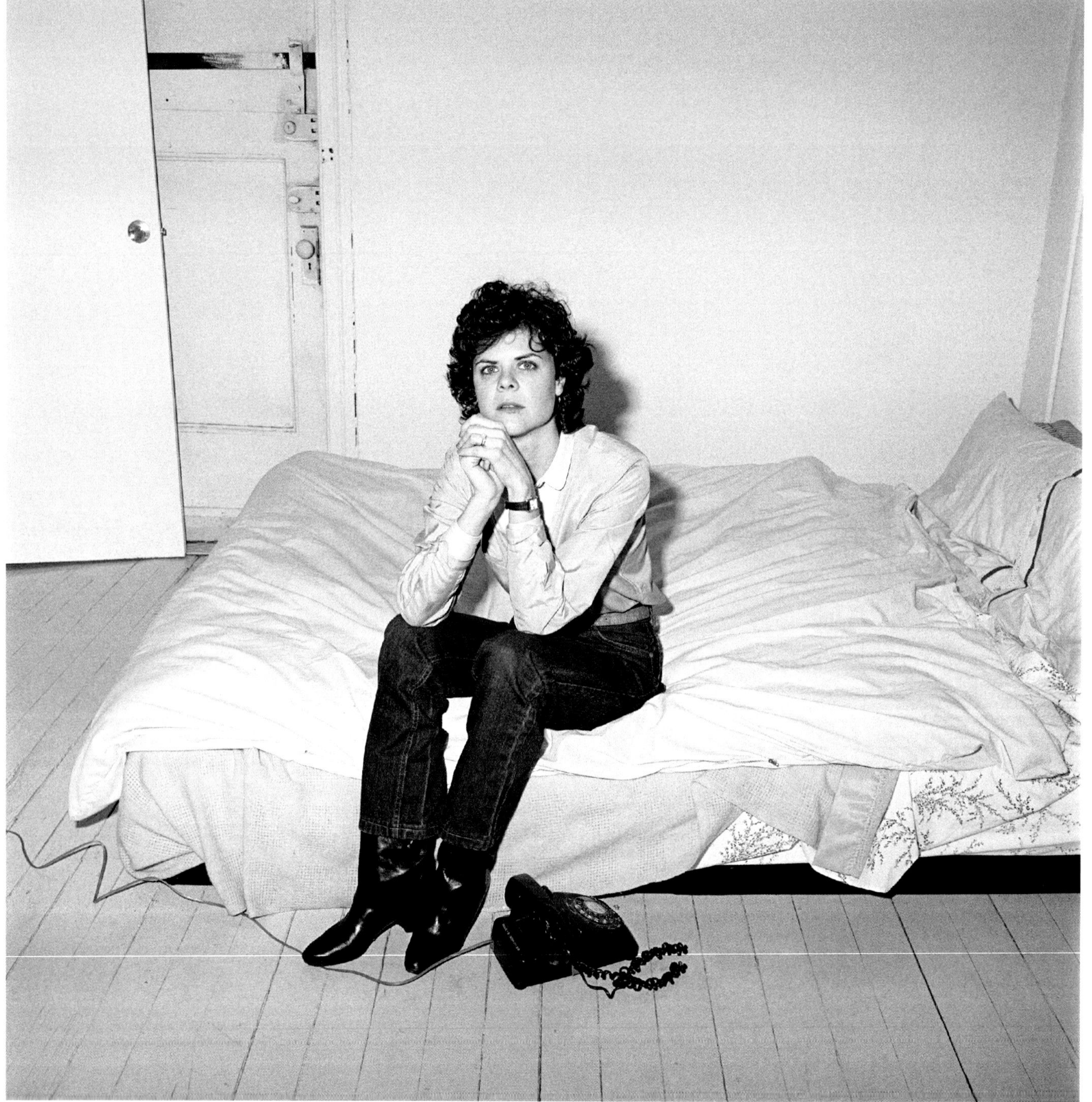

Bill Eggleston's Cousin, Mississippi, 1977

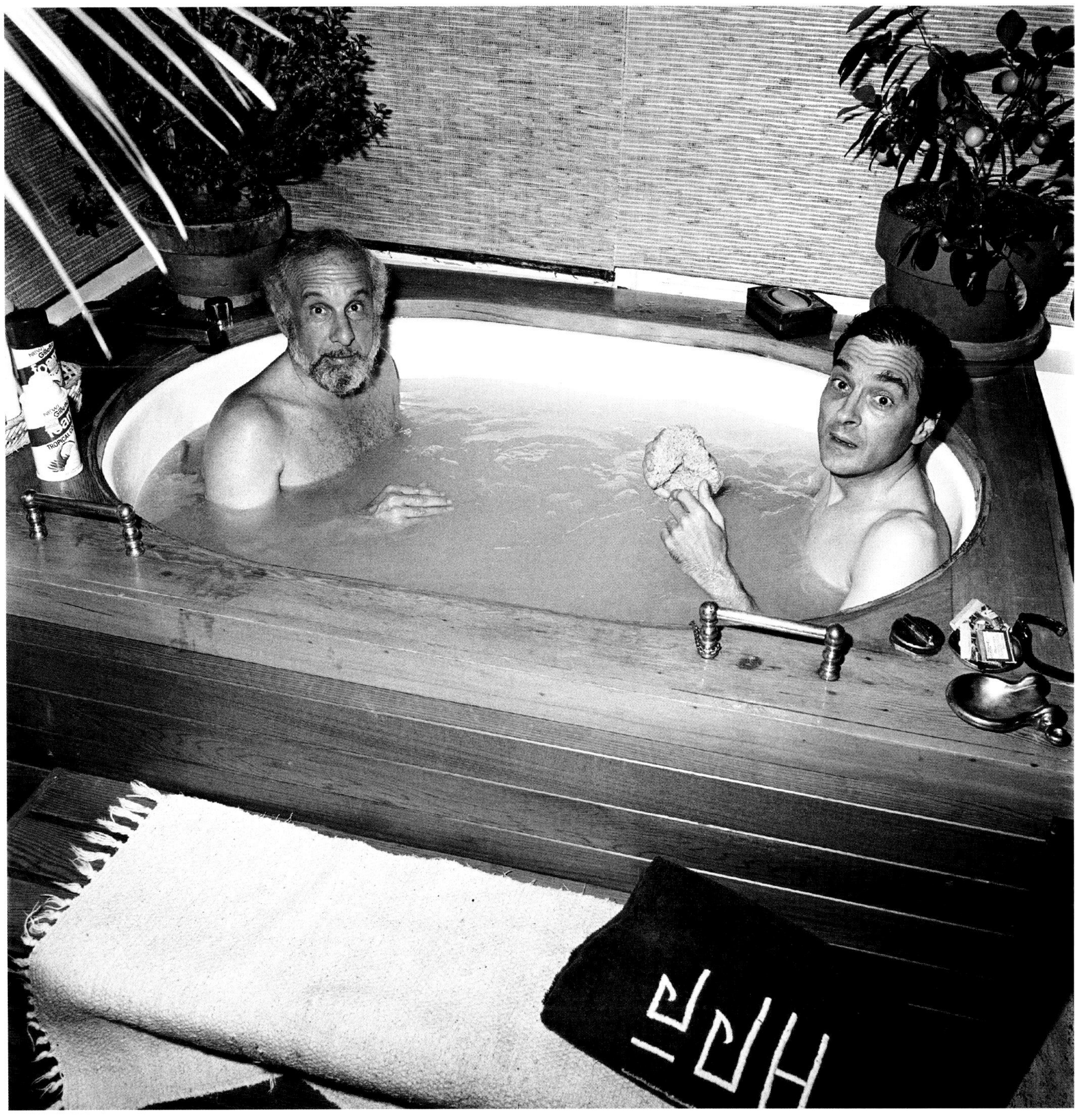

Collector and Artist, **Memphis, Tennessee, 1977**
All photographs © the artist/MUUS Collection

who lived as an outcast in Greenwood, Mississippi. In 1980, Fox Solomon would return to Mississippi to photograph the charred remains of Boring's home; he had died in a fire that year under mysterious circumstances. "Bill loved, I think, the wildness about Tom," one of Eggleston's friends told Fox Solomon, who was clearly curious about that wildness herself. "There's an overlap between an intellectualism and a kind of craziness," the friend said—he was talking about the Memphis bar scene, but he might as well have been describing Eggleston's whole strange demimonde, with its polite bubble baths, its dilapidated toys, its simmering tensions. Fox Solomon's photographs live in that overlap: They present a manicured exterior from which something unnamable is trying to escape.

Dan Piepenbring is the New Books columnist for *Harper's* magazine.

Curriculum
Nick Knight

To call Nick Knight a "fashion photographer" is an understatement. For four decades, the British image maker has explored the medium's bleeding edge through collaborations with the likes of Alexander McQueen, Björk, and Yohji Yamamoto. This year marks the twenty-fifth anniversary of SHOWstudio, the first platform to livestream fashion shoots and a creative nucleus for Knight's practice, which channels sculpture, painting, film, augmented reality, and artificial intelligence through his singular, hyperdigital vision.

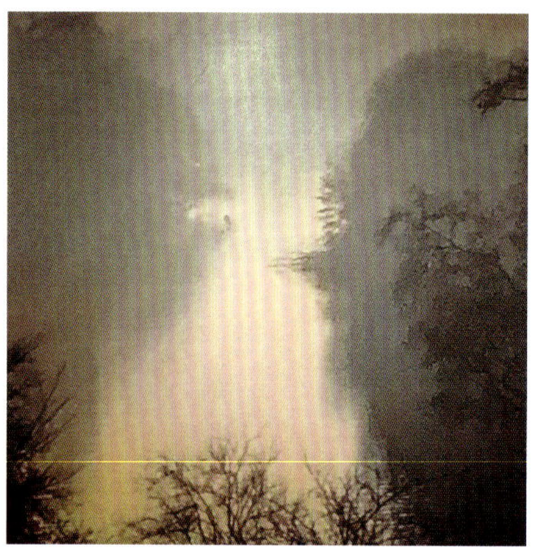

THE VIEW FROM RICHMOND HILL
Studying science at university, I often felt miserable and frustrated as I realized I had taken the wrong path with my studies. My student accommodation was on the eleventh floor of a tower block looking out over West London, and I would spend hours watching the skies, clouds, and setting sun while imagining pictures I wanted to take if I ever became a photographer. I left university after a year and enrolled in art college. The view over West London from Richmond Hill was painted many times by J. M. W. Turner and, surprisingly, has hardly changed since. It's very similar to the view I used to see from my student window.

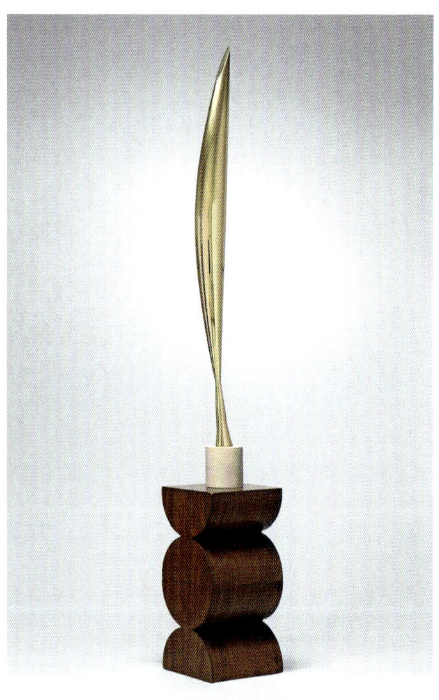

BIRD IN SPACE
Sculpture has increasingly become a passion for me. I'm extremely excited by creating sculptures as part of my own work, but my first love was Constantin Brancusi, especially *Bird in Space* (1932–40). He managed to make the form seem weightless and to give it the feeling of power and grace—almost of divinity. Brancusi concentrated not on the physical attributes of the bird but instead created a work all about the idea of flight.

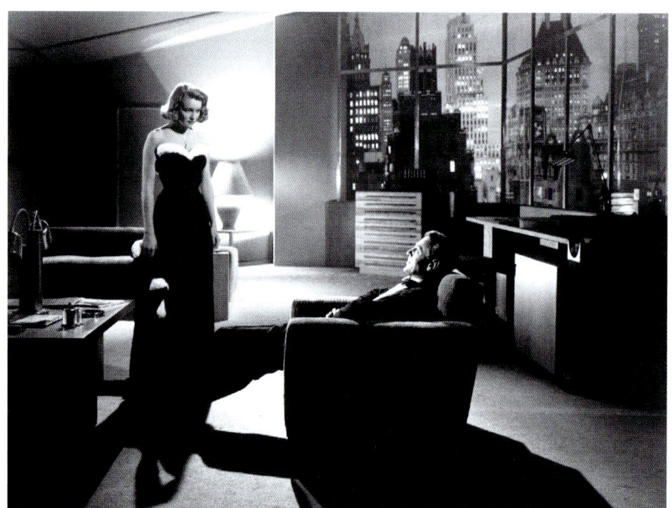

THE FOUNTAINHEAD
Apart from the really interesting narratives about man playing God in this 1949 film, it has always stayed with me because the scenes are so spectacularly lit. Working on fashion films, where every frame must be as beautiful as a still photograph, I have always appreciated and admired the incredible mastery of light in this film.

See page 6 for image credits.

THE THIRD WAVE

What if civilization, far from ending, has really just begun? In this 1980 book, Alvin Toffler describes a cresting "third wave" marked by reshaped family structures, remote work, and greater individualism, arguing that these shifts will require updated value systems. He also says that the path and transition to a new society will be bumpy, because the old power structures will not want to lose their control. This appears to be exactly what we are currently experiencing in so many conflicts across the world.

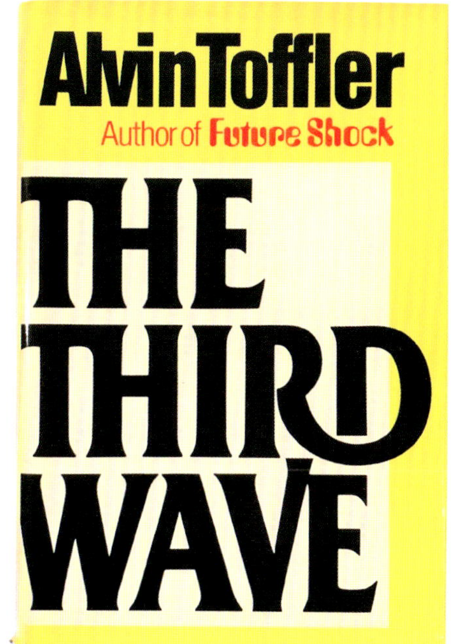

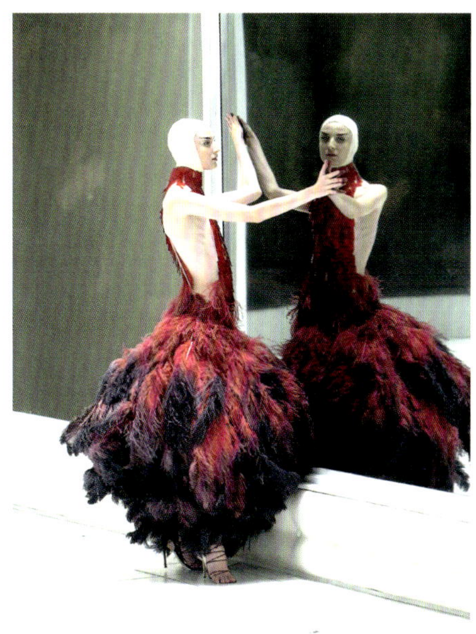

ALEXANDER MCQUEEN VOSS COLLECTION

One of the most powerful pieces of fashion theater or performance art I have ever seen! For his spring/summer 2001 *Voss* collection, Alexander McQueen had the whole of the front row—*Vogue* editors, actors, and all the most important people in fashion—sit for almost an hour staring at their own reflections in the mirrored surface of a huge cube in which he was presenting his show. The natural reaction was to eventually look down toward your feet, to avoid your own, and others', gaze. He got the whole fashion world to bow to him. Eventually, the lights went off in the room and on inside the two-way-mirrored glass box, turning the tables. Now the audience was invisible in the dark, like predators in the night, while their "prey"—the spectacle of models wearing McQueen's collection—was in full view.

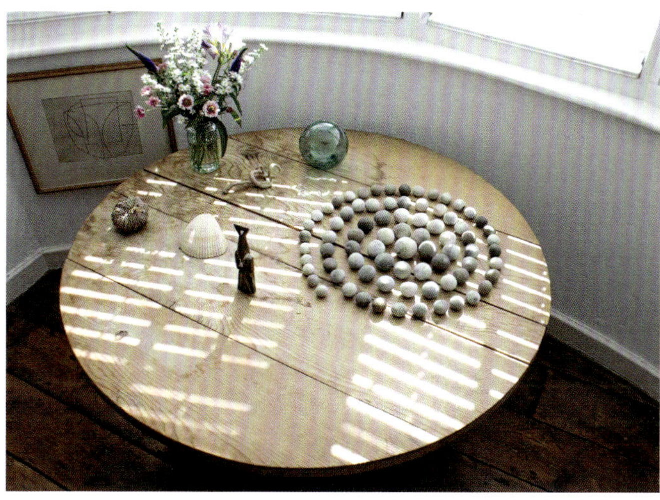

KETTLE'S YARD

Kettle's Yard in Cambridge always seems to me like the right way to see art, as opposed to in most galleries, which make it feel like a commodity. The space was previously the home of Jim Ede, a former assistant curator at the Tate, and his wife. Ede's friends would come to stay and often leave their art as gifts. His friends and acquaintances just happened to be some of the most amazing artists of the twentieth century. Ben Nicholson, Barbara Hepworth, and Constantin Brancusi are all on show, blended in with bowls of pebbles and little vases with fresh garden flowers. It is this feeling and approach to experiencing art that inspired me when I opened the SHOWstudio Gallery.

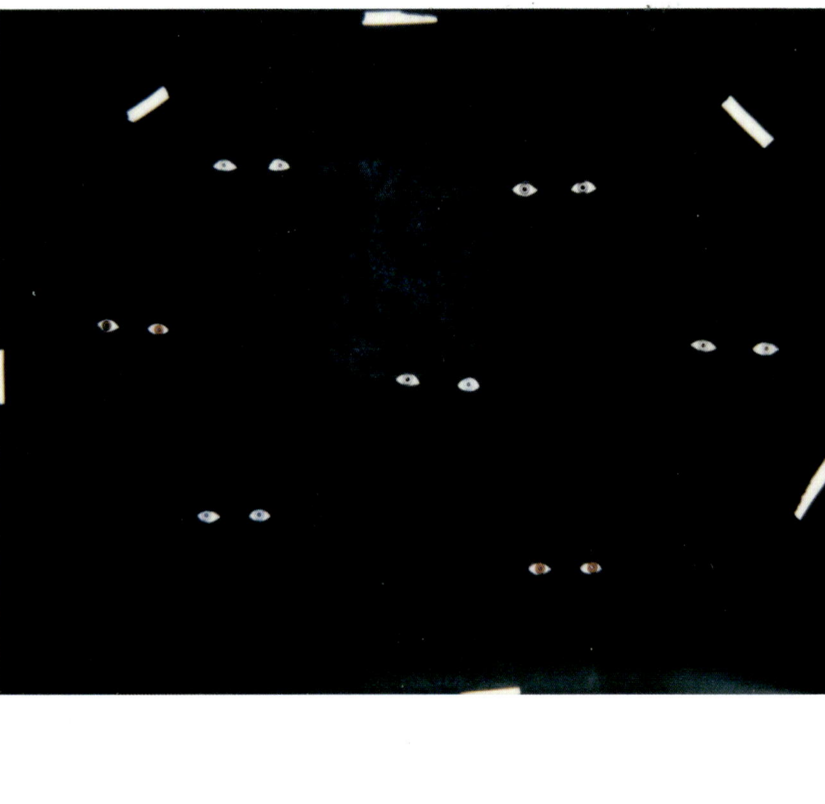

Sarah Charlesworth, *Test Frame (Eyes)*, ca. 1992–93

Secrets

We live in a strange, shape-shifting time, where the contours of an agreed-upon reality are in flux. On social-media feeds churned by data-driven AI, the plot thickens until it shatters into a thousand pieces. Conspiracy, once the precinct of supermarket tabloids, is becoming common sense. Against a backdrop of fractured politics, the intrigue around the Epstein files offers a lingua franca, an unsavory point of consensus that an illuminati have circled their Gulfstreams to protect their own.

Power, as the artist Taryn Simon has shown, is less a spectacle than a system. Simon has spent her career documenting the unseen structures that shape institutions, from flower arrangements to nuclear storage sites. "I've never been looking to expose, I've been looking carefully to understand," she tells us in these pages. It's a line that speaks to how photographs have always existed in a kind of gap between revelation and concealment.

Not all secrets are pernicious, of course. In an age of oversharing and eroded privacy, a well-guarded secret takes on a new currency, a means of opting out of a system that wants to know everything about you. The photographers featured in this issue show how a secret can be a powerful bond, a shared symbology among workers, a form of play, the basis of a riveting whodunit, or something that can't easily be put into words. Sarah Charlesworth and Alix Cléo Roubaud both left behind enigmatic bodies of images shrouded in open-ended questions. Charlesworth set her beguiling pictures up like magic tricks, only without a big "reveal." Roubaud delighted in the sorcery of the darkroom. "I want to make everything come up to the surface," she said. Like that of all the artists gathered here, her work asks not only what is hidden, but how and why we choose to look.

Dark Rooms

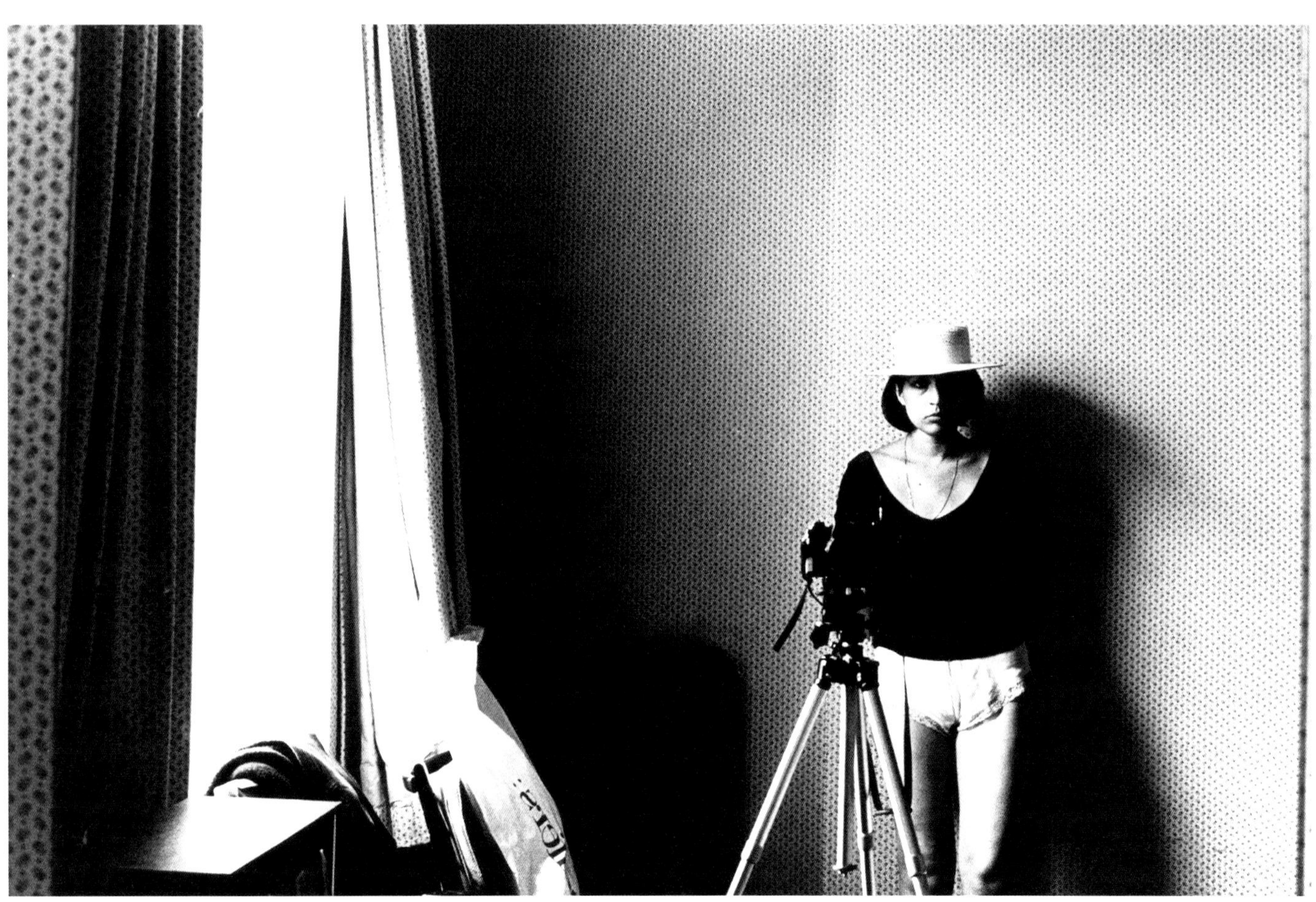

Alix Cléo Roubaud

Lou Stoppard

Alix Cléo Roubaud lived her life at the threshold, in states of in-between. Born in Mexico in 1952, she grew up in a nomadic way. Her father was a Canadian diplomat, and as a child she moved frequently. The family left Mexico when she was four, cycling through year-long stints in Egypt and South Africa before returning to Canada and then setting off again for postings in Portugal and Greece. She had an unplaceable accent, no clear first language. She spent her career, if one can call it that, in a state of transition—a perpetual state of *becoming* a photographer. She achieved no real success, being rejected by various galleries and critics before her death from a pulmonary embolism at thirty-one. She spent years of her youth wondering if she would be a poet or a novelist or a philosopher, and even after making the choice to focus firmly on photography in 1978 she sometimes found herself, especially when faced with dismissal, returning to thoughts of some other, different path.

Roubaud liked to work in the middle of the night. Her journal describes a basically nocturnal darkroom schedule: coming back from parties and printing from three to six in the morning, or five to eleven. She called these hours "my private night." After her 1980 marriage to the celebrated poet Jacques Roubaud, some twenty years her senior, she lived between the marital home and her own separate apartment one street away in Paris, moving back and forth, between happiness and despair, marital fulfillment (the pair often shared moments of intimacy as he was waking up for the day, and she was finally settling down to bed) and a cycle of love affairs, togetherness and solitude. She was often drunk, often depressed—both states that allow for a fundamental detachment from the world. To her, living was hard and full of mysterious, irreconcilable dimensions. Her images reflect this. Writing of a perfect summer day, a clear sky, a swimming pool, she remembered a recent suicide attempt and noted "the reasons for living have no overlap with the reasons for death."

In 1980, Roubaud wrote in her journal a thought directed to her husband: "Would that we could be the dark-room for one another." The journal is an odd, slippery document: a semipublic, semiprivate endeavor that was both personal diary and rolling letter to her husband, though he was forbidden from reading it in her lifetime. It was, he wrote in his introduction to the parts of it he published in 1984, her "secret expression." (The paradox of this phrase, given his decision to publish, further complicates the document's already unusual status and intentions).

The book, *Alix's Journal*, has come to be the best-known thing about her—alongside the film *Les photos d'Alix* (*Alix's Pictures*, 1980) by her friend Jean Eustache, which won the 1982 César Award for Best Short Film—giving Roubaud a notability that eluded her in her lifetime, despite the fact it represents only a small fragment of her life. Roubaud had kept a journal from adolescence, but her husband chose to publish only the later entries written between 1979 and 1983, during their relationship, thus framing her within the confines of their marriage. Our understanding of her life remains stunted, full of misunderstandings, secrets, and confusions, much like the interior world she inhabited and pictured. Her photographs offer visions that are dizzying and sliding: a wine glass spilling multiple times, a floating face, a dissolving body, nothing ever quite what it seems. In *Alix's Pictures*, Roubaud sits in her apartment and describes her photographs to a

Opposite:
University Arms Hotel, Cambridge, 1980

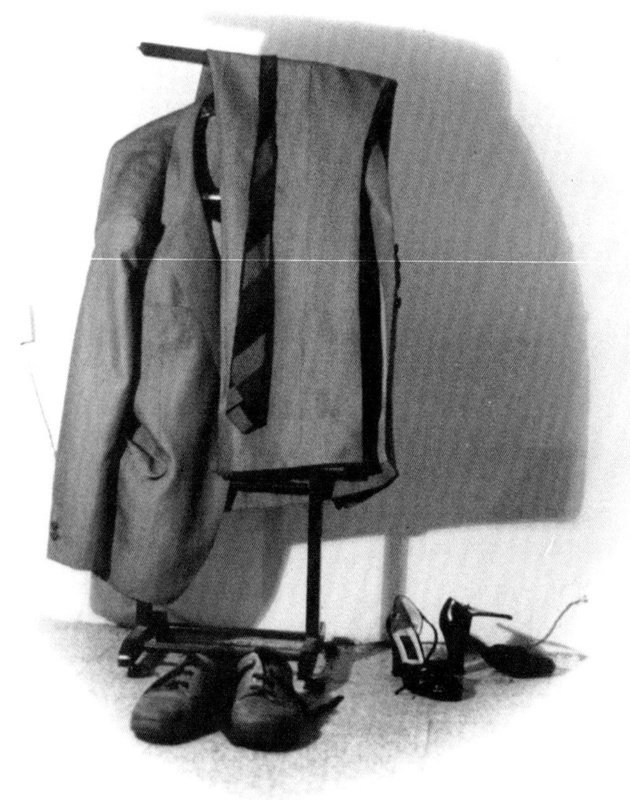

Venise, le 27 avril 1979–Paris, le 14 juillet 1979, 1979

young man, Eustache's son. Gradually her words depart from the images we see on-screen. A shoe is described as a self-portrait, a pillow as a beautiful body. The viewer is left confused, frustrated, amused, unsure of exactly at what point things fell out of sync.

Roubaud's thought to her husband is a complex assertion: A dark room is a solitary space, where one retreats, hidden. But it is also a space defined by emergence—by an activation of sorts, as things, images, become open, real, living. Roubaud referred to negatives as being like a "painter's palette" and sometimes spent up to ten hours on a single print, reveling in the chemical process. Writing in *Alix Cléo Roubaud: A Portrait in Fragments* (2024), Hélène Giannecchini—who as director of the Alix Cléo Roubaud Foundation has done much to organize the work and writings into a coherent archive and bring new attention to the photographer's practice—describes her techniques as varied and ambitious, making use of inks in chemical baths and applied toners, and even scratching her negatives or drawing directly on the print's surface. "For Alix the darkroom was a crucial step in the material and symbolic making of a photograph," she writes. "Everything that happened before that was of little importance. The quality of a photograph depended very little on the shot itself. It was at the developing and printing stage that Alix came close to the final work." "I told you," Roubaud herself wrote, "I want to make everything come up to the surface."

As objects, photographs often reveal themselves like secrets unearthed—bolts of information or memory, stumbled upon in "biscuit boxes or chocolate boxes, photographs in brown envelopes," as Roubaud wrote in her journal of finding a trove of her husband's childhood family photographs. But they spark mysteries too. What is it that they depict? Not the future, not the past. As Roubaud herself put it, "When you see this, it will no longer be." As soon as the image is made, the scene or person it depicts is gone, lost, already finished, already dead, ungraspable.

Roubaud was never formally trained—she completed a single short course at the photography school in Arles—but was already pondering the conundrums of the medium from a young age. Writing in a letter to a childhood friend at age fourteen, her words are probing and startingly mature, anticipating her later voice and style. She describes receiving a new photograph of her friend, grown-up, taller, more beautiful than she remembered: "And faced with an image on a piece of paper, my eyes falter, stubbornly persist, try desperately to come to terms with the mobile reality that it represents. Weary of this futile effort, I tuck the photo away into my purse, unsatisfied."

Lou Stoppard is a London-based writer and curator.

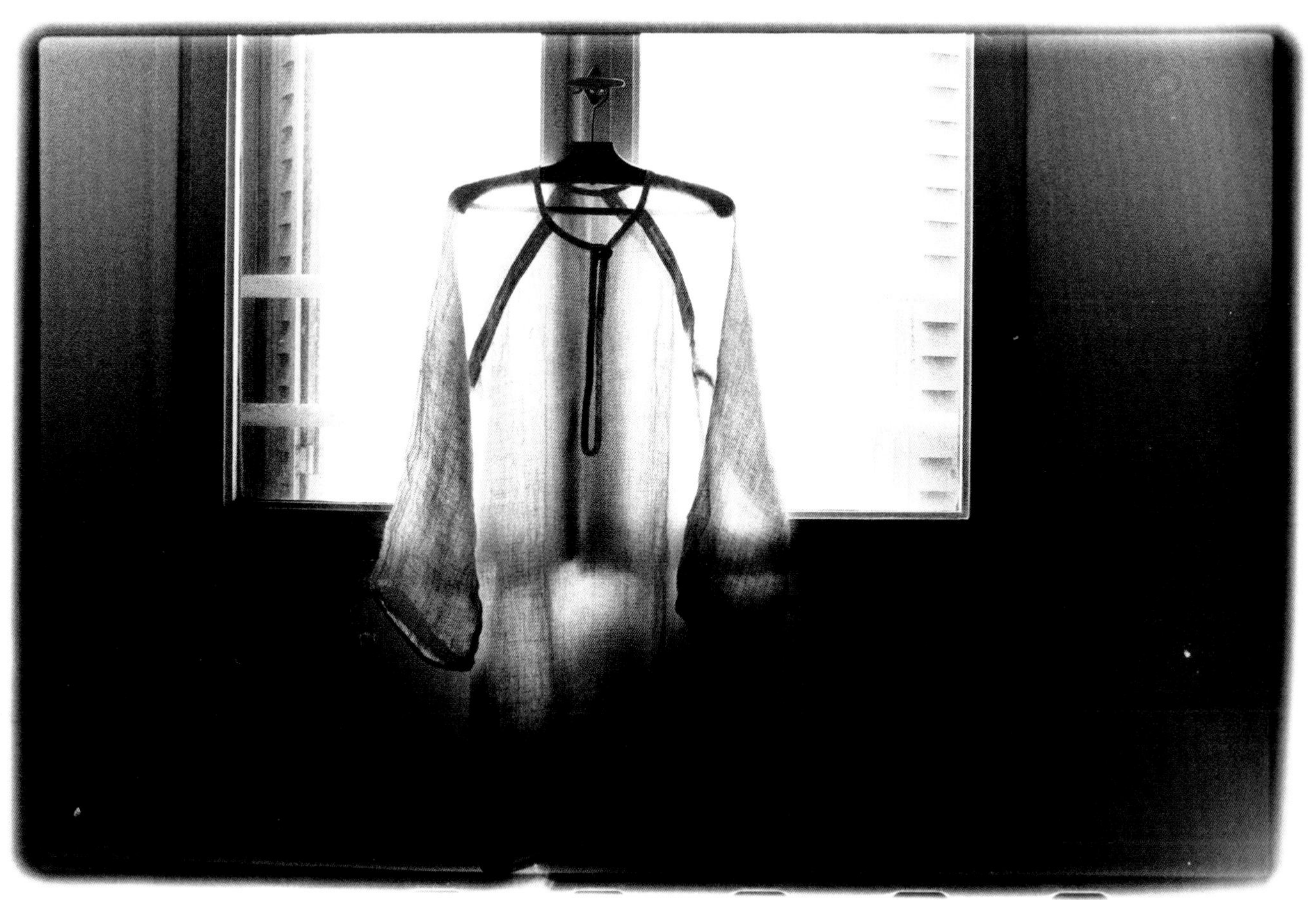

Untitled, 1980

Non contact theory,
1980–81

The mother's eyes, 1981

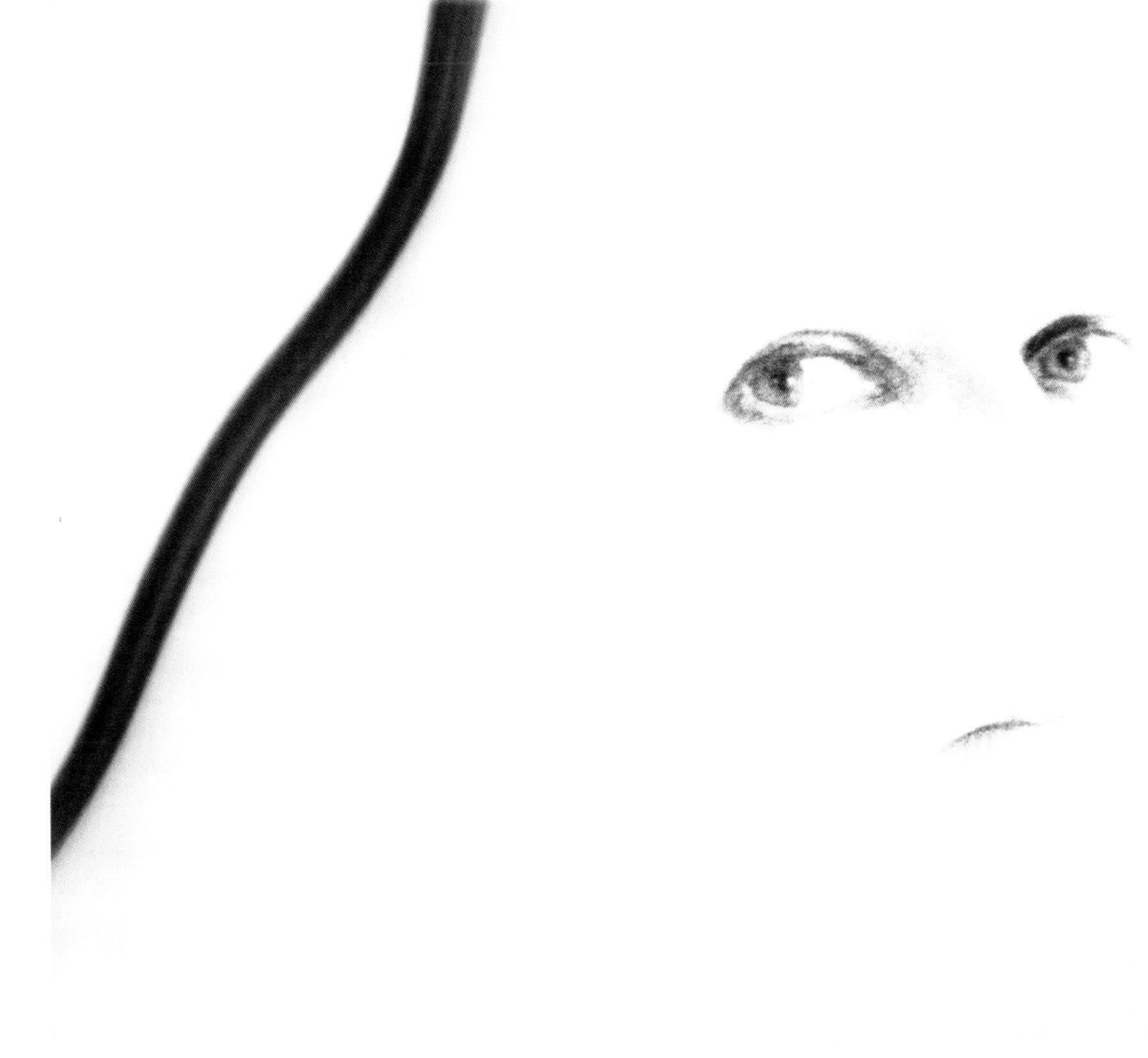

Untitled, 1979

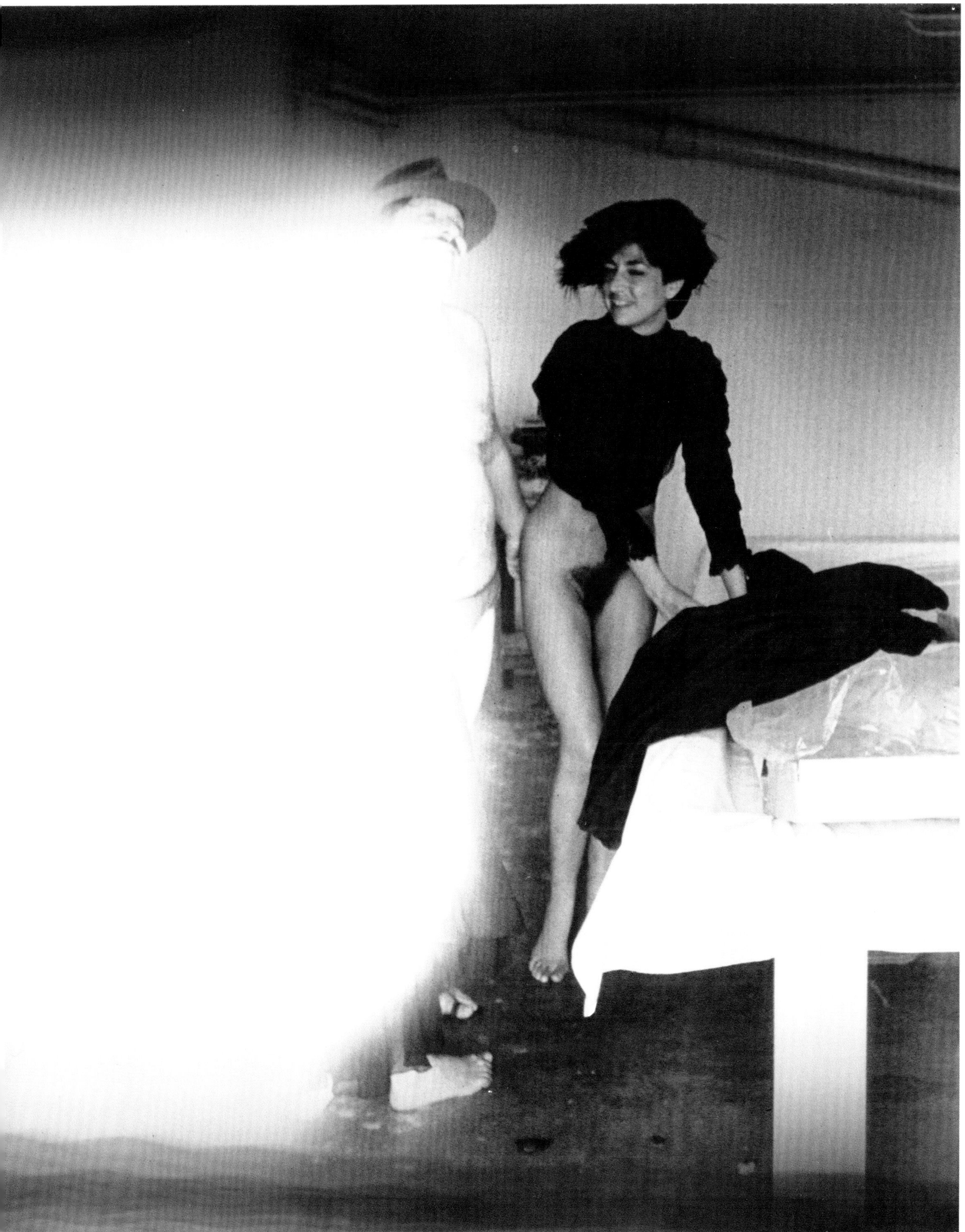

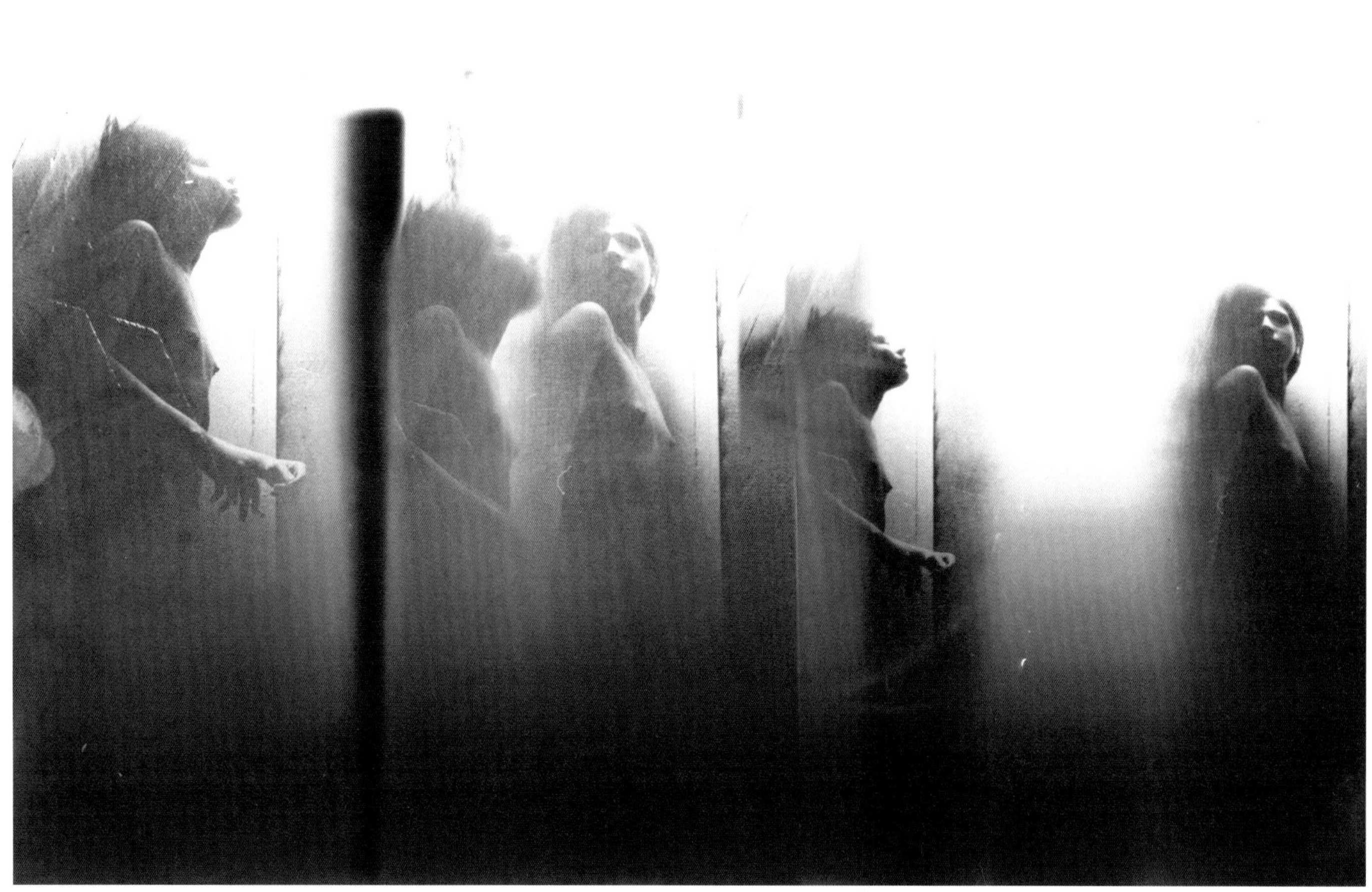

Untitled (Correction of perspective in my bedroom), 1980

The Last Room, Ottawa 1973–Paris 1979, 1979

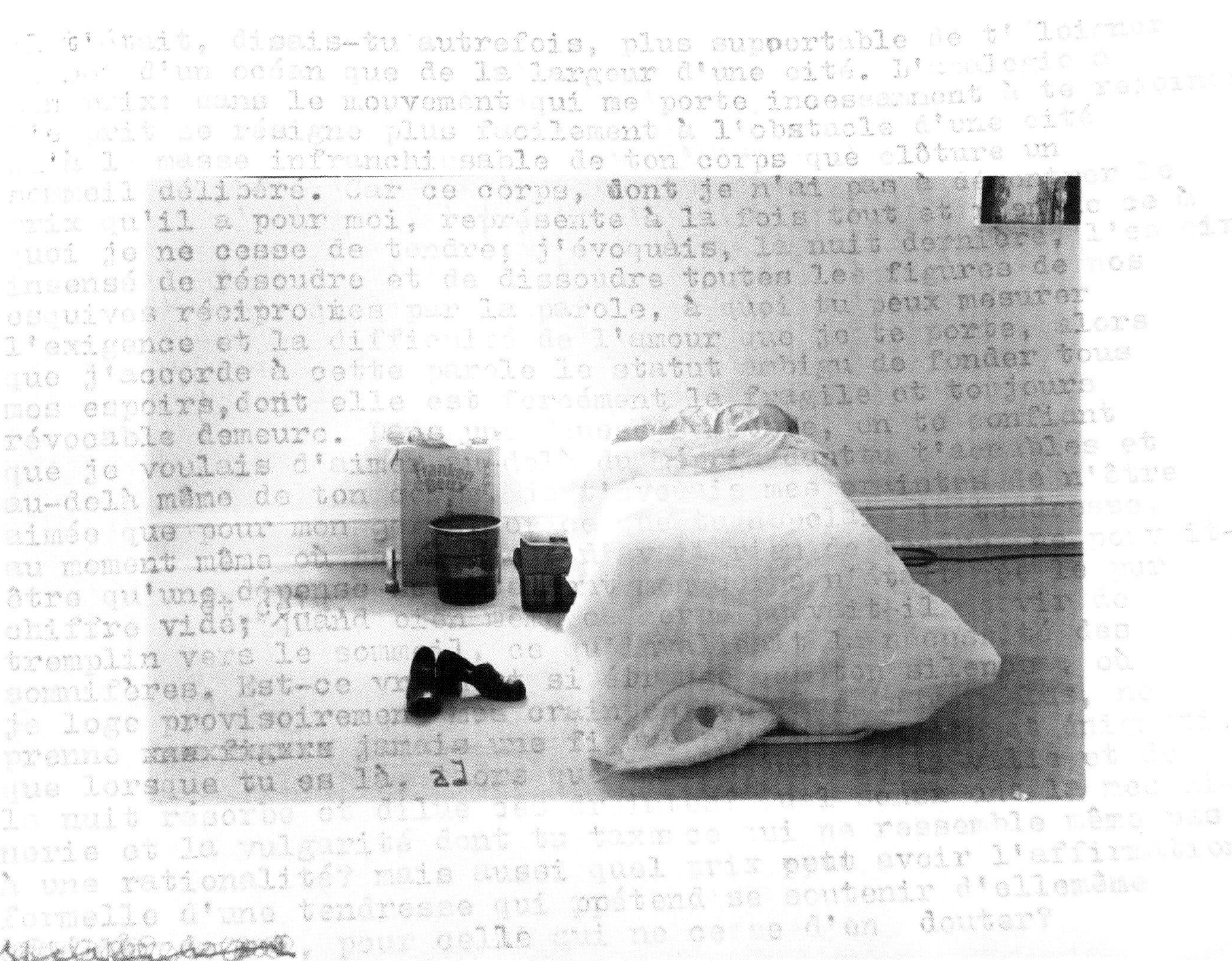

Pornographie bourgeoise, 1981

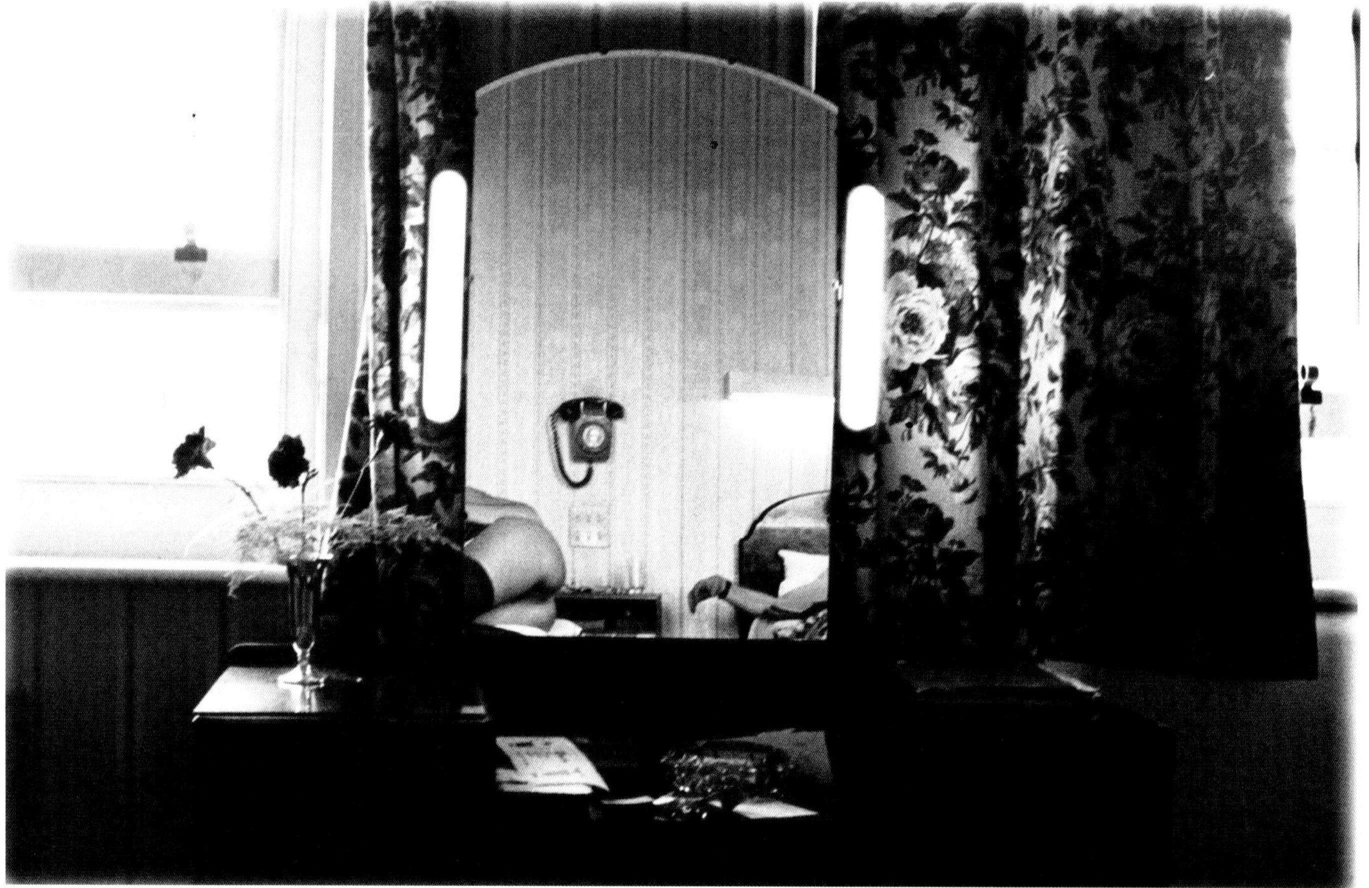

***Two sisters who are not sisters*, 1980**
All photographs courtesy Estate of Alix Cléo Roubaud and Galerie Buchholz

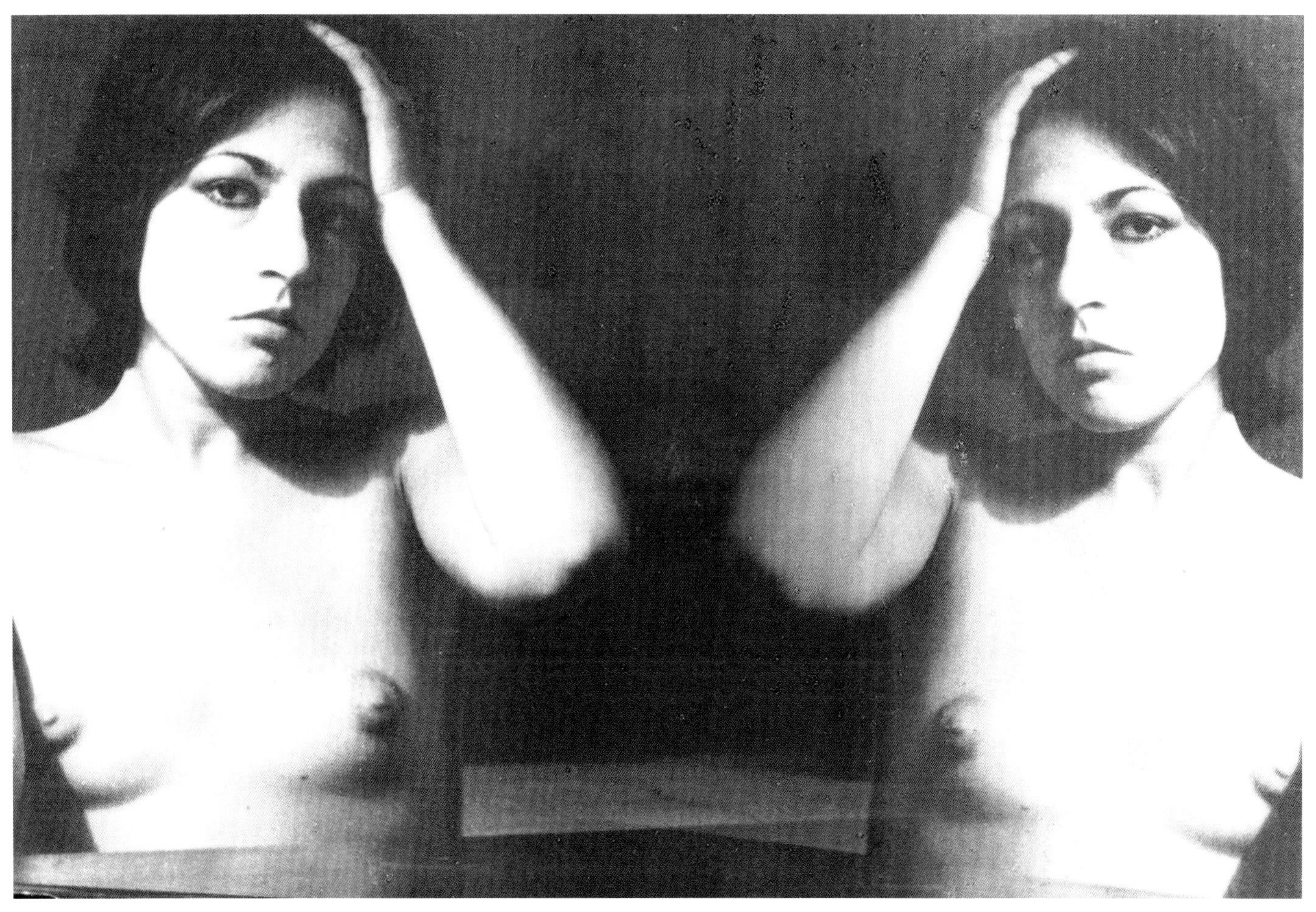

Iñaki Bonillas
Barragán's Closets

Ana Karina Zatarain

When I visited Luis Barragán's home and studio, it struck me as an ode to the ennobling quality of solitude. Years later, I shared this thought with a man I was dating, who countered that, during his own visit, he had been overwhelmed by the sense that the home was the physical manifestation of a repressed sexuality. Looking back now, I can see that our interpretations revealed more about each other than about the architect or his house, though it is indeed rumored that Barragán lived a closeted life, and his closets, as it happens, are what this piece is about—sort of.

Casa Luis Barragán sits on a dead-end street in Mexico City. Its architect, arguably Mexico's greatest, lived there alone for four decades, until his death in 1988. Six years later, it was opened to the public for visits; ten years after that, it was enshrined as a UNESCO World Heritage Site. Today, the immaculately preserved home receives hundreds of monthly visitors, many of them meekly reverent architecture students hoping, almost praying, for the pilgrimage to unlock in them some profound understanding of Barragán's masterful design language. Casa Luis Barragán harbors many secrets. Its flat facade is unpainted and unassuming, its labyrinthine interiors possessed of a beauty at once familiar and inscrutable—like your grandmother's house, if it was all warmth and texture but devoid of the often ugly utilitarian objects on which domesticity relies.

So where did Barragán store his unsightly essentials? "In all the closets," the artist Iñaki Bonillas told me recently. We were discussing the 2016 exhibition *Secretos* (Secrets), in which Bonillas stealthily placed art objects and photographs inside the house's many closets, drawers, and obscured corners. By being itself hidden from view, the exhibition pointed to the idea of secrecy. The eponymous book, not so much a catalog of the show as an extension of it, opens with black-and-white photographs that evoke the project's detective-like nature: Shots of various corners of the house are illuminated by the circular glow of a flashlight. Other images show close-ups of the imprints left by pieces of furniture over carpets and rugs, exposing the contrast between surfaces worn by time and those protected from it.

Most of the photographs document the works that Bonillas planted around Casa Luis Barragán: various conceptual pieces that reference art history and pop culture as they relate to the space. "I approached this project thinking that my dialogue was with Barragán and the house," said Bonillas, "but soon after, another presence appeared: the ghost of Marcel Duchamp." Duchamp's female alter ego, Rrose Sélavy—a homophonic pun on the French phrase for "eros, that's life"—came to Bonillas's mind while he wandered the house of a man whose sexuality remained veiled but whose architecture, devoted as it is to the mysteries of intimacy, is often read as erotically charged. In one drawer, Bonillas laid a print of Hieronymus Bosch's *The Garden of Earthly Delights* below a magnifying glass that highlights a mussel shell; in a separate closet, he placed a plate full of the same bivalves, symbols of lust and entrapment. "Because Barragán's sexuality is so taboo, so difficult to discuss without offending the sensibilities of many scholars of his work, it becomes the thing one most wants to talk about when one is inside his house," said Bonillas.

Perhaps my ex-boyfriend was right all along. And yet, *Secretos* confronts eros subtly, indirectly, adding to the tension of the space rather than defusing it. In this sense, Bonillas amplifies Barragán's architecture by refusing revelation. Something always remains hidden.

Ana Karina Zatarain is a writer living in Mexico City.

All photographs from the series *Secretos* (Secrets), Casa Luis Barragán, Mexico City, 2016
Courtesy the artist and Estancia Femsa

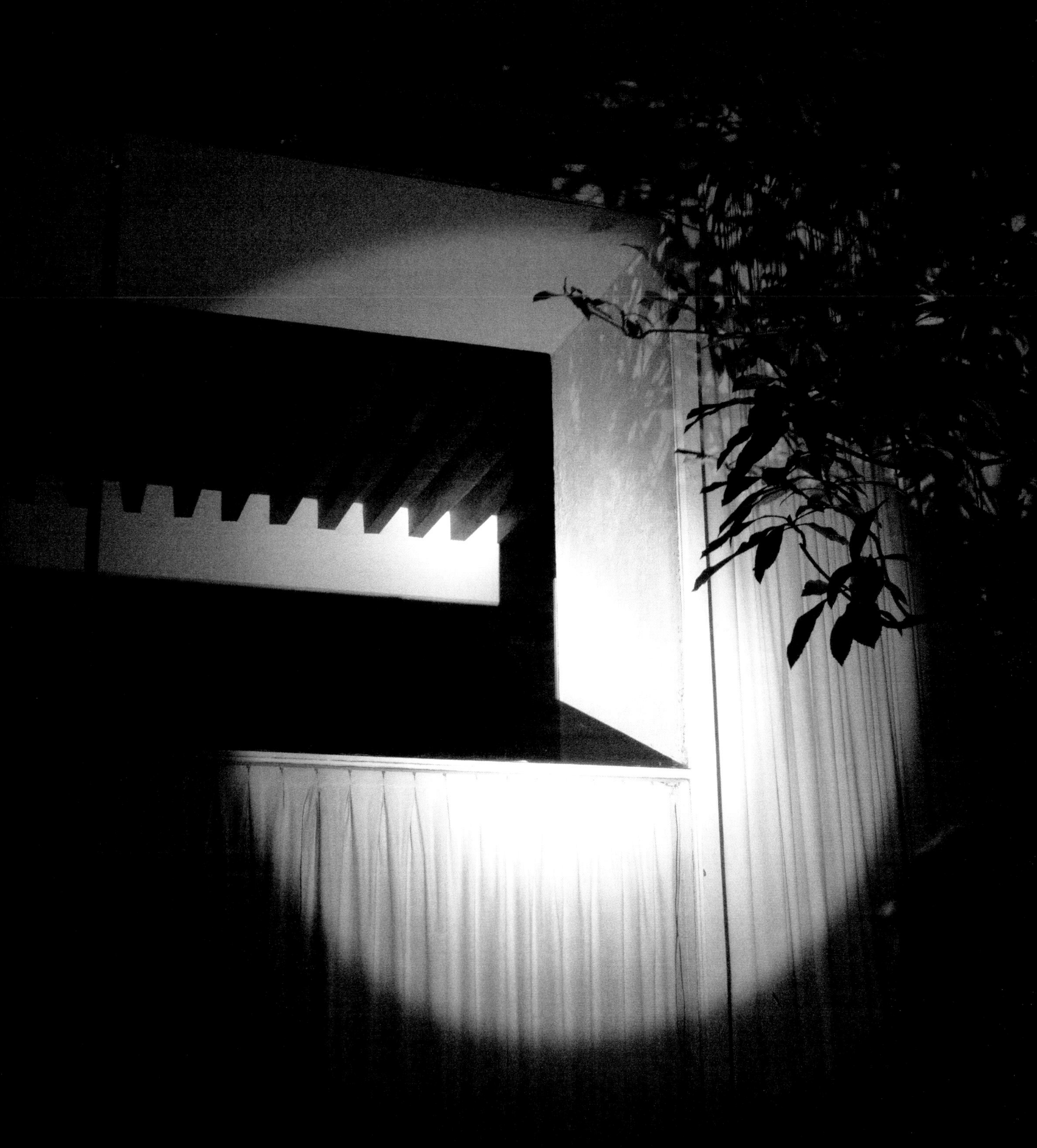

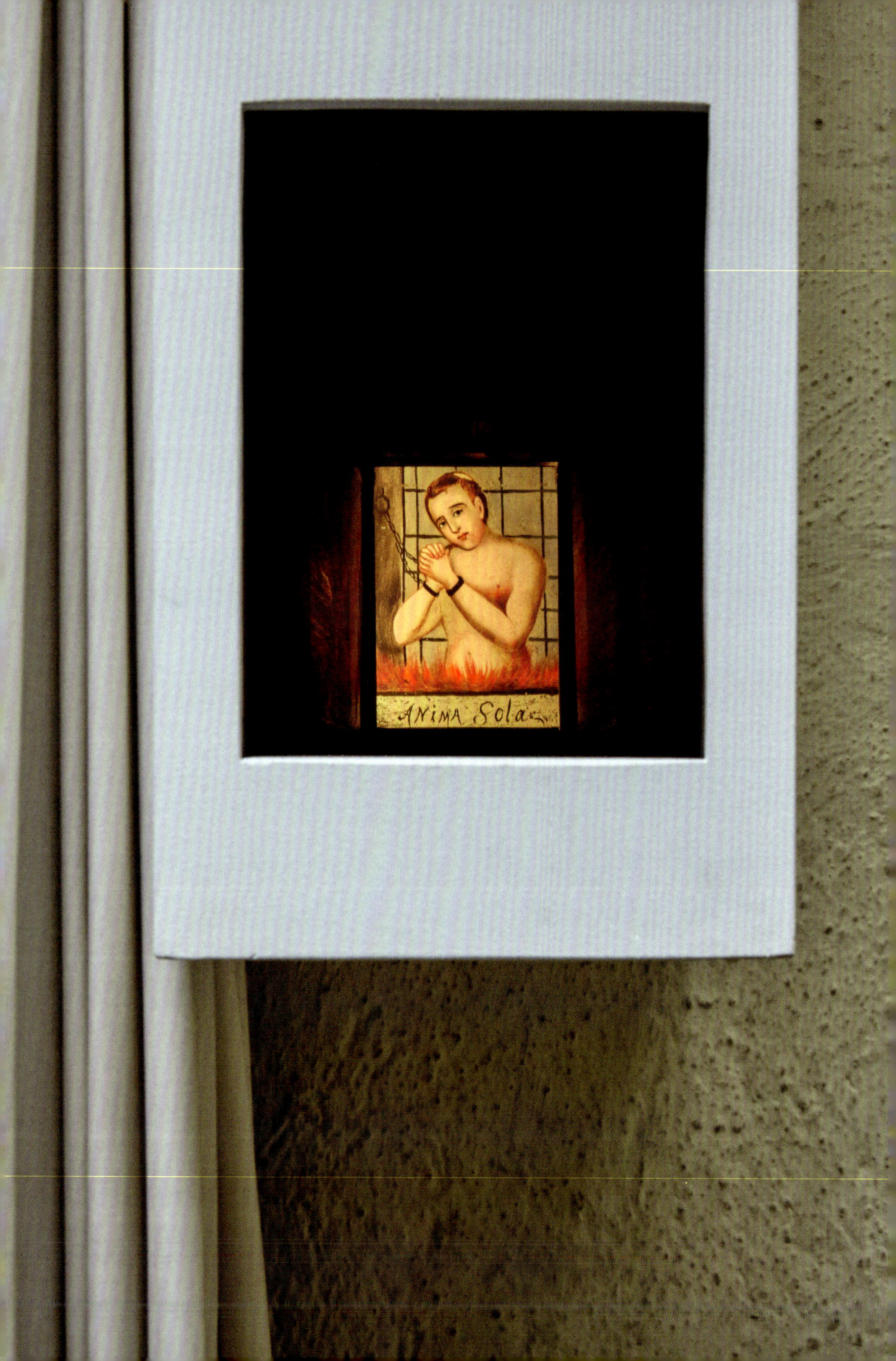
ANIMA Sola

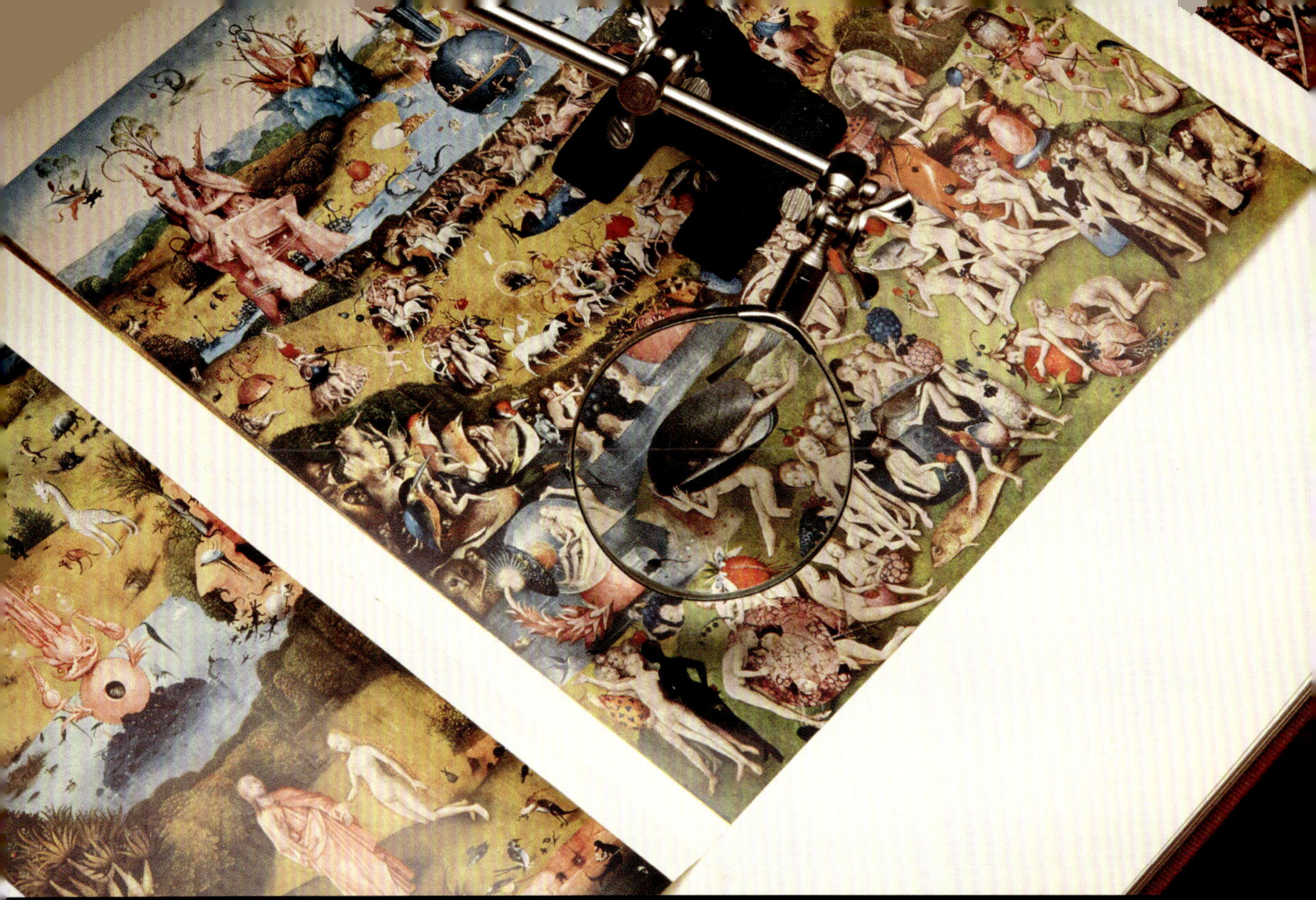

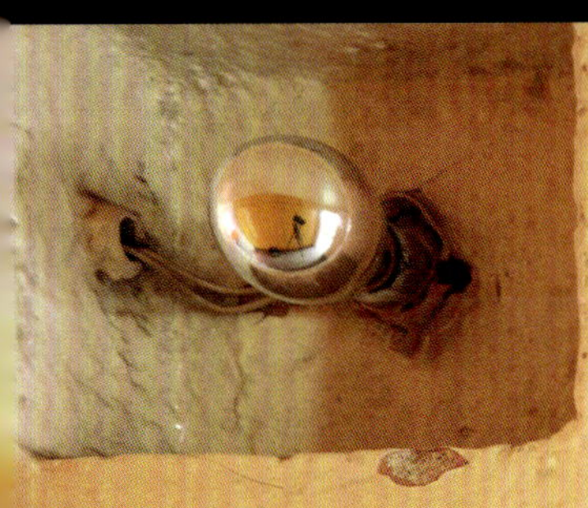

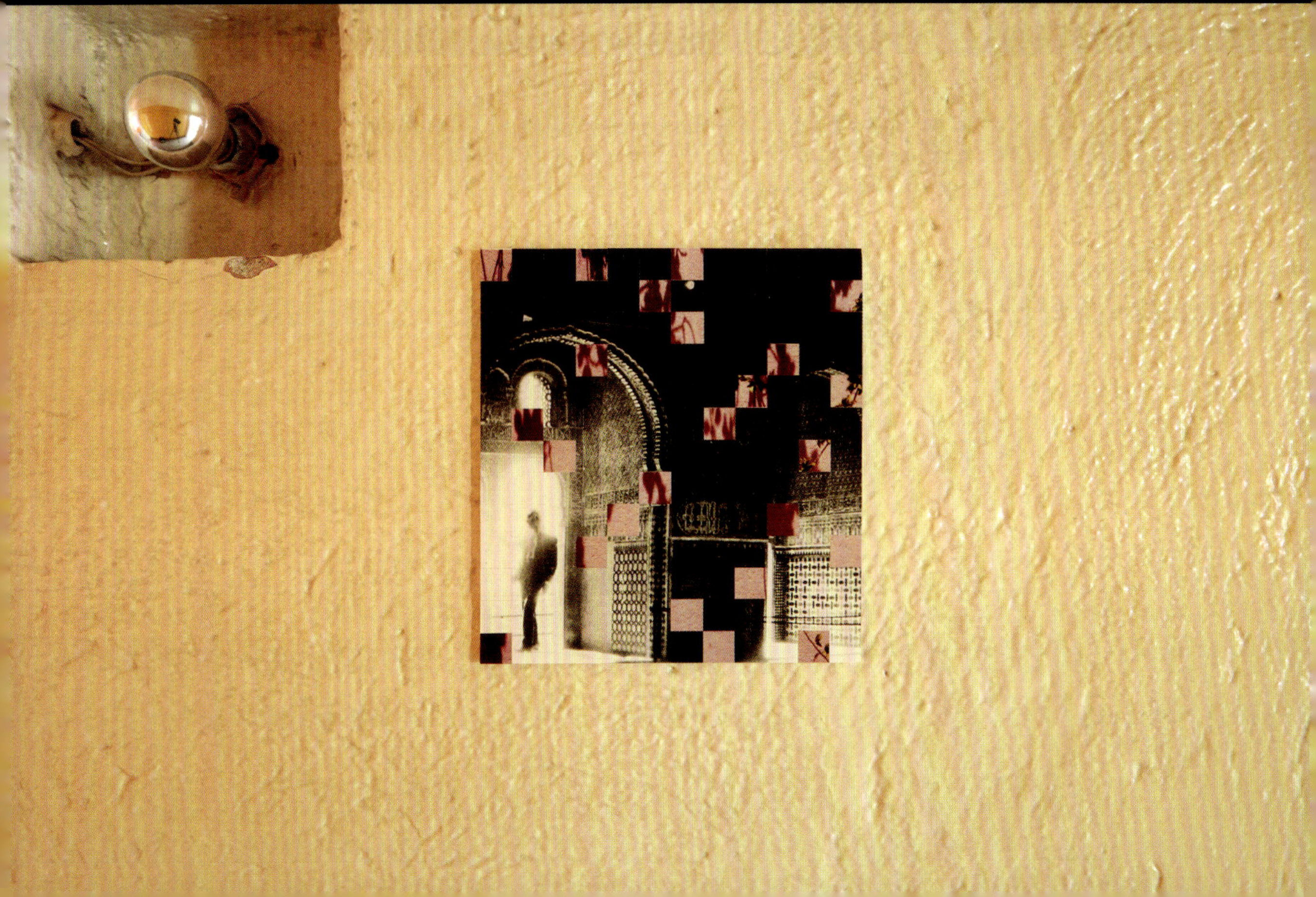

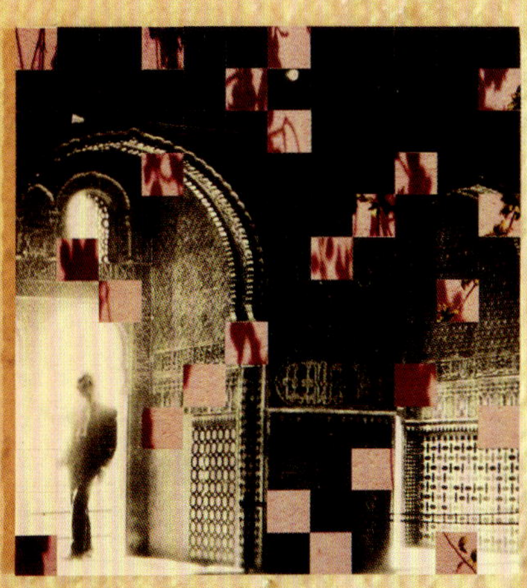

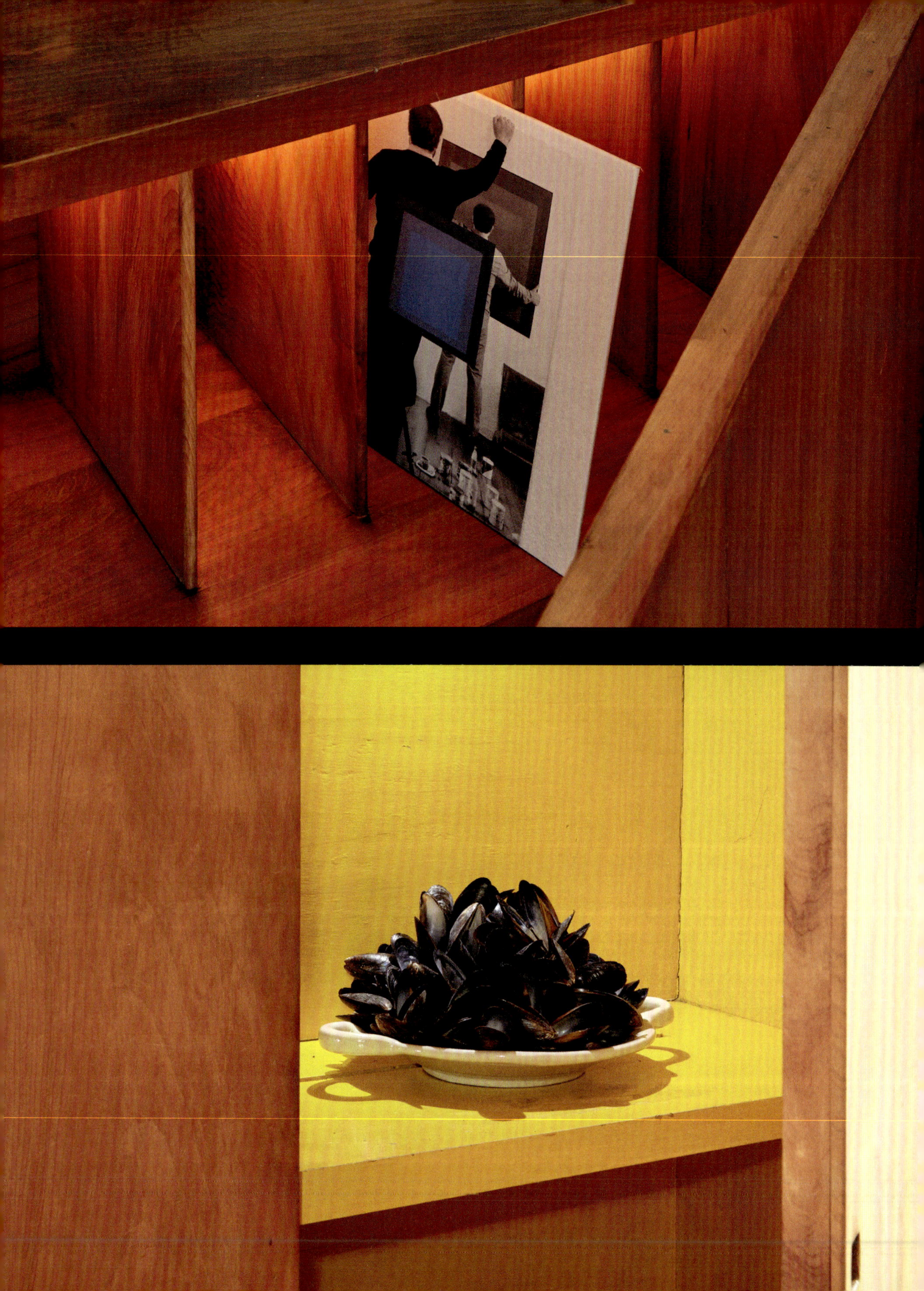

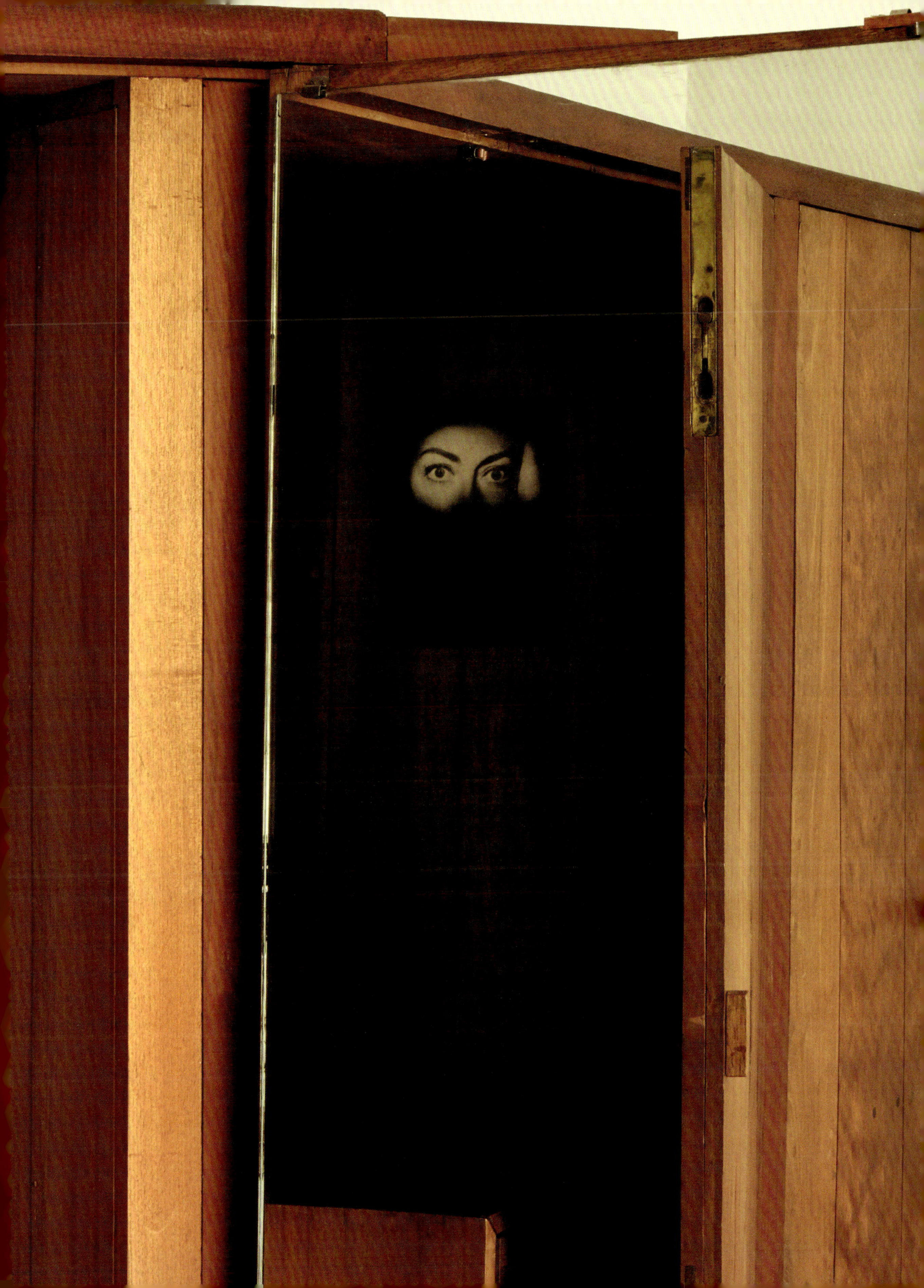

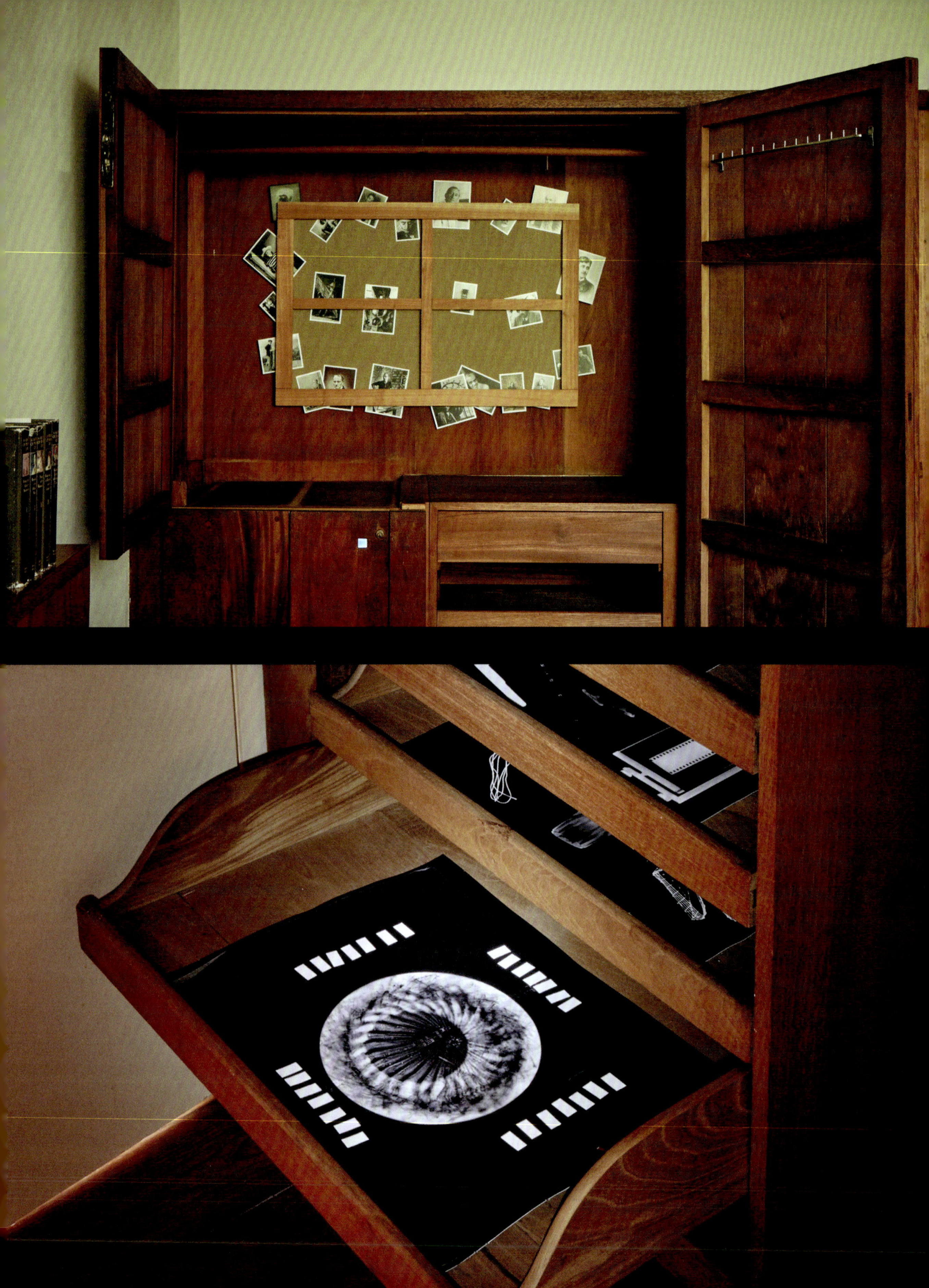

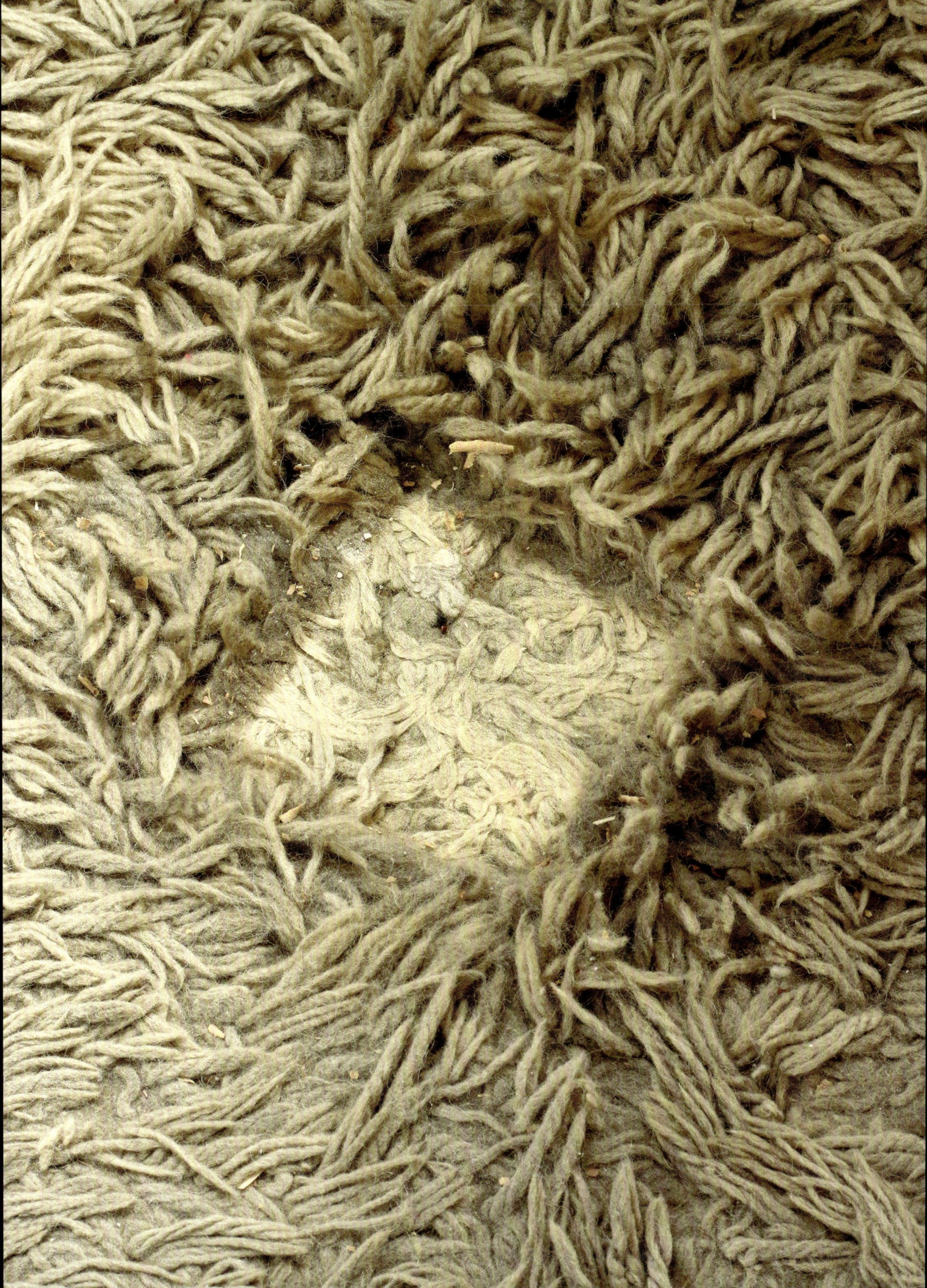

Polly Brown *Signs & Signals*

Thessaly La Force

Certain gestures intended for discretion can, paradoxically, become known. When, for example, Queen Elizabeth II wanted to end a conversation, she would twist her gold wedding band, alerting her minders to interrupt. Or consider the airplane stewardess who would flash her hands—palms forward, fingers out—in front of her forehead like they were antlers, signaling to her colleagues that a bachelor party (or *stag do*, as it's commonly called in England) was onboard. These are just a couple of the gestures that the British photographer Polly Brown began researching, documenting, and visually reinterpreting over the last several years, resulting in a portfolio published here for the first time. To her, they operate like secrets, intended to communicate an idea, action, or status to the indoctrinated.

Photographed in soft light against a flat paper backdrop with models dressed in similar anonymous-looking attire, Brown's images appear to belong to a vintage textbook, a manual one wishes actually existed for navigating the real world (Bruno Munari's charming 1958 taxonomy of Italian hand gestures also comes to mind). Her discoveries span centuries—my favorite might be the specific way two Romans used to greet each other: by gripping the other's forearm to check that neither was carrying a knife. Or how a casino spotter, with the subtlest downward swipe of an index finger, signals to a blackjack player to "twist," or take a hit. Others are more personal, such as the way Brown's two children interlock their index fingers to make a pact not to talk about something.

If Brown's starting point was a variety of secret handshakes, she eventually found them less intriguing. After all, many were fairly obvious, and not that secret anymore. "If you're going to do something secret, not only must the gesture be secret but the thing you are saying should be super secret too," she told me. This led her to explore different professions in which essential information must be communicated in front of others but without anyone knowing, from thieves to croupiers, waiters to cruisers to spies. A tug at a collar. A flick of a wrist. A finger lodged in a specific pocket.

Brown delights in language but also its garbled codes, as seen in an earlier project of hers exploring the wide-ranging universe of idioms. The Japanese, for example, have an expression to describe when one feigns friendliness or naivete: "putting on a cat". Brown's accompanying image, of a young woman holding a black cat over her head, is both playful and strange, rendering the idiom into a funny kind of literalness. "I was interested in how the body's been used in theater, imagery, and paintings to stand for a greater narrative or another secondary reading to something. And that took me to hand symbols and signals," she explained. If our faces can give everything away, our hands may be our best means of keeping it strictly between a trusted few.

Thessaly La Force is a writer living in New York.

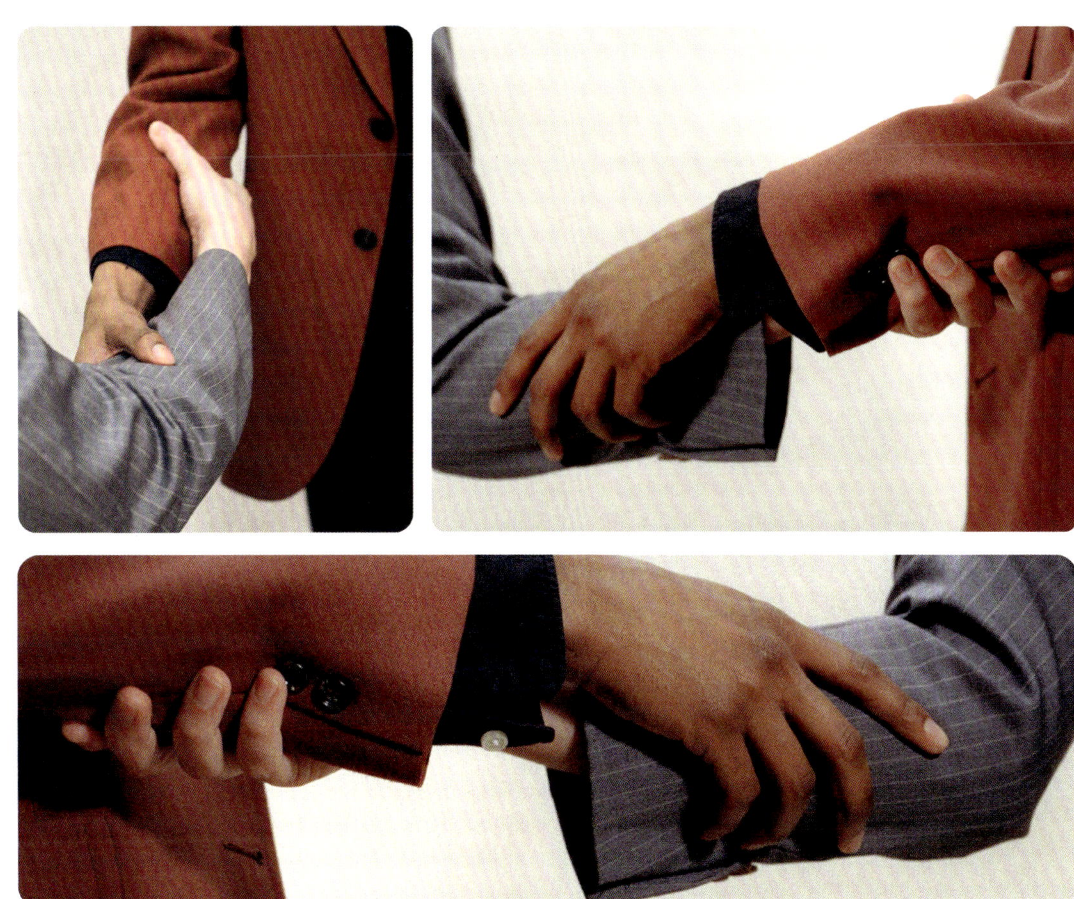

No Knife

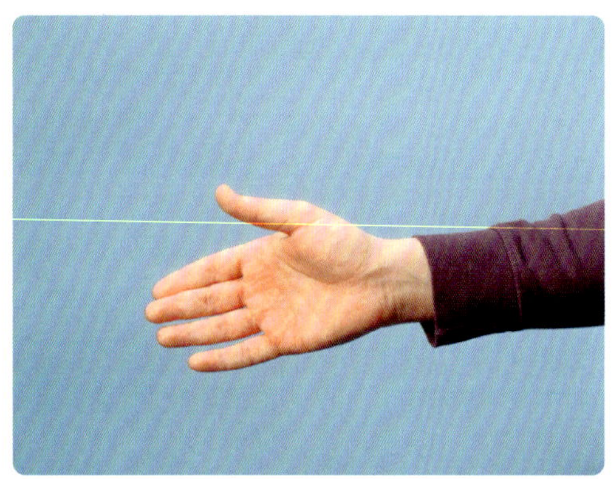

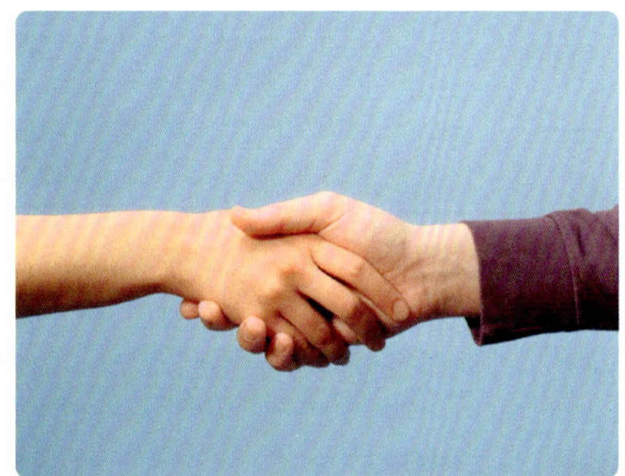

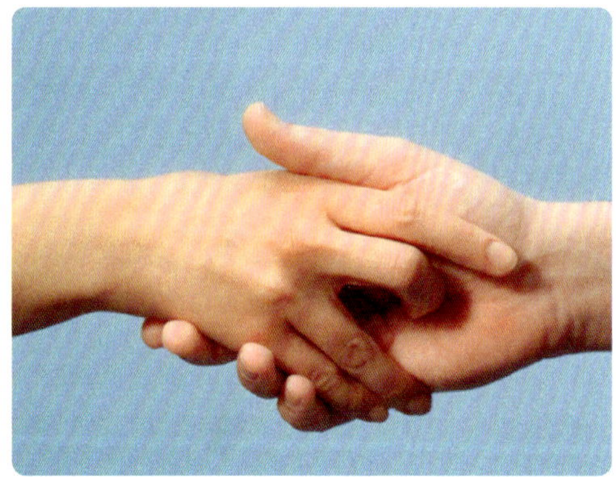

"The Tickler"
(Interested)

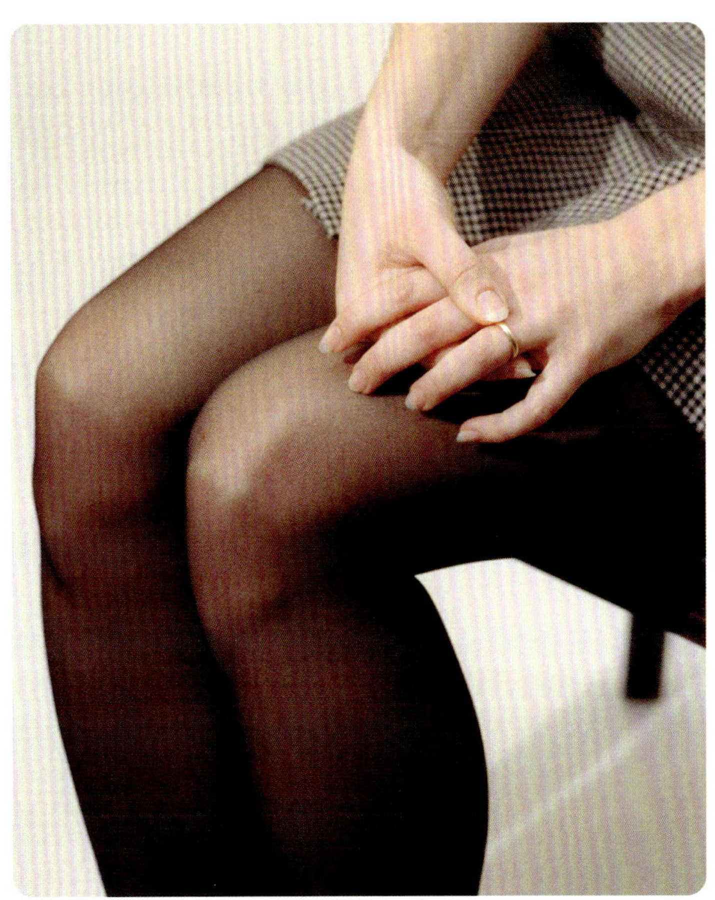

Interrupt

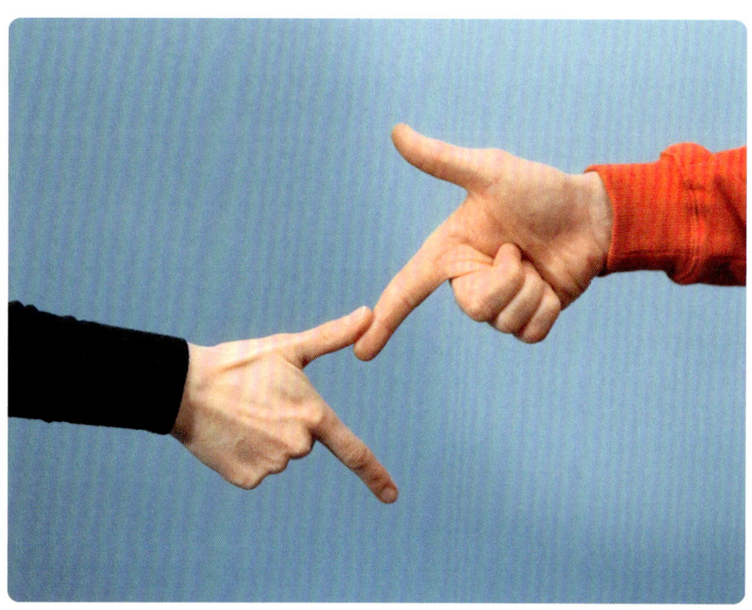

Top / Bottom

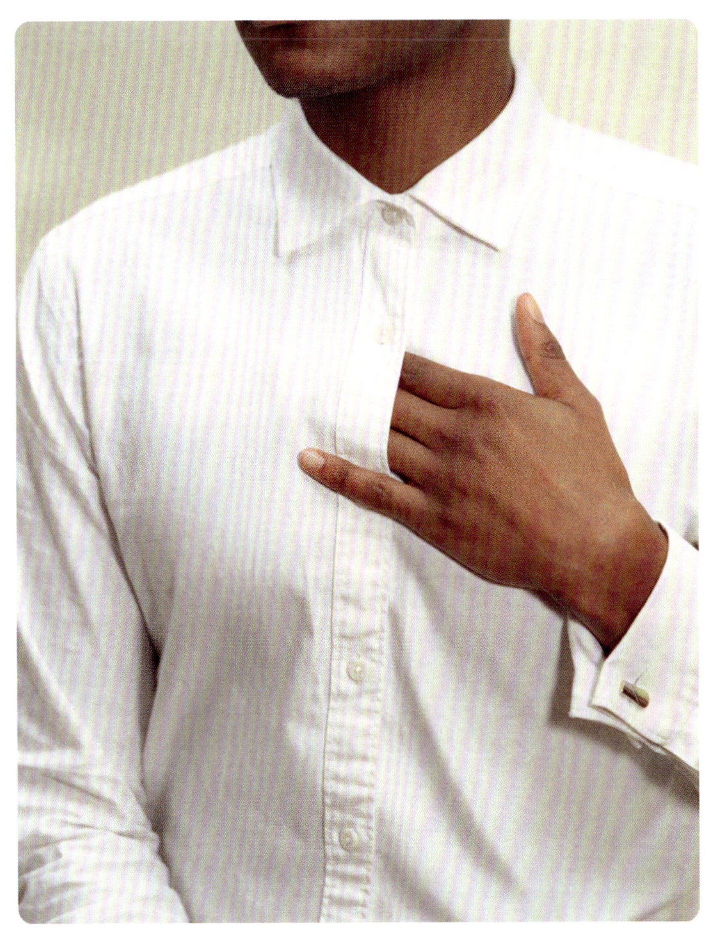

Big Spender

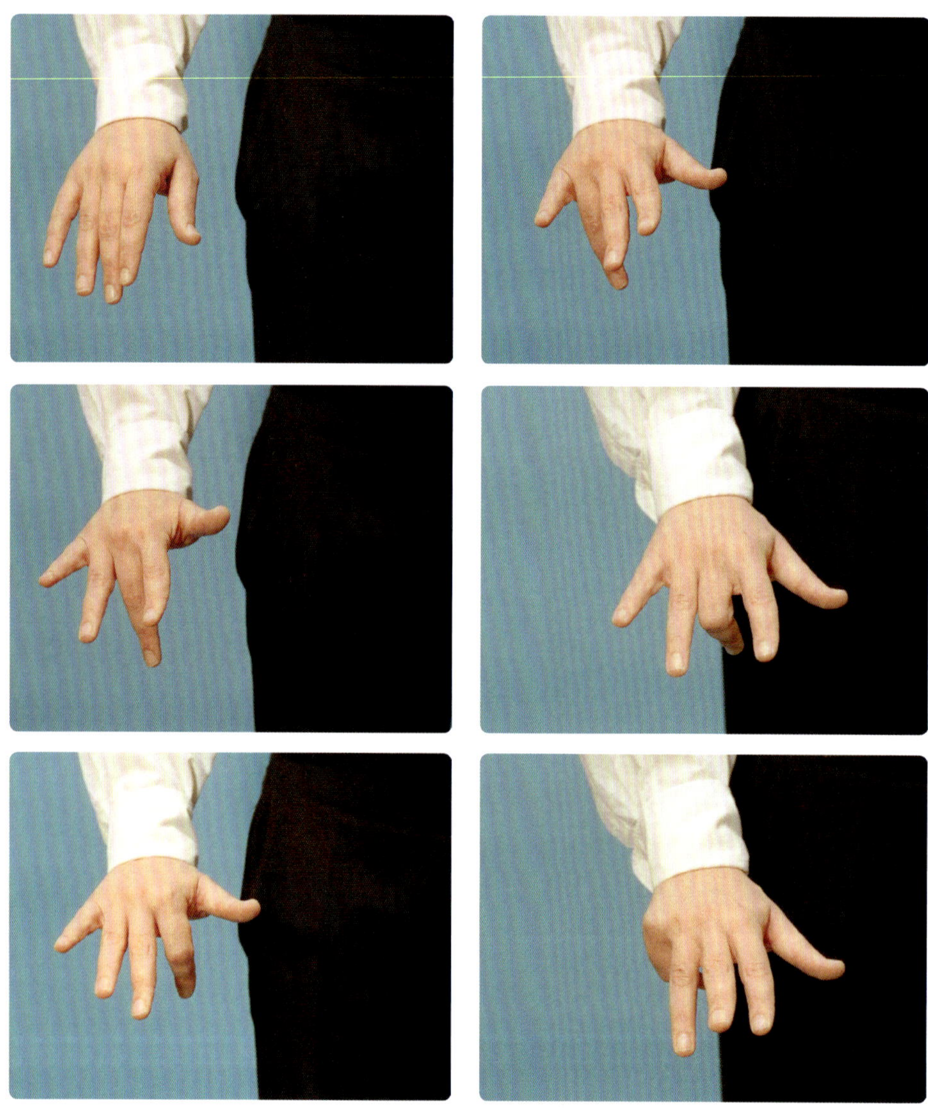

Fizzy Water

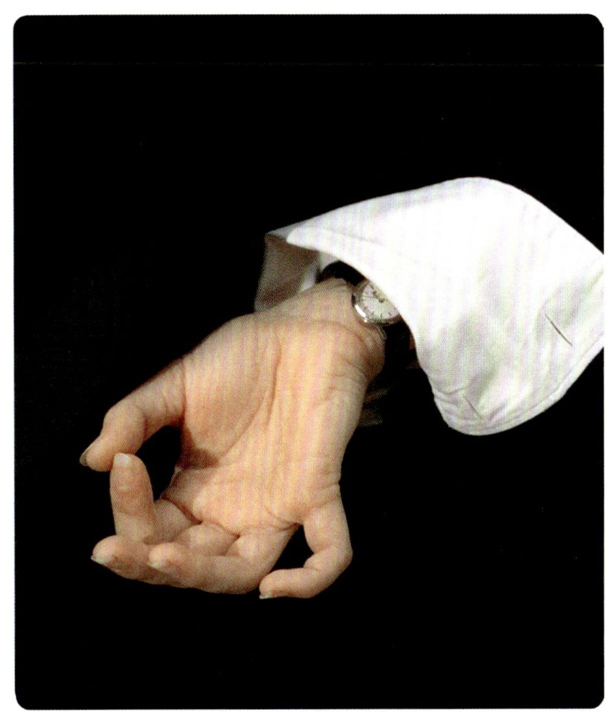

Make the Play

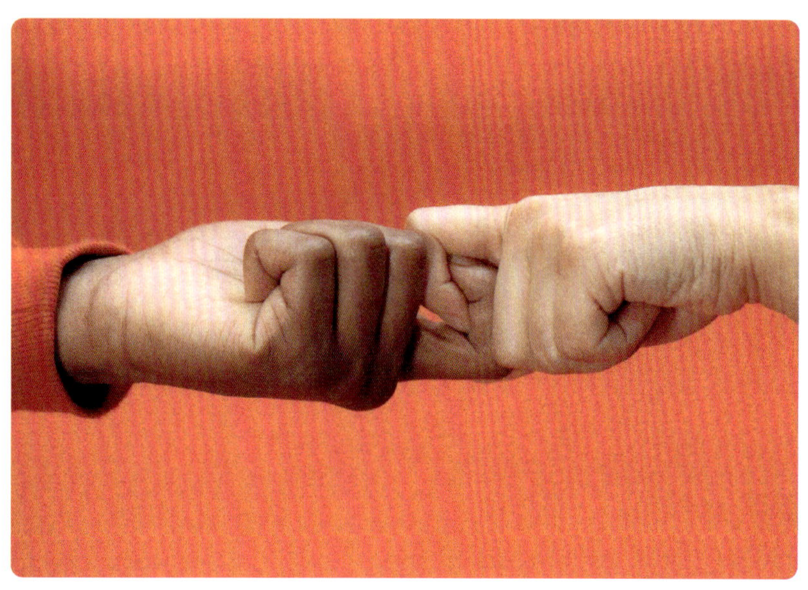

Keep Quiet

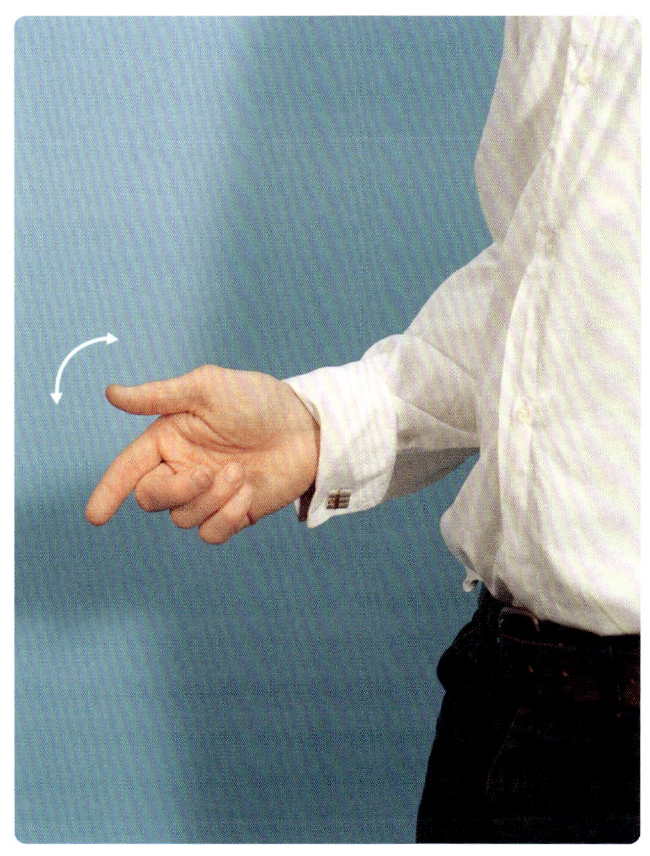

Twist

All photographs from the series *Secret Gestures*, 2026

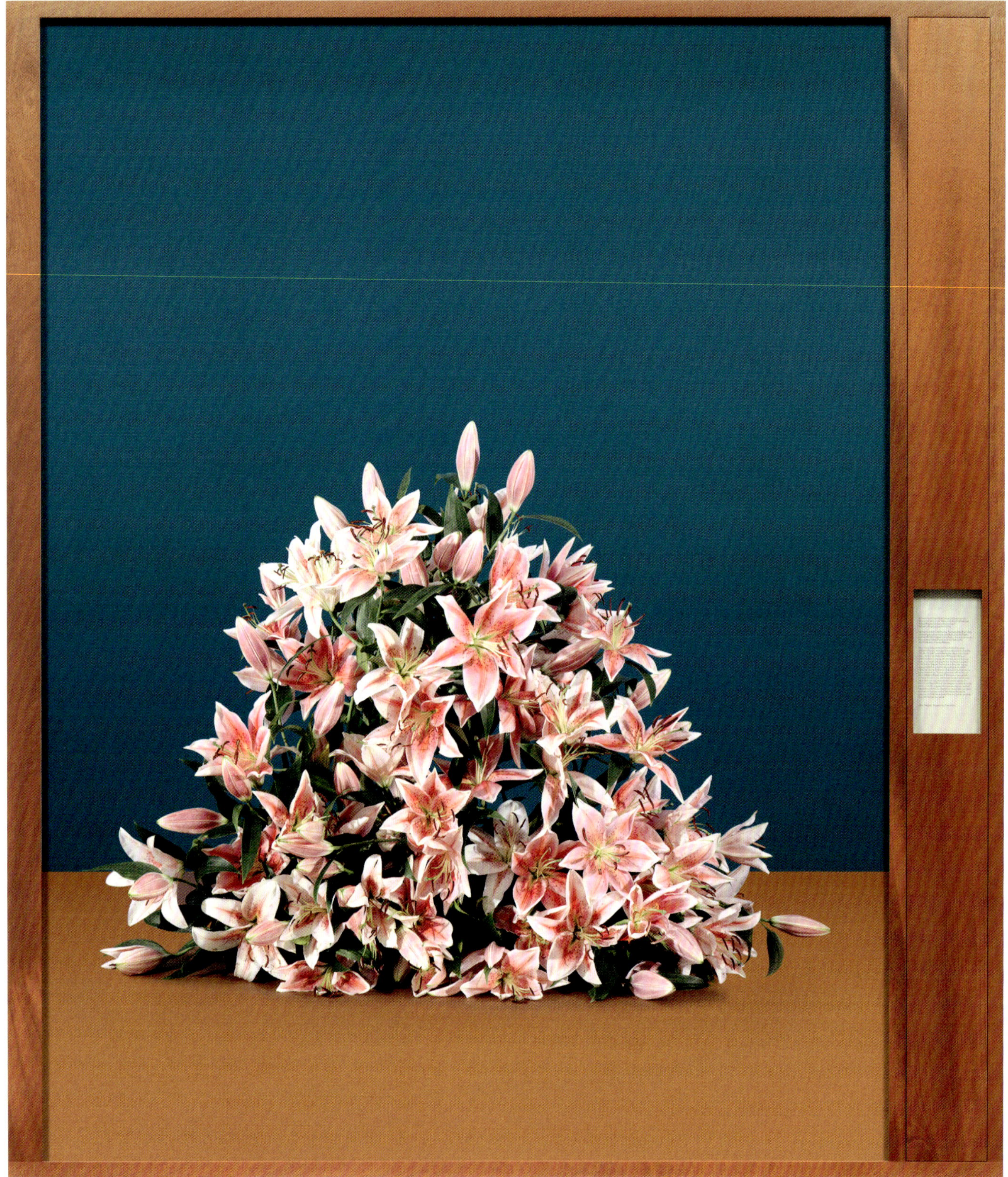

Memorandum on Security Assurances in Connection with Ukraine's Accession to the Treaty on the Non-Proliferation of Nuclear Weapons (Budapest Memorandum) Budapest, Hungary, December 5, 1994

Ukrainian president Leonid Kuchma, Russian president Boris Yeltsin, United Kingdom prime minister John Major, and United States president Bill Clinton signed a memorandum on security assurances that completed Ukraine's accession to the Treaty on the Non Proliferation of Nuclear Weapons.

From *Paperwork and the Will of Capital*, 2015

Taryn Simon Out of Sight

A Conversation with Christopher Glazek

"I want to see everything," Taryn Simon once said. This could serve as her artist statement in a nutshell: For over twenty years, the American photographer has pulled back the curtain on the hidden structures that shape everyday life. Rather than isolating individual subjects, she draws our gaze to the ordering systems—forensic investigations, flower arrangements, bloodlines—through which power quietly takes shape. Whether documenting CIA art collections, nuclear waste storage, or a checkpoint in the West Bank, Simon's painstakingly researched work denies the emotional catharsis and moral authority typical of an exposé. Her restrained photographs tend to depict sites of control that are intact, ongoing, and eerily beautiful.

In the decades since Simon rose to prominence, public trust in institutions is at a nadir. We live in a world of echo chambers, limited hangouts, rampant artificial intelligence, and a fourth estate under siege. Surveillance is omnipresent, and conspiracy has gone mainstream. This September, Simon will premiere a sweeping body of images throughout the spiraling rotunda of New York's Guggenheim Museum. Leading up to that exhibition, the artist agreed to speak about her prescient oeuvre and what transparency means today with the journalist Christopher Glazek on the condition that the new work wouldn't be discussed—she wanted to keep that a secret.

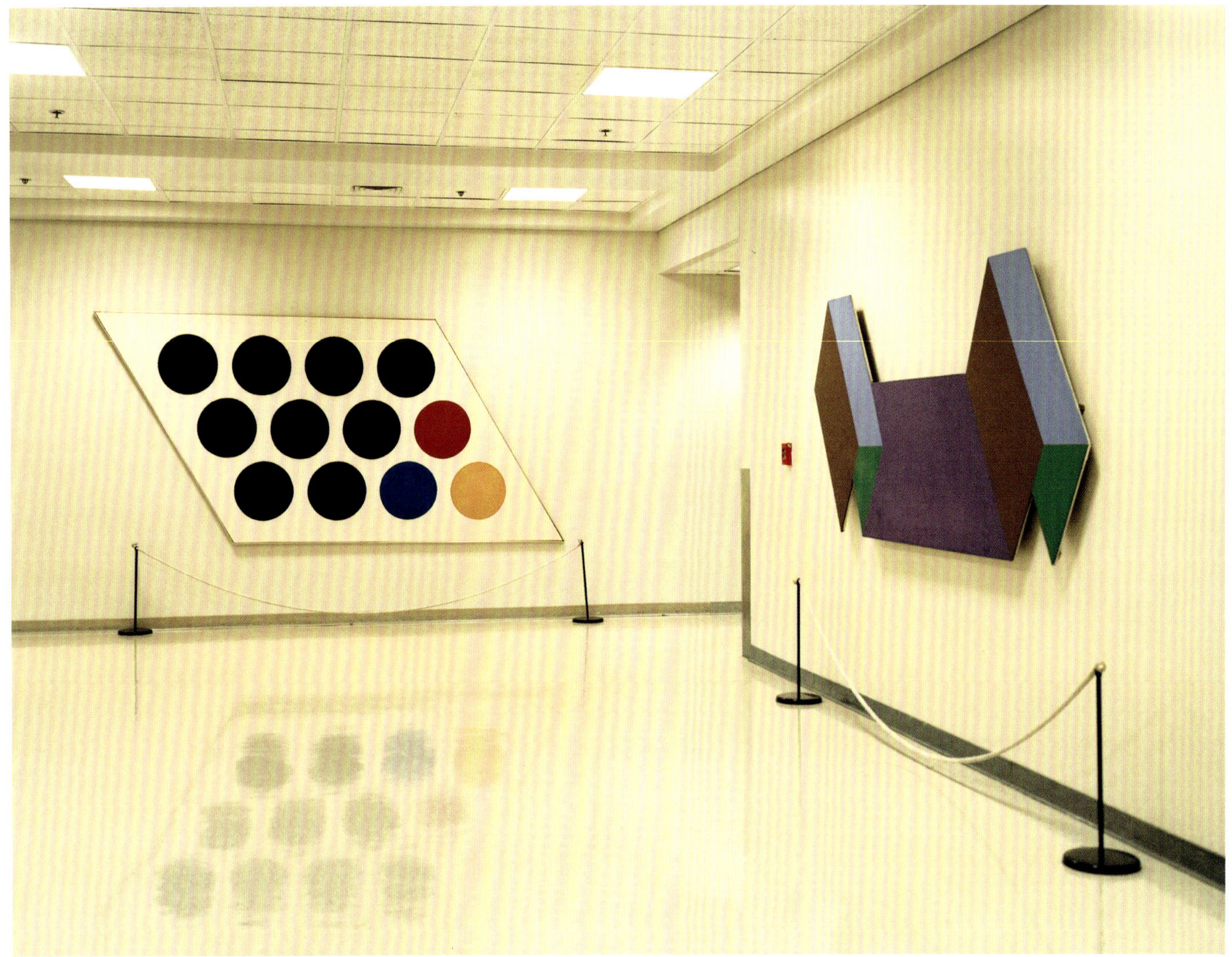

The Central Intelligence Agency, Art
CIA Original Headquarters Building
Langley, Virginia

The Fine Arts Commission of the CIA is responsible for acquiring art to display in the Agency's buildings. Among the Commission's curated art are two pieces (pictured) by Thomas Downing, on long-term loan from the Vincent Melzac Collection. Downing was a member of the Washington Color School, a group of post-World War II painters whose influence helped to establish the city as a center for arts and culture. Vincent Melzac was a private collector of abstract art and the Administrative Director of the Corcoran Gallery of Art, Washington DC's premier art museum.

Since its founding in 1947, the Agency has participated in both covert and public cultural diplomacy efforts throughout the world. It is speculated that some of the CIA's involvement in the arts was designed to counter Soviet Communism by helping to popularize what it considered pro-American thought and aesthetic sensibilities. Such involvement has raised historical questions about certain art forms or styles that may have elicited the interest of the Agency, including Abstract Expressionism.

From *An American Index of the Hidden and Unfamiliar*, 2007

Christopher Glazek: **When I think of so many of your works—*An American Index of the Hidden and Unfamiliar* (2007), *Contraband* (2010), *Paperwork and the Will of Capital* (2015)—you're photographing things that are ordinarily kept out of sight, be it restricted sites, seized objects, hidden machinery of the state. Lately, though, it feels like a lot of power operates in public—shamelessly, performatively. Does exposure matter anymore?**

Taryn Simon: I've never been looking to expose, I've been looking carefully to understand. Sometimes that directs me to distractions or the periphery. I think the secret will always prevail, it just finds different hiding spaces. It relocates. So many of the brazen and performative reveals today are just that. Power has a way of reorganizing itself behind new language and performances. I'm interested in what quietly persists.

CG: **Your work has done so much over the years—thinking of series like *The Innocents* (2000–3) and *Image Atlas* (2012)—to highlight how meaning is produced, how authority is exercised, by an infrastructure of images. Now, though, we live in a world where millions of amateur detectives practice open-source sleuthing every day, typically on unmoderated platforms. We're drowning in screenshots, dossiers, forensics—sometimes persuasive, often delusional, usually with a strong aesthetic overlay. Has ordinary online culture taken possession of the tools of archival critique? Do those methods then become defanged or devalued to you?**

TS: I don't know. I've always liked to approach material like a child who is learning but with a fact-checking skeleton of an old woman who's seen the holes. I guess it's all in the approach and intention, how it all yields.

CG: **On that topic, a lot of your work brings me back to the classic Eve Sedgwick essay, "Paranoid Reading and Reparative Reading." On a podcast last week, Elon Musk answered a question about whether we should fear AI manipulation by reasoning, "People say, 'What if the AI tricks us into doing stuff?' Actually, humans are doing that to other humans all the time! Propaganda is constant. Every day is a new psy-op." I'm curious how you think about the relationship between paranoia and critique.**

Paranoia is often how wisdom is labeled.

TS: He's right. Humans have done a pretty good job of making a somewhat organized mess of what could be a utopia. But we are that very image in our bodies and brains. Our internal makeup and survival depend on nested realities. Our brains and bodies remain operational through a balance between what you could call good and bad. Why would what we yield in the world look any different. And we are very advanced computers. Paranoia is often how wisdom is labeled.

CG: **The last twenty years have seen violent swings in popular attitudes about the carceral state, with reformist impulses gaining steam throughout the 2010s and seemingly reversing in the 2020s. What has surprised you most about this evolution?**

TS: Just how fickle everything is. There is a profound regression to the idea of future. Things quickly shifted from transformation to containment.

CG: **Your work often treats media systems as environments, sometimes governed by rules, sometimes chaotic. I wonder if you agree, though, that film and art have struggled when it comes to depicting social media. Is there something about social media that makes it aesthetically resistant? Where are the great works of art about social media?**

TS: It's ambient, adhesive, self-updating—less like earlier technologies and more like weather or atmosphere. It easily feels redundant or inert when used. It's a third skin—but also a metabolic system digesting and emitting images in real time. Trying to aestheticize it can feel like aestheticizing vomit: The act itself is already complete, already excessive. The raw event outperforms its reenactment.

CG: **In a world where the marginal cost of creating digital content is approaching zero, we're often told the value of live experiences is rising. You've increasingly experimented with live experiential elements in works like *An Occupation of Loss* (2016), *A Cold Hole* (2018), and *Kleroterion* (2024). I'm curious what you've learned about the difference between photographic**

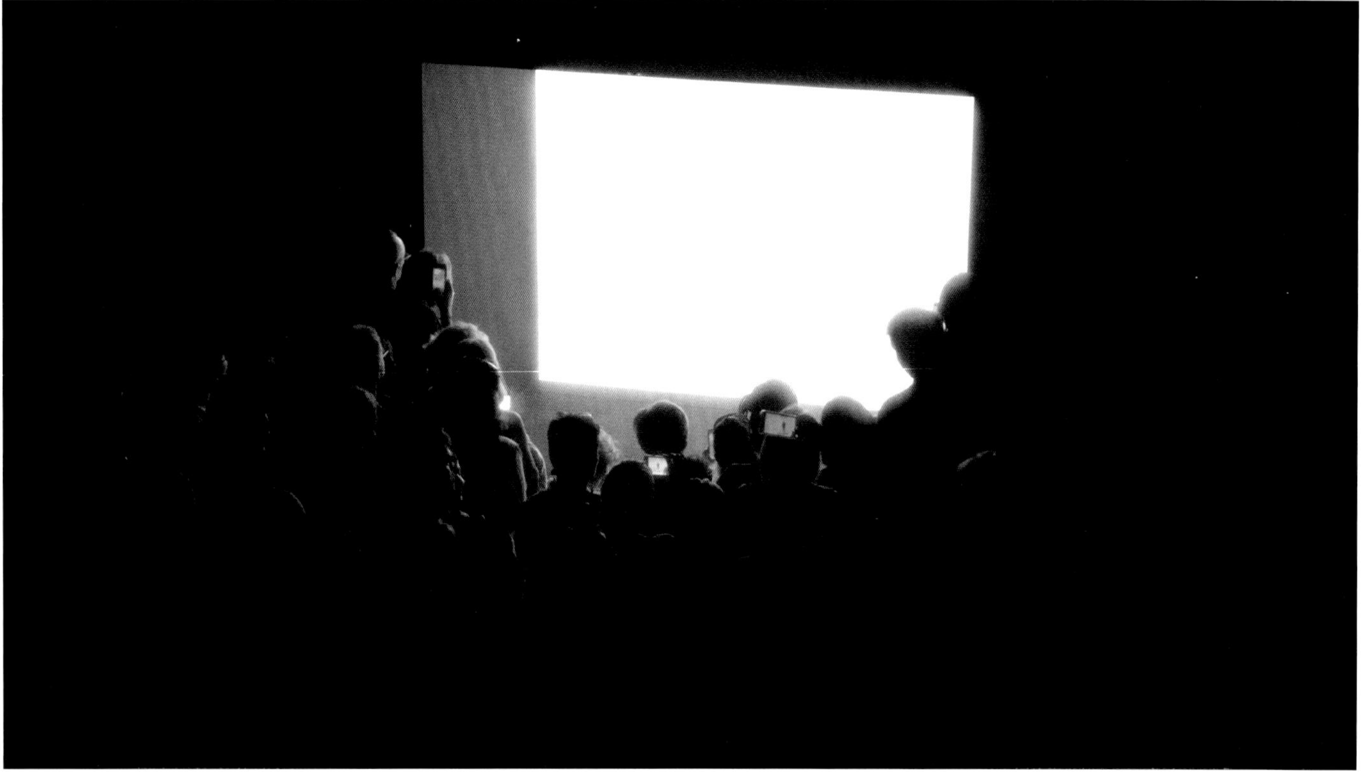

A Cold Hole, 2018
Courtesy the Massachusetts Museum of Contemporary Art; photograph by David Dashiell

systems, working with "documents" versus building living situations?

TS: There's a loss of control, predictability and longevity built into live experience. You get something that can't be repeated, something that doesn't exist elsewhere, the undistributed. At the end of the day everyone just wants something special and impossible. Their birthday, a kiss, the sun, a shooting star, immortality. Photos stick around in ways a performance can't. They freeze time and avoid death and forgetting.

CG: **In the last few years, the cultural institutions of the art world have become flash points, over labor, donors, speech—and especially over the war in Gaza, which has put greater stress on the art world's social contract, perhaps, than any other event in living memory. What will it take to heal these wounds? Are you optimistic?**

TS: Nothing sits still. But some wounds don't heal. Some rupture, some fester in quiet. Even in the act of healing, scars grow and over time stretch, becoming part of the body's structure.

CG: **A lot of your work brushes up against desire and erotics indirectly. Have you ever wanted to make a work that addresses eroticism directly? Do you think you already have?**

TS: Many, many times.

CG: **Your work shows powerful emotion but steers clear of easy catharsis. Why do you think contemporary art often treats sentimentality as taboo, while tolerating other emotional manipulations—trolling, irony, shock, even the aesthetics of the sacred? Is sentimentality always cheap? Can it be rigorous?**

TS: I feel the most when I'm not told what to feel—when something changes the air, adds pressure and density, and then steps back without the need to persuade.

Christopher Glazek is a critic and journalist based in New York.

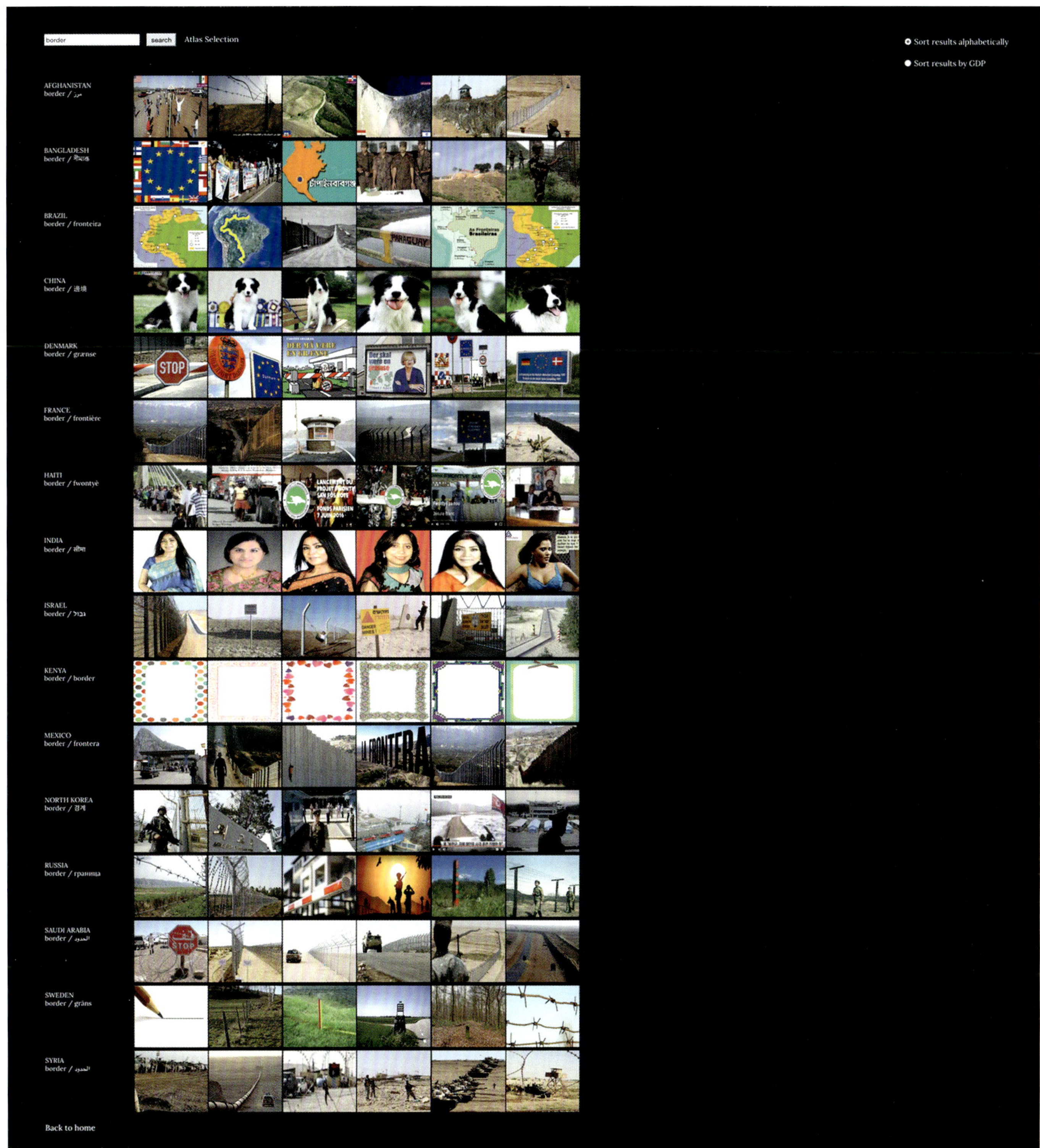

Border, *Image Atlas*, 2012
All photographs courtesy Gagosian

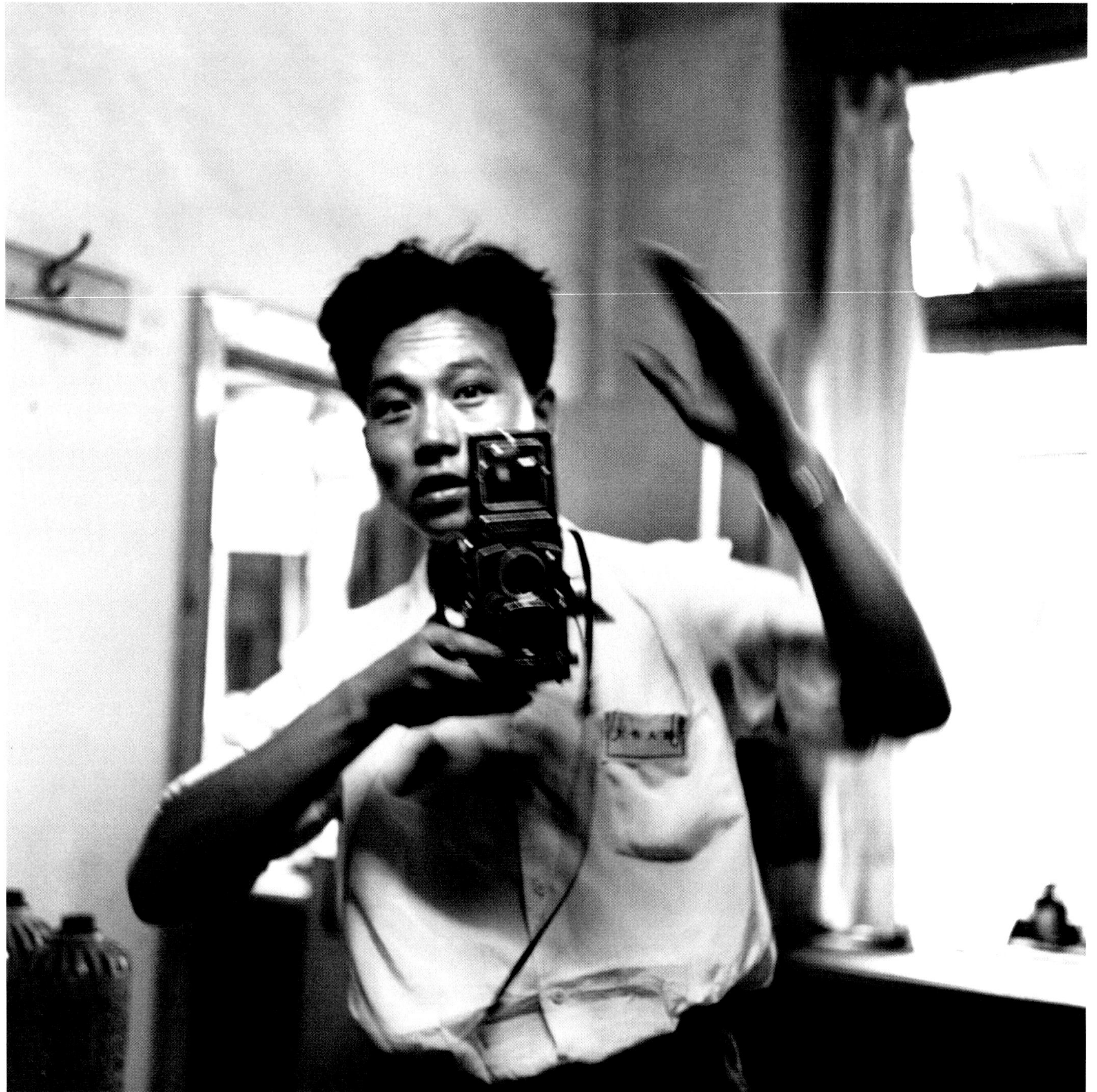

Li Zhensheng,
Self-Portrait, 1967

Witness Li Zhensheng

A state photographer during China's Cultural Revolution quietly made images that contradicted official mandates. Fearing discovery, he hid his negatives for decades beneath his floorboards.

Yechen Zhao

WHEN HE WORKED AT THE *HEILONGJIANG DAILY* during the Chinese Cultural Revolution, Li Zhensheng always left the last few frames of each film roll unexposed after shooting an assignment. He told his colleagues he was reserving them in case something happened on the way back to their offices, but in reality Li saved those extra frames for himself. Using his office as a makeshift studio, he secretly posed for self-portraits. Some look hurried, as if Li had only a few moments to snap the shutter unobserved. Others are more carefully staged, like one in which the photographer displays his Red Guard armband—the prized symbol of the Cultural Revolution's vanguard. When Mao Zedong launched this mass movement in May of 1966, he directed all of Chinese society to vanquish "reactionary bourgeois ideas" by finding and eliminating the "counterrevolutionary revisionists" behind them. Li earned his armband by forming a revolutionary cell at the *Daily*, which gave him a degree of political power that not only allowed him to photograph without harassment but also shielded him from scrutiny. Reflecting on this period, he later admitted: "Everyone looked very revolutionary from the outside, but deep down, it was often another story." Everyone, including Li, had their secrets.

During this paranoid period of Chinese history, the photographer repeatedly witnessed the dragging of private lives into public view, where they were transformed into incontrovertible proof of a person's guilt. In 1965, he covered the trial of a local farmer accused of being a "rich peasant." The farmer's home was turned into a propaganda museum, where his family's possessions were put on display to warn others against succumbing to bourgeois pleasures. Li photographed the exhibition, which included a radio, leather shoes, and a pair of silk stockings.

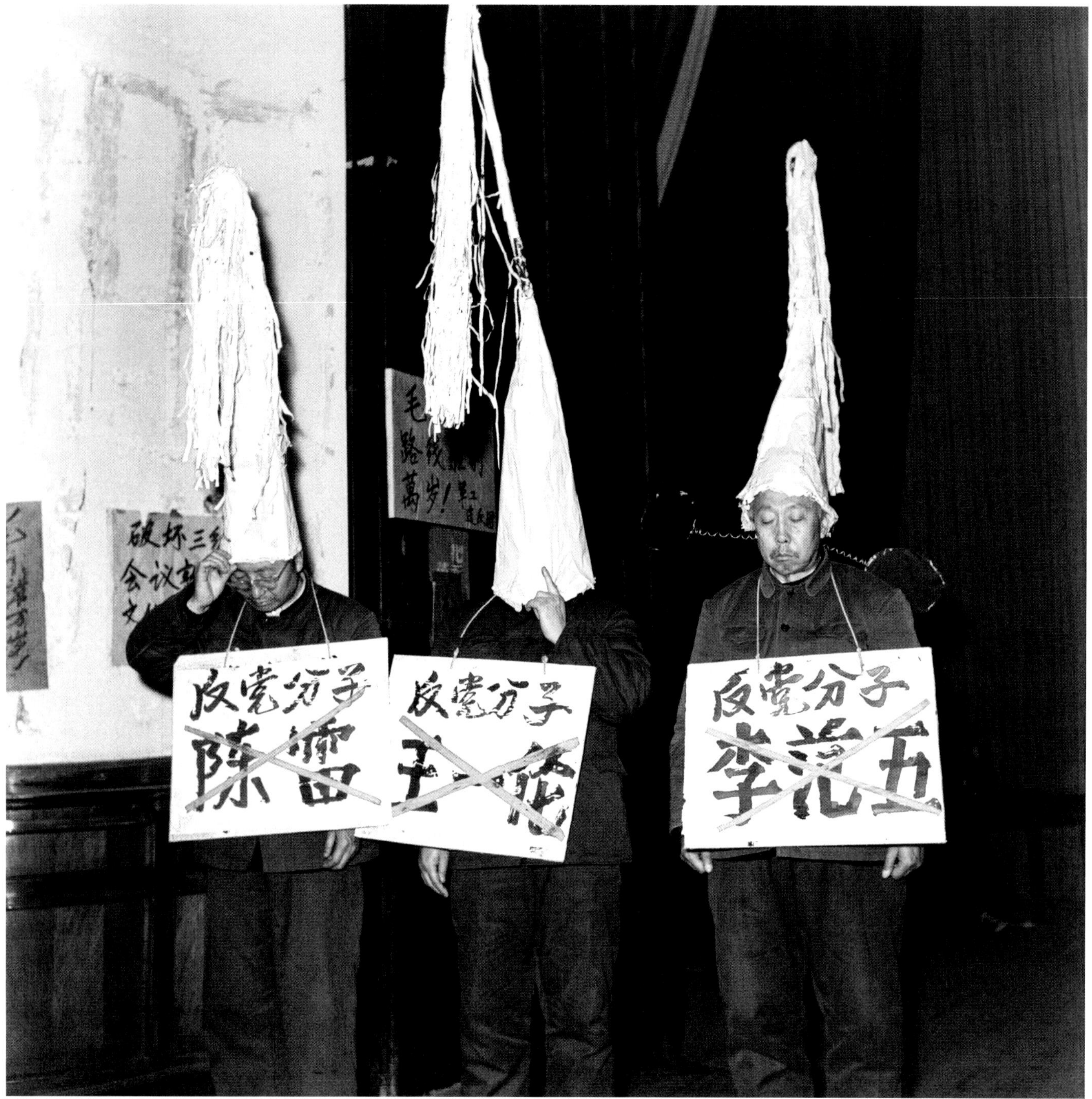

A year later, while Heilongjiang's governor was on public trial for corruption, Li turned his camera away from the shouting masses and snapped a picture of the incriminating evidence, which consisted of a few wristwatches and leather bags. Li had his own small cache of contraband at home—a stamp collection that included reproductions of Francisco Goya nudes and some coins bearing the Nationalist leader Chiang Kai-shek's likeness—but he kept his biggest secrets on government-issued film.

Li quietly chose to make photographs that fell outside, if not outright contradicted, the official mandates of his job. Photographic production under Mao was tightly controlled by the government, which employed people to take photographs that served political needs. Li diligently served the cause, making pictures of cheering crowds holding up portraits of

This page:
Harbin, Heilongjiang province, 1966. At the Harbin Workers' Club, Party secretaries are forced to wear oversized dunce caps during a criticism session.

Opposite:
Harbin, June 9, 1967. This man was photographed four days after a deadly skirmish with rebel factions over the control of a broadcasting bus.

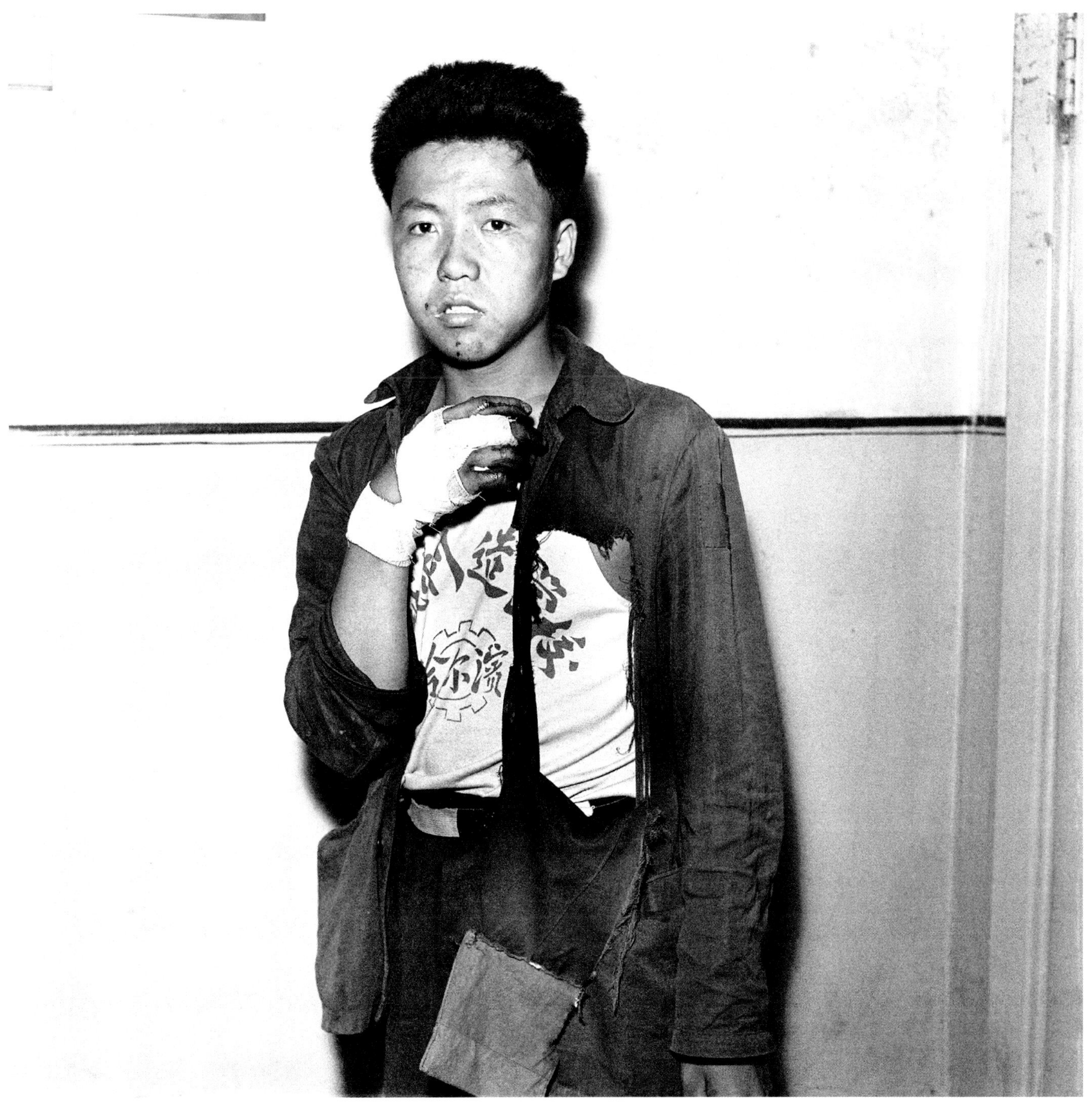

the Chairman, workers studying the Little Red Book, and performances of revolutionary operas. However, personal ambition drove him to do more with the camera than just follow the party line. Li was inspired by his mentor Wu Yinxian, the photographer and filmmaker who stood by Mao as the Communist Party came to power in the 1940s, and he wanted to capture all aspects of a movement that seemed to have world-historical significance. Li never failed to produce the idealized images that his bosses required, but he also documented the chaos of the Cultural Revolution: public trials where the accused were forced to stand with heads bowed for hours on end while wearing signs proclaiming their guilt, piles of books ransacked from libraries, defaced statues in Buddhist temples, Red Guards bloodied from street fights with rival factions.

Making self-portraits with state resources was already a violation, but using precious film to photograph the violence carried out in Mao's name was a serious crime. This was a time not only when colleagues, friends, and family members spied on one another but when Red Guards would force their way into people's homes to search for evidence of political dissidence. Li knew that his colleagues had noticed him taking extra pictures while on assignment and had likely seen some of his offending negatives drying in the darkroom. He took the film home before it could be used against him and hid it in a secret compartment that he and his wife, Zu Yingxia, had cut into the floorboards.

Li's caution in stashing away the negatives proved warranted when, two years into the Cultural Revolution, he became the

Chaoyang commune, Shuangcheng county, December 17, 1974. Peasants till and irrigate frozen land in preparation for the season's planting.

target of a political investigation. Red Guards visited his hometown, combed his records from primary school all the way through university, and eventually subjected him to the same kind of public denunciation he had photographed so many times before. They finally searched his home on a cold December night, pulling out his stamp collection, personal photographs, and love letters. When Zu objected to their confiscation, one of the guards smugly declared: "A Communist Party member has nothing to hide."

Of course, Li was hiding something. That night during the search, he stood for hours in front of a desk he had moved to cover the compartment holding his negatives, which the Red Guards never discovered. Though Li and his wife were sentenced to hard labor, when they returned to their home two years later the film was still there. The photographer kept his secret through the end of the Cultural Revolution, in 1976, and the early years of China's reform era. Despite loosening restrictions on personal expression, Deng Xiaoping, the country's new

"Everyone looked very revolutionary from the outside, but deep down, it was often another story," Li said.

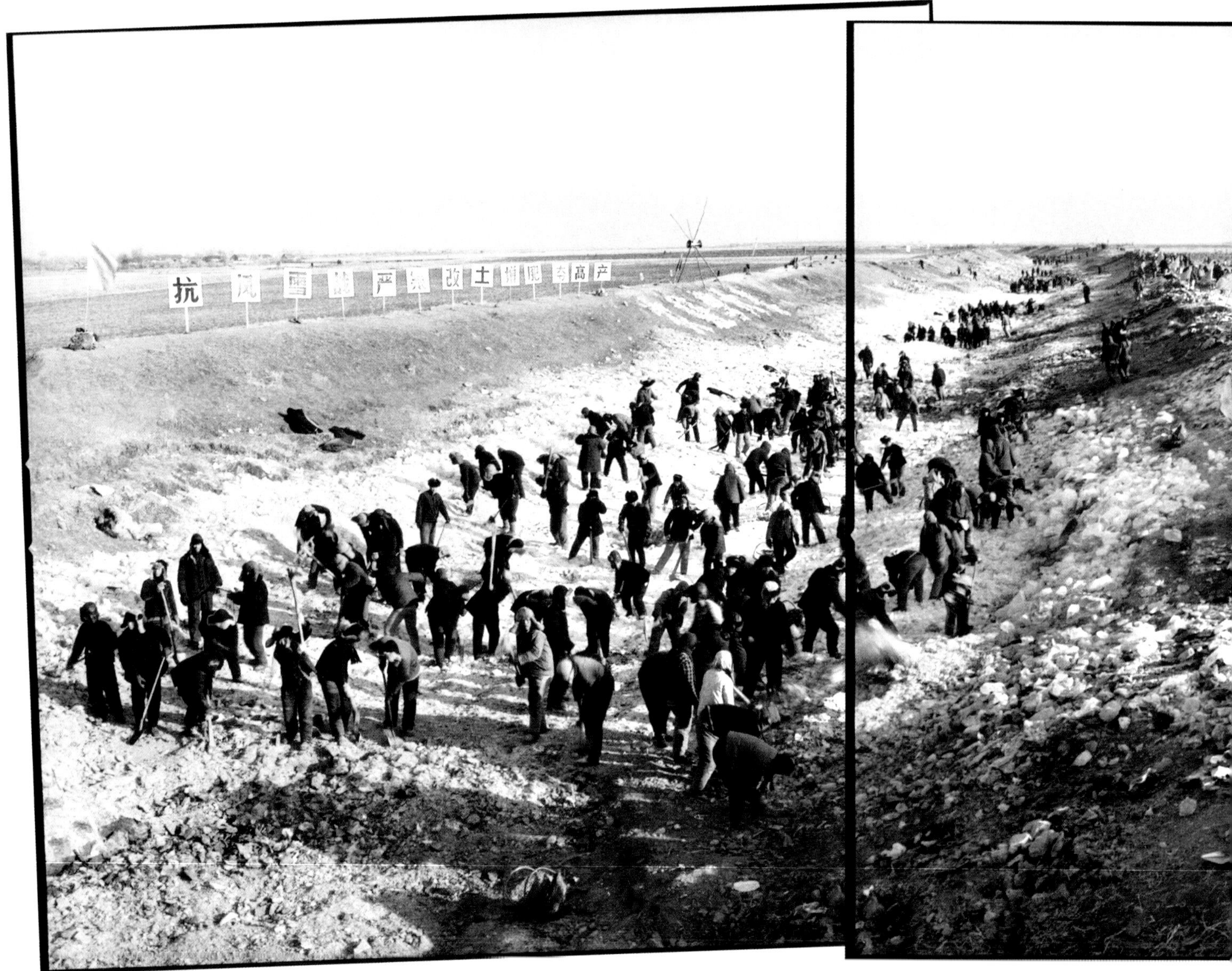

leader, quashed any nuanced discussion of the past by issuing a terse official account of the revolution as a ten-year disaster, attributing its chaos to a miscalculation by Mao and treachery committed by his advisors. But the effort to extinguish any remaining grudges through a blanket pardon of all Chinese people—regardless of the violence they had committed, witnessed, or failed to stop—left everyone uncertain about what they could and could not share. The Cultural Revolution had become a public secret, leaving Li reluctant to puncture that silence with his photographs.

In 1988 he had to be begged to submit his photographs to a competition in Beijing. Now teaching photography in the capital, Li relented and chose twenty of the approximately sixty thousand pictures he made during the revolution. His work attracted the attention of Robert Pledge, the founder of Contact Press Images, who immediately sought to collaborate on a book. Their hopes were dashed by the 1989 violent repression of protestors at Tiananmen Square and the ensuing political crackdown, but the two reconnected in 1996, when Li was invited to lecture in the United States. Over the next several years, Li delivered thousands of negatives to Pledge's New York office. At first he carried them from China surreptitiously, but soon realized he could travel with little fear of their seizure or his arrest. Was the need for secrecy over?

Yes, to an extent. By then, China's market-based economy had developed to a point where the Cultural Revolution was fueling a "culture industry" that included books, films, and even a television drama. This groundswell of interest was further propelled by the *zhiqing* (educated youth), the generation of teenagers who were sent to live and work in rural China during the revolution. In 1998, a small publishing house put out *Zhiqing Old Photos*, a collection of 150 pictures that showed beaming youths doing farm labor and military training in the countryside. Although the government still exercised substantial control over public representations of the Cultural Revolution, it now competed with a burgeoning private sphere that sold memories

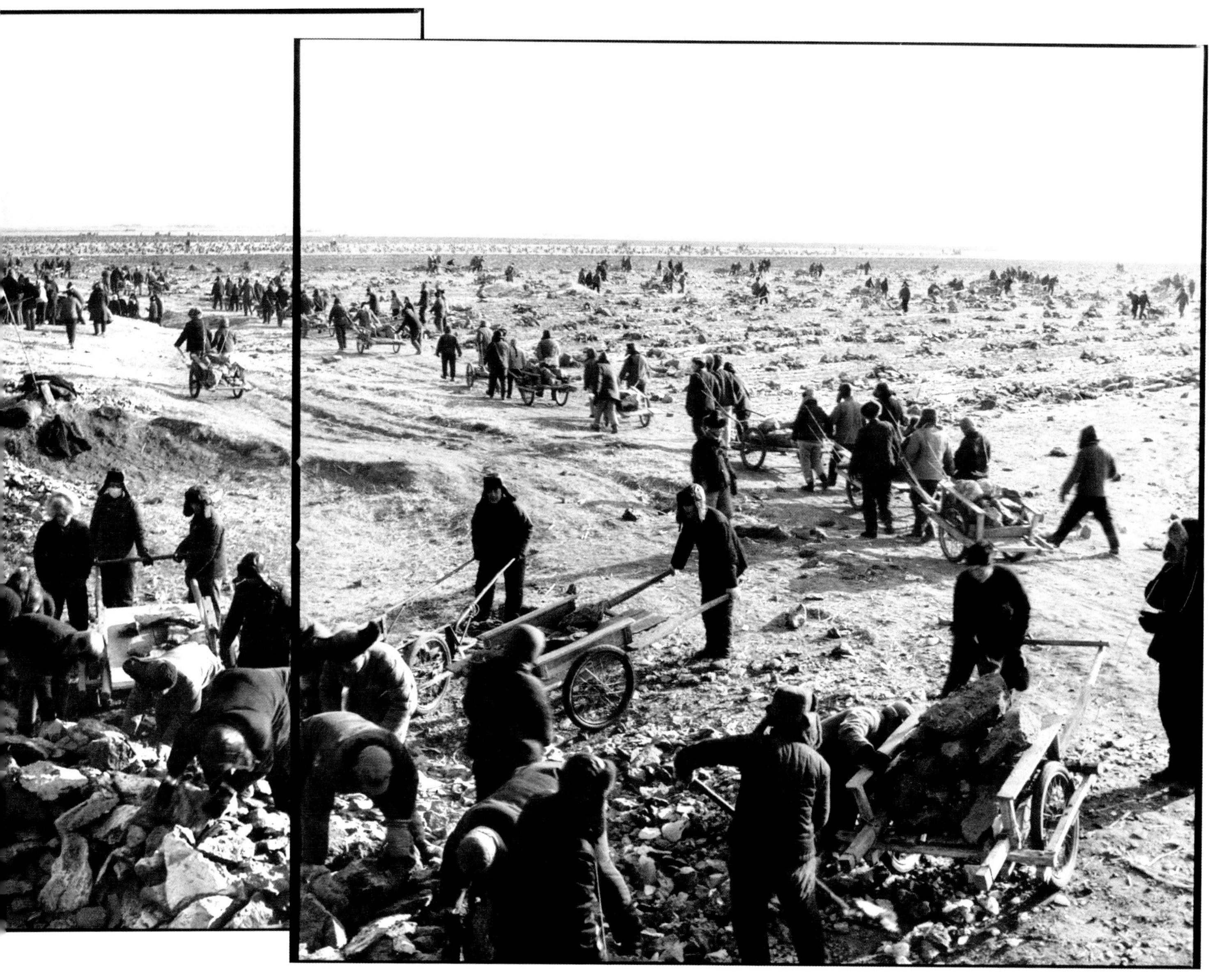

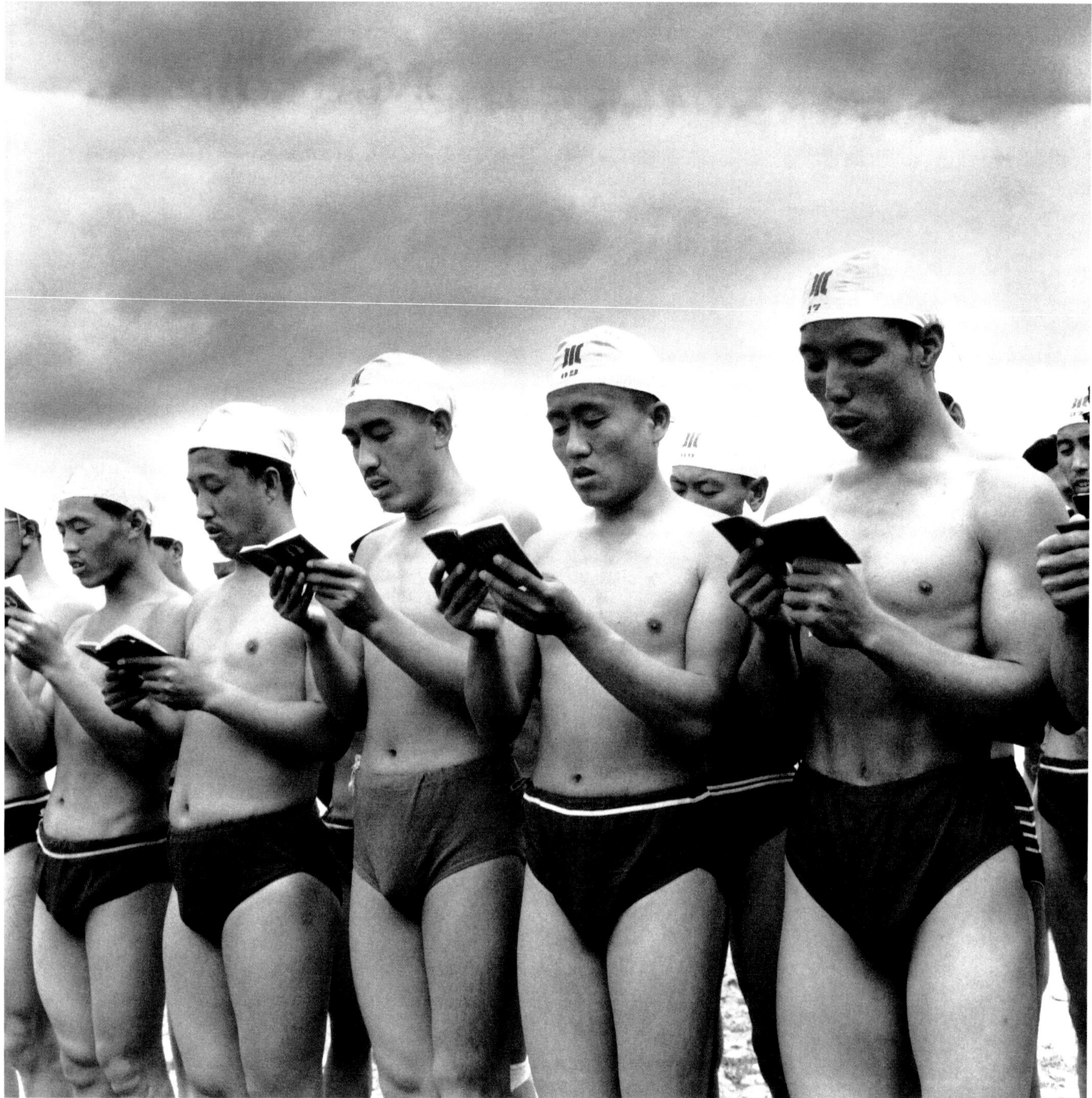

of the past. When *Red-Color News Soldier*, Li's book of photographs, appeared in 2003, it added to a growing effort to examine more critically the Cultural Revolution through photography: In the 1990s, Wang Tong documented fading images of Mao and big-character posters across China, Hai Bo was working with revolution-era family photographs in his series *They* (1997–2000), and Shao Yinong and Mu Chen had begun photographing the assembly halls used for political meetings during the revolution.

Li passed away in 2020. Sixty years have now elapsed since Mao began the Cultural Revolution, which remains at once very known and very secret. Although Li's pictures of public denunciations and executions stunned the world just over twenty years ago, they remain revelatory because they belong to the photographer's larger pursuit of individual subjectivity in a period of mass mobilization, when such reflection was considered at best a luxury and at worst a form of political subversion. Even though an entire nation listened to the same broadcasts, saw the same operas, and gathered in the same assembly halls, the artist Shao Yinong reminds us that each person's memory of these scenes is different: "My father never forgot seeing two counter-revolutionaries being killed at the chairman's platform, and my brother remembered his first love of a schoolmate backstage." More than just a clandestine recorder of history, Li held those secrets until they crystallized into a magisterial yet personal account of a period that has yet to be fully reconciled. Ultimately, his self-portraits remain most revelatory because they show the photographer secretly refusing

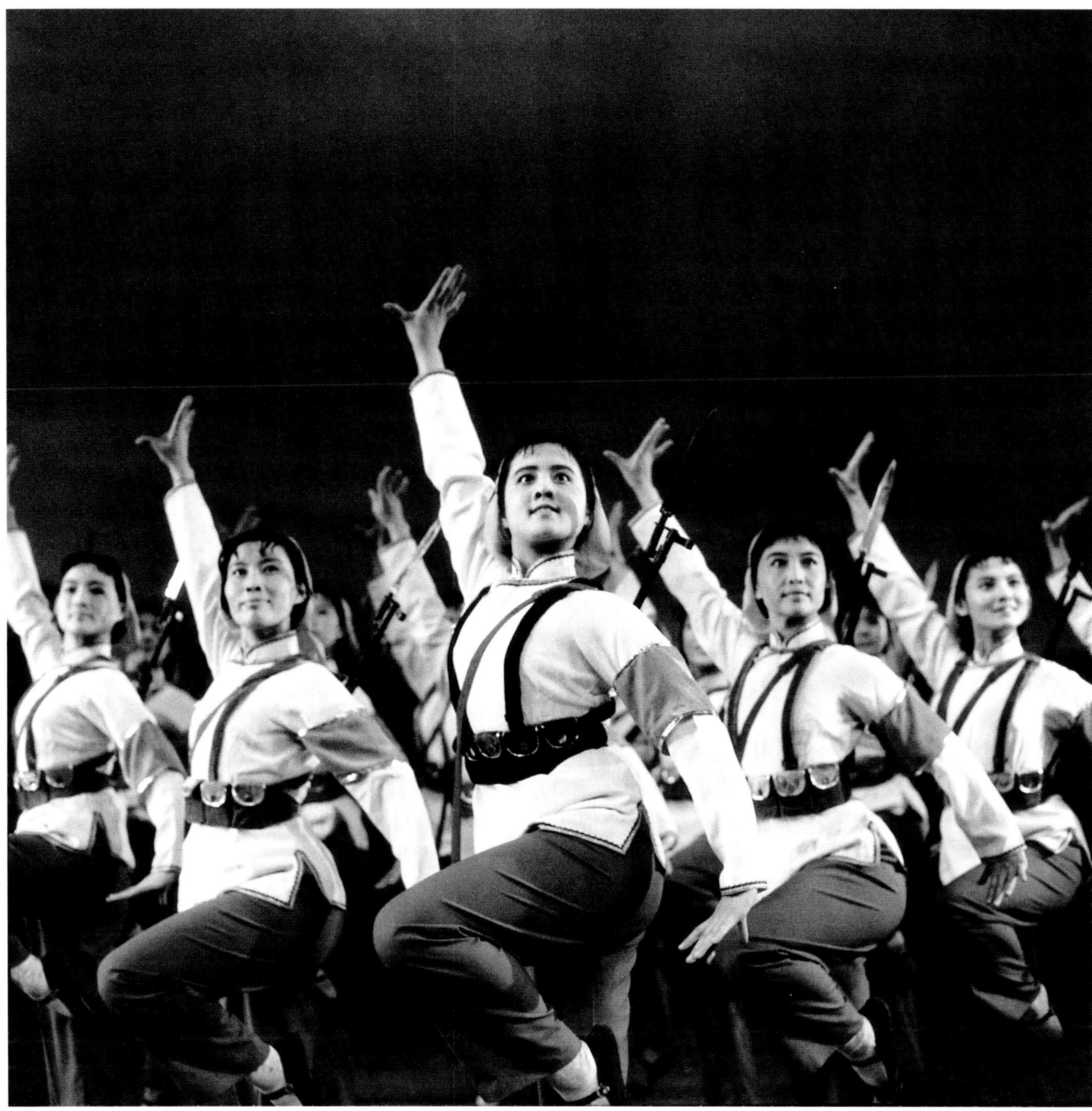

This page:
Dancers from the Heilongjiang Song and Dance Company perform *Militia Women*, a piece about women training to join the fight against reactionaries.

Opposite:
Swimmers prepare to plunge into the Songhua River to commemorate the second anniversary of Mao's swim in the Yangtze River.

All photographs from *Red-Color News Soldier*, 1966–76

to derive a sense of self from collective identity. Indeed, Li credited his "rebellious nature" as the motivating force behind all his work: "If I achieved something, including these photographs, I would say the reason is that I always believed I should make it by myself."

Yechen Zhao is the Karen Frank Assistant Curator of Photography and Media at the Art Institute of Chicago.

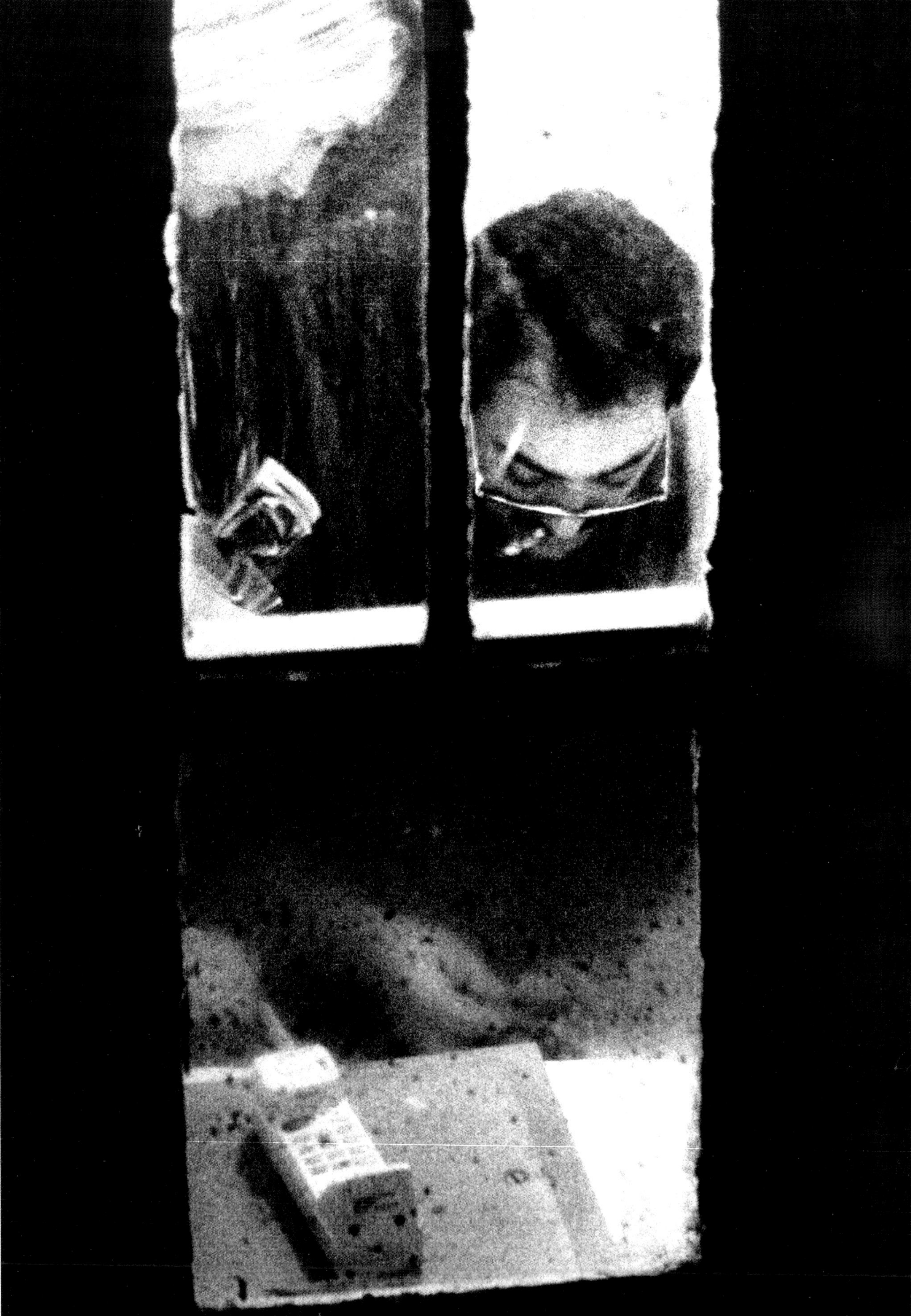

Perfect Strangers

Photography and voyeurism have long been entwined, yet the person most exposed is often behind the lens.

Emily LaBarge

THEY ARE GRAINY, BLACK AND WHITE, UP CLOSE BUT taken from afar, which is to say zoomed in, hence the grain, which adds a kind of softened patina, not quite like a Hollywood noir filter but let's say almost, because the images, each bisected in some configuration by the dark T-bar of a window sash, are not graphic or sordid or perverse, as people have sometimes described them—particularly then but sometimes still now—even if the 1993–94 series by the New York–born photographer Merry Alpern is, after all, called *Dirty Windows*.

"I had watched, for so many days, the pastimes of perfect strangers," Alpern said of the series, which attracted controversy

Page 78, this page, and opposite: Merry Alpern, from the series *Dirty Windows*, 1993–94

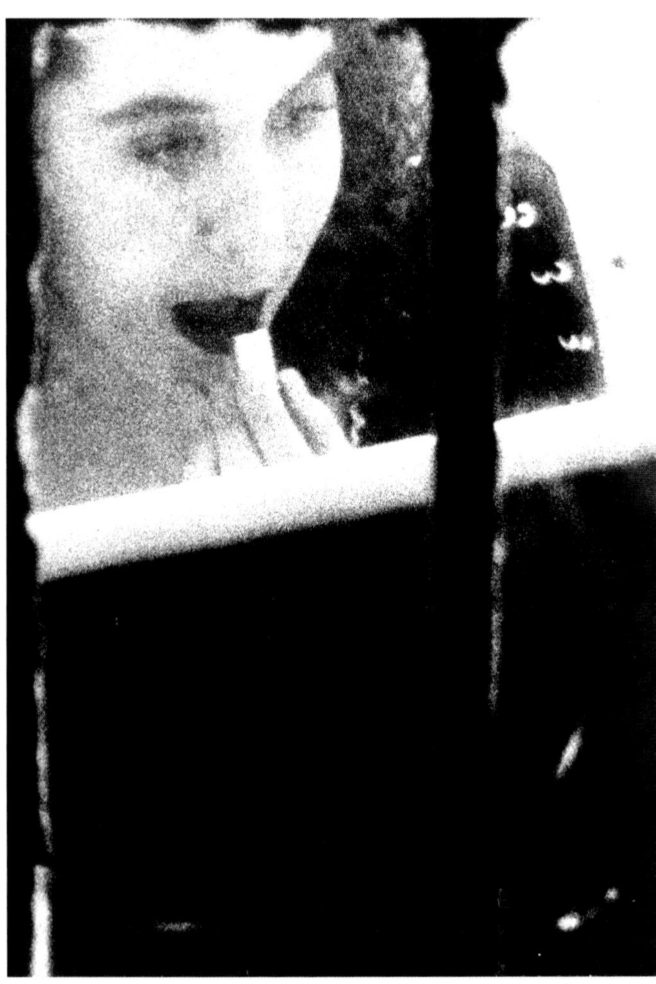

almost immediately. From behind, a woman peeling off a studded thong. A different woman (or the same? or is it just the angle, the light, a reflection, or a shadow?) dressed in dark clothing, leaning forward, long hair and dark lips, left hand (painted nails) holding a thin straw. An arm outstretched, but this time disembodied, coming in from the left of the image, palm upward, pallid and slender against the lower torso of a man of whom little is discernible but a shiny watch. Yet another woman, in a lacy dark shirt (or brassiere) and a pale pleated skirt, bent over, purse in right hand, soft cleavage just visible, an elegant pose this one, the image somehow bringing to mind Edgar Degas's backstage ballerinas, whom he painted as if through a keyhole—a secret scene, something private, a subject glimpsed unawares and never looking back at the viewer, who is left to imagine what they have stumbled upon.

Late in 1993, when Alpern was at a friend's loft in New York's financial district, he led her to a back room from which, across a dark air shaft, one flight down, a rectangle of light was visible. "I saw a bathroom window and felt the vibrations of a pulsing bass track," Alpern told curator Pauline Vermare when *Dirty Windows* was included in the International Center of Photography's 2016 exhibition *Public, Private, Secret*. "Suddenly, a body in a sparkling harness appeared, then disappeared." A low-rent, probably illegal private lap-dance club had recently opened, and its workers and patrons frequently used the bathroom to do business and keep the party going: Money changed hands for drugs and sex, and for several weeks over the next six months Alpern sat in the dark, dressed in black, covered in blankets to ward off the cold, with her telephoto lens sticking out the window and trained on the illuminated fragments of bodies moving in and out of view.

Because of the dim light, she had to use fast black-and-white film, giving the resulting images a coarse, sfumato quality that might read as illicit, peep-show-like, or with a kind of soft, almost romantic eros. Alpern was never entirely sure what she had captured, which gave her gaze an uncertainty driven as much by the thrill of the chase ("I felt like a trophy hunter waiting in the blind") as by an experiment in composition. The question was not only who or what might appear and transpire but how would it be framed? What might we see or not see? (Faces were obscured, usually, because of the downward angle.) What, exactly, is the line between observing and intruding? And perhaps more difficult to ascertain, especially in art: Who decides?

Photography and voyeurism have long been linked, sometimes in an accusatory charge, other times with pride by the person behind the viewfinder, who considers it their job to record the world as they see it—a calling that doesn't require permission. "Stare. It is the way to educate your eye, and more. Stare, pry, listen, eavesdrop. Die knowing something. You are not here long," advised the prolific American photographer Walker Evans, who documented the Great Depression but also surreptitiously recorded, using a Contax and shutter release, subway riders of New York between 1938 and 1941. People appear lost in thought or conversation, peeking sideways to read a neighboring traveler's newspaper, staring into the middle distance, sometimes making eye contact with the photographer, though oblivious of his camera.

Born two decades after Evans, Diane Arbus described her work in similar terms: "I always thought of photography as a naughty thing to do—that was one of my favorite things about

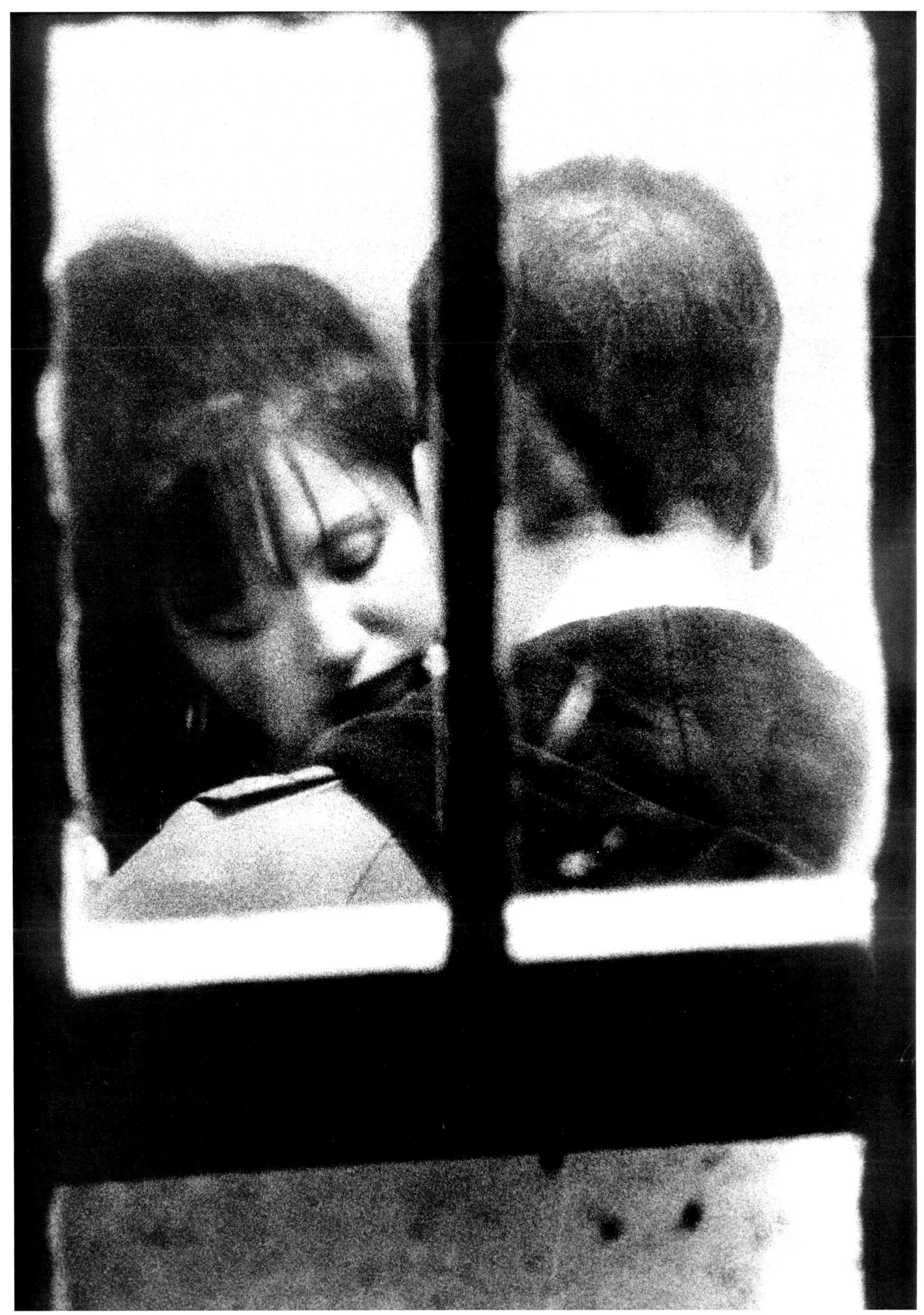

Shizuka Yokomizo, *Stranger No. 1*, 1998

it, and when I first did it I felt very perverse." Some find this statement and her work in general morally offensive. In an essay collected in *On Photography* (1977), Susan Sontag pits Evans and Arbus against each other as polar opposites. "America, Seen Through Photographs, Darkly" was originally published in 1973 in *The New York Review of Books* under the title "Freak Show"—"genetic freaks" is Sontag's term for Arbus's subjects (which range from babies and women in hats to tattooed carnival performers and nudists), along with "monsters," "dwarfs," "border-line cases," "members of the sexual underworld," "deviates," "people who are pathetic . . . pitiable . . . repulsive," "taboo, perverse, evil."

Though few would contest Sontag's assertion that photography, like the act of looking itself, engages in a power dynamic, the essay has aged, if not badly, then bizarrely. (If you find yourself asking of any person if they know how grotesque they are, that might be what we now call a "you problem.") And yet Sontag's critique of Arbus and her argument in *On Photography* that "to photograph is to appropriate the thing photographed," always a top-down exercise of power, still hangs heavy over practices that might be considered to transgress an invisible ethical boundary.

I thought about "Freak Show" while reading reviews of Alpern's *Dirty Windows* from the mid-1990s to recent times (among other group exhibitions over the past decade, the work was presented as a solo show in London last year). In 1994 and 1995, a spate of articles highlighted Alpern when, along with the artists Andres Serrano and Barbara DeGenevieve, she was selected to receive a grant by the National Endowment for the Arts, only to have it rescinded by the NEA's advisory council, who were considered to be pushing a conservative agenda. It was the subject matter—strippers, sex workers, drugs (not, presumably, Wall Street professionals)—that was the problem, the unseemly, as if not seeing it would somehow solve a (confected) moral panic; and Alpern was, like Arbus, perverse for revealing it.

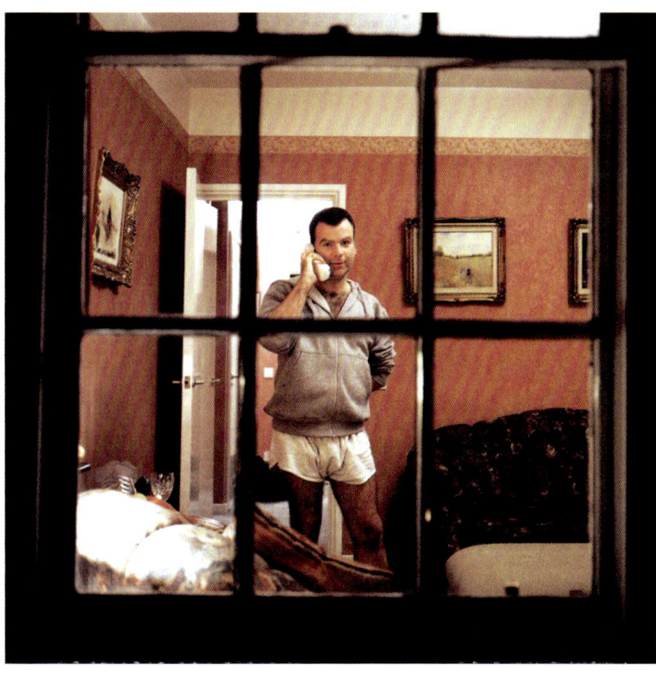

But no gaze is unidirectional. Every gaze can be returned (just think of Manet's peerless *Olympia*), and with artworks the gaze of the viewer is always part of the project, a triangulation, a relational web that spreads and multiplies. And anyway, no one's interior life can be read on their face or any other part of their body. Alpern noted her fascination, and identification, with the women she could see in glowing flickers—not like a peep show but like a ticker tape reel of details that hinted at a wider narrative about the ways women survive the world as it is, and how people find means to connect in any circumstance. "The smallest details of the couples' interactions became obsessively interesting," she said. "Although the notion of the 'female gaze' has never really interested me, as a woman I could project some of my own experiences onto the pantomime in the window. I recognized the ruse when a dancer reached in her purse and brandished a tampon in the face of an overeager, undesirable patron."

Other women photographers have similarly negotiated the "female gaze"—too commonly thought of, depressingly, as simply the inverse of the "male gaze" popularized by Laura Mulvey in her 1973 essay "Visual Pleasure and Narrative Cinema," as if that's all women can manage—in a way that explodes conventional ideas of voyeurism. The term, defined most basically as "the practice of obtaining sexual gratification from observing others," originated in France in the late nineteenth century,

Kohei Yoshiyuki, *Untitled*, 1979
© the artist and courtesy Yossi Milo, New York

when the possibility of paying to observe brothels through a peephole (remember that scene in Proust) became well-known. Some photographers have used the idea of the camera lens as illicit peephole to fascinating ends. In the 1970s, Kohei Yoshiyuki visited Tokyo's public parks at night, documenting clandestine trysts using infrared film and a flash: Bodies in various states of undress and amorous embrace appear pale and spectral. More surprising is that the images also illuminate shadowy onlookers, like a *mise en abyme* of voyeurs upon voyeurs—glimmers of nocturnal intimacy in the cold metropolis.

What is the line between observing and intruding? And perhaps more difficult to ascertain, especially in art: Who decides?

For photographers such as Shizuka Yokomizo, Nan Goldin, and Sophie Calle, the female photographer's gaze seems to afford something different: not an othering or a looking from without but a reflecting back on the self. In her series *Dear Stranger* (1998–2000), Yokomizo penned anonymous letters to strangers asking them to appear in their window at a certain date and time if they wished to be photographed and asking them to make eye contact: "I needed these people to look back and recognize me equally as a stranger," she said. In Goldin's vast oeuvre, her own inclusion in the work changes the dynamics of its frank intimacy: "There is a popular notion that the photographer is by nature a voyeur, the last one invited to the party," she has said of her epic slideshow *The Ballad of Sexual Dependency* (1983–2008). "But I'm not crashing; this is my party. This is my family, my history." Calle has spent a lifetime making projects that have involved snooping through people's belongings (*The Hotel*, 1981), following and documenting strangers (*Venetian Suite*, 1980), and reconstructing a person's identity via a found

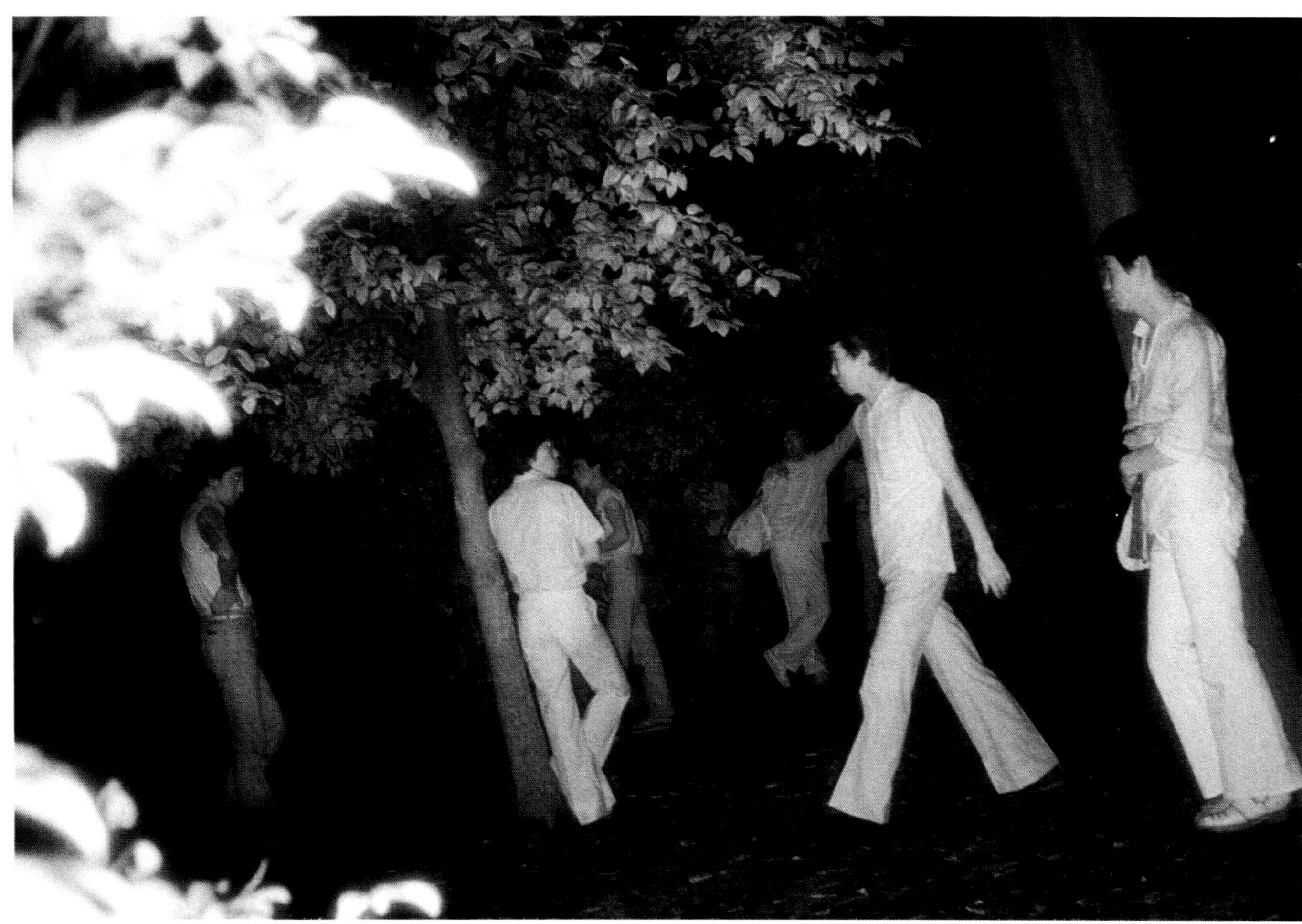

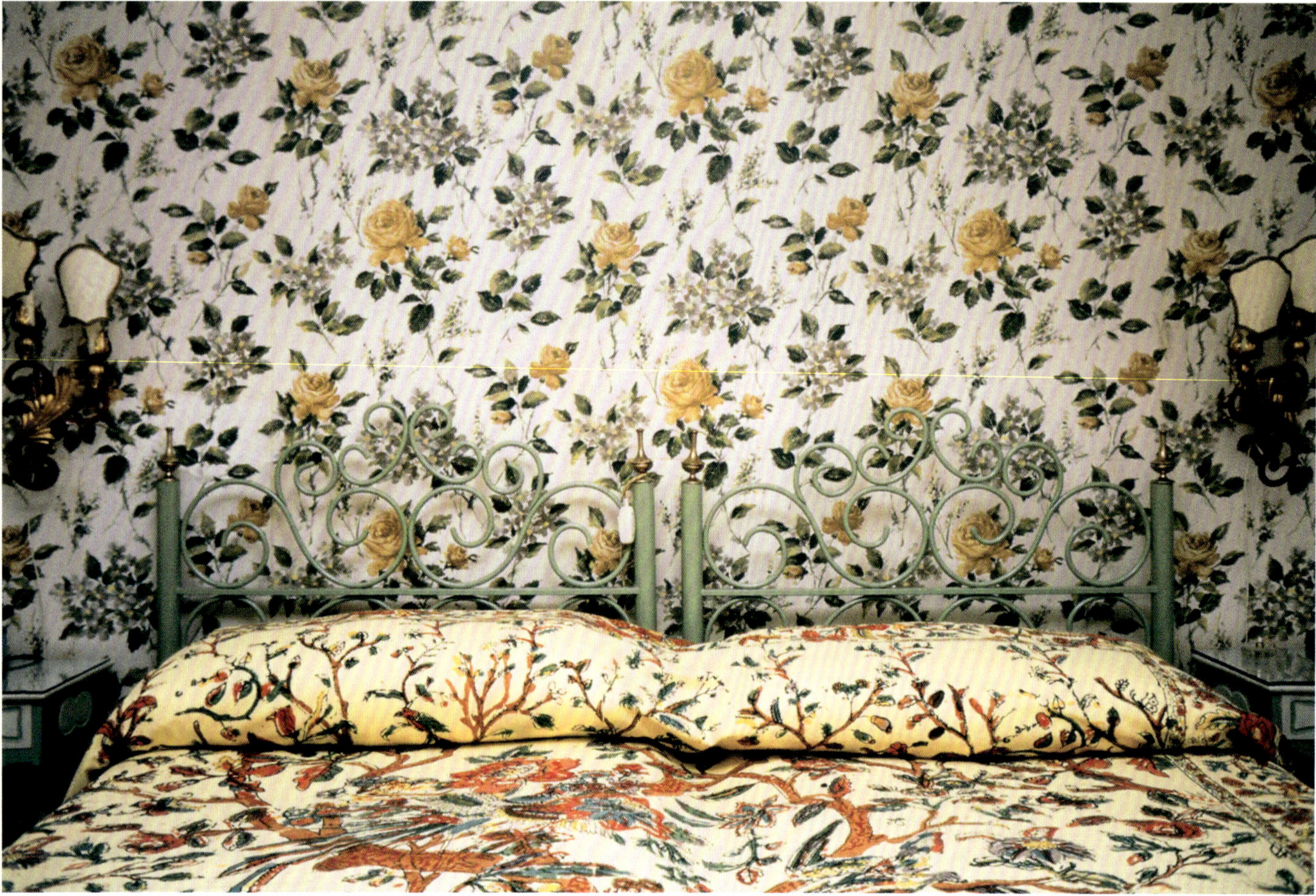

This page:
Sophie Calle, *The Hotel, Room 26, February 28* (detail), 1983
 and courtesy Paula Cooper Gallery, New York

Opposite:
Merry Alpern, from the series *Dirty Windows*, 1993–94
All photographs by Merry Alpern courtesy the artist and Galerie Miranda, Paris

address book and publishing it in a national newspaper (*The Address Book*, 1983), but also employing a private eye to follow her (*The Shadow*, 1981) and asking a novelist to dictate her behavior using a fictional character (*Double Game*, 1999, with Paul Auster). "It is for 'him' I am getting my hair done. To please him," she writes happily in *The Shadow*, as if to be momentarily relinquished of a singular identity were a sweet relief.

Ultimately, it's not the act of looking, of prying, staring, eavesdropping that makes the photograph—it's the camera, whose lens is in fact different from an eye, and which offers more than simply a gaze, desired or not. It captures things unseeable by the naked eye. "A photograph is a secret about a secret," Arbus said. "The more it tells you the less you know." Of all that she discovered making *Dirty Windows* Alpern wrote, "Finally, there's nothing left to do but examine my motivations: Why am I sitting alone again in a darkened room, waiting to watch strangers fuck?" As with all compelling works of art, the less you know, the more you might have to ask yourself.

Emily LaBarge is a Canadian writer based in London.

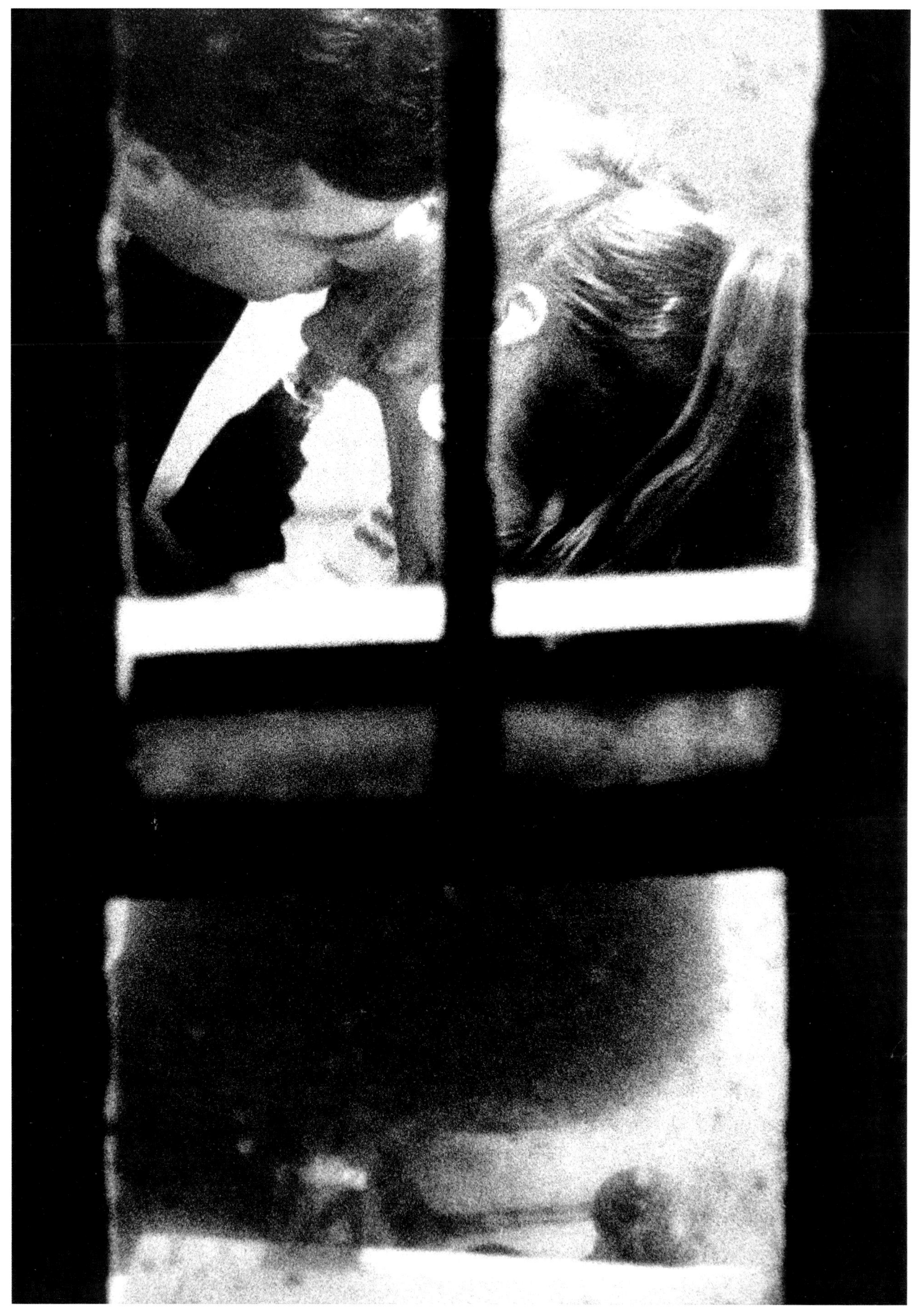

John Divola
The X-Files

Chloe Wyma

Since the early 1990s, John Divola had wanted to photograph sites where miracles were said to have happened. But, as he later recalled, such places were scarce in the United States. He pivoted to American mythology, photographing Walden Pond and the battlefields at Gettysburg and Little Bighorn. Back home in Los Angeles, he trained his camera on storefront churches, adult bookshops, liquor stores, and psychic parlors—vernacular spaces promising an "intensity of experience" beyond the banalities of the "instrumental universe," he told me. Still, his original idea lingered.

Miracles may be rare in American life, but they were a routine occurrence on *The X-Files*. Week after week, special agents Fox Mulder (David Duchovny) and Dana Scully (Gillian Anderson) probed the veil of the ordinary, investigating a shadow government conspiring with extraterrestrial colonizers while encountering paranormal phenomena from alien abduction to angelic visitation, immaculate conception to resurrection. In 2001, Divola ran into a former student working as a production designer on the cult television series. He gained access to the soundstages on days between shoots and, with that, to the miraculous by other means: a prime-time transcendentalism torqued by UFO religion, millenarian anxiety, and the anti-institutional posture of Gen X.

"In large part, our aggregate representational knowledge of the world is based on planted and fabricated evidence." This bite of Mulderish paranoia is, in fact, a line of Divola's from *Continuity*, his 1997 book of 1930s set stills—found images once intended to ensure seamless transitions between frames. Such showbiz dross was pervasive in the postwar LA of Divola's youth. As a kid, he roamed an old movie ranch in the hills around Calabasas. As a young man, around the time he composed the derelict seascapes of his breakthrough *Zuma* series (1977–78), he photographed MGM's crumbling New York back lot as it was slowly dismantled.

When Divola chanced upon *The X-Files*, its heyday was likewise past. The show's woo-woo metaphysics and will-they-or-won't-they romance (spoiler alert: they will) were no match for the invasion of prestige TV and the bipartisan credulity of the emerging War on Terror. "Even if *The X-Files* hadn't self-destructed, it still would have been pushed into irrelevance by the events of Sept. 11," went a postmortem in *The New York Times*, printed ahead of its would-be finale. (Unwilling to let good IP go to waste, Fox reopened *The X-Files* for two seasons in 2016 and 2018. A third is reportedly in development with Ryan Coogler.)

Evacuated of narrative clues and actorly charisma, the images in Divola's *X-Files* series (2002) exude the clinical chill of forensic photography. The camera treats illusion and apparatus with equal interest: A bedroom papered in grisly crime-scene photographs exposes its particleboard backside; a painted backdrop of a sinister, infinitely regressing hallway looms over a utility shelf stocked with paint buckets and other tools of the prop master's trade. Duchovny was largely absent from the show's final seasons due a contract dispute, and dedicated *X*-philes will recognize Mulder's deserted subbasement office, its acoustic drop ceiling riddled with yellow pencils.

Wandering the steely bowels of the show's soundstage for the FBI's Hoover Building, Divola happened upon a surprise: a cluster of kitschy 1970s interiors that looked like sets from *The Brady Bunch*. And, in fact, that's what they were. Furnished with fieldstone veneer, high-pile shag, and an avocado dinette, these rooms appear in the original *X-Files*'s penultimate episode, in which a lonely man psychokinetically transforms his mangy bachelor pad into the Bradys' cheerful mid-century ranch, haunted with phantoms of the happy family he never had. But the split-level dreamworld exacts a bodily price. Lest his organs fail, he must relinquish the simulacrum and learn to live—and love—in the real world.

Scrape off some of the after-school-special syrup and you might find a parable about the trap of nostalgia, the toll of AI, or the tenacity of Divola's art, which, for all its self-conscious sophistication, insists on contact with the world at the very moment when illusion becomes most seductive. "I'm old-fashioned," Divola told me. "I see all of my work as artifacts of a lived life, and I want my work to be representative of my time, place, and circumstance in the world." Truism though it may be, the truth is out there still.

Chloe Wyma is the deputy editor of *New York Review of Architecture*.

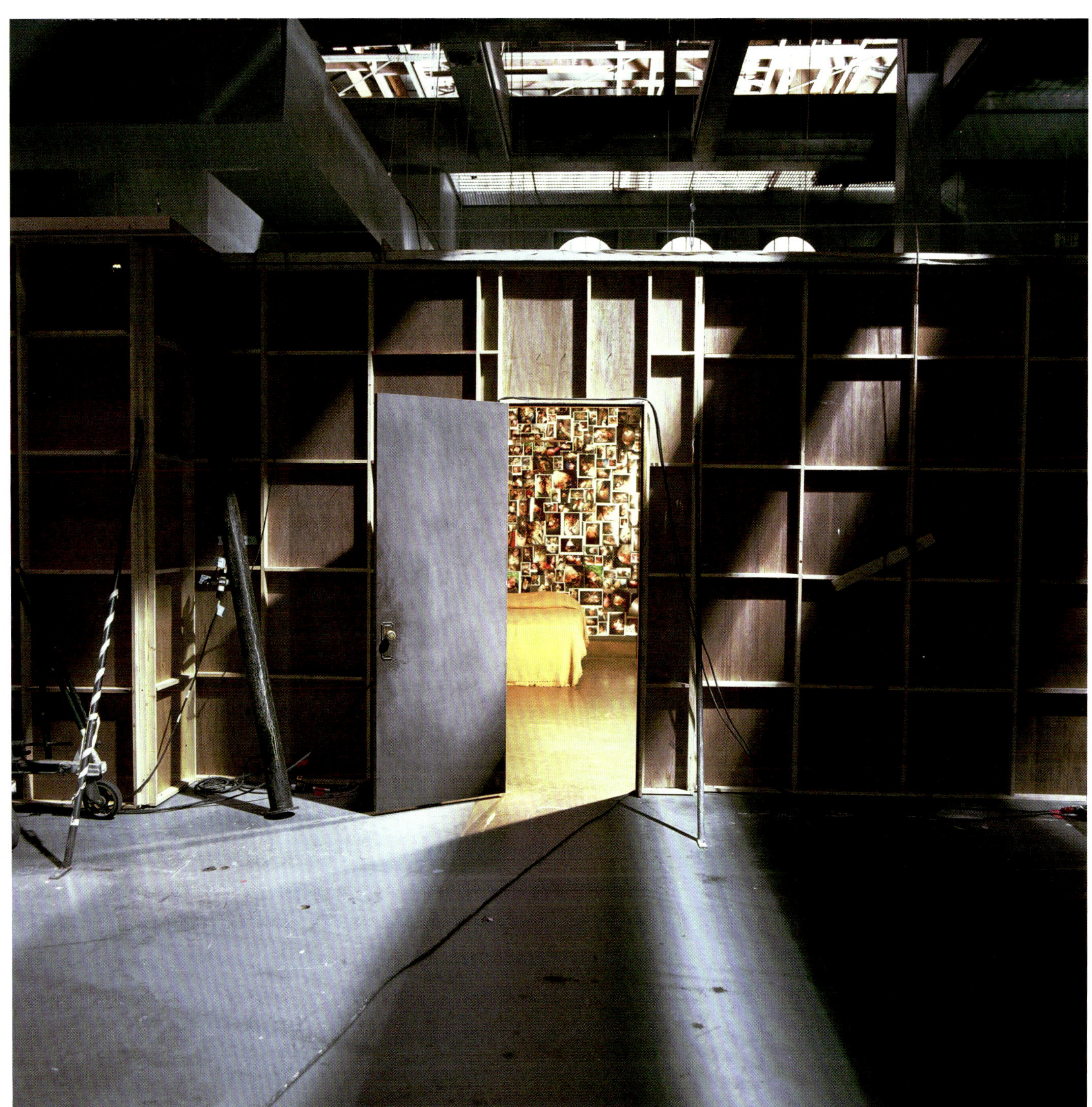

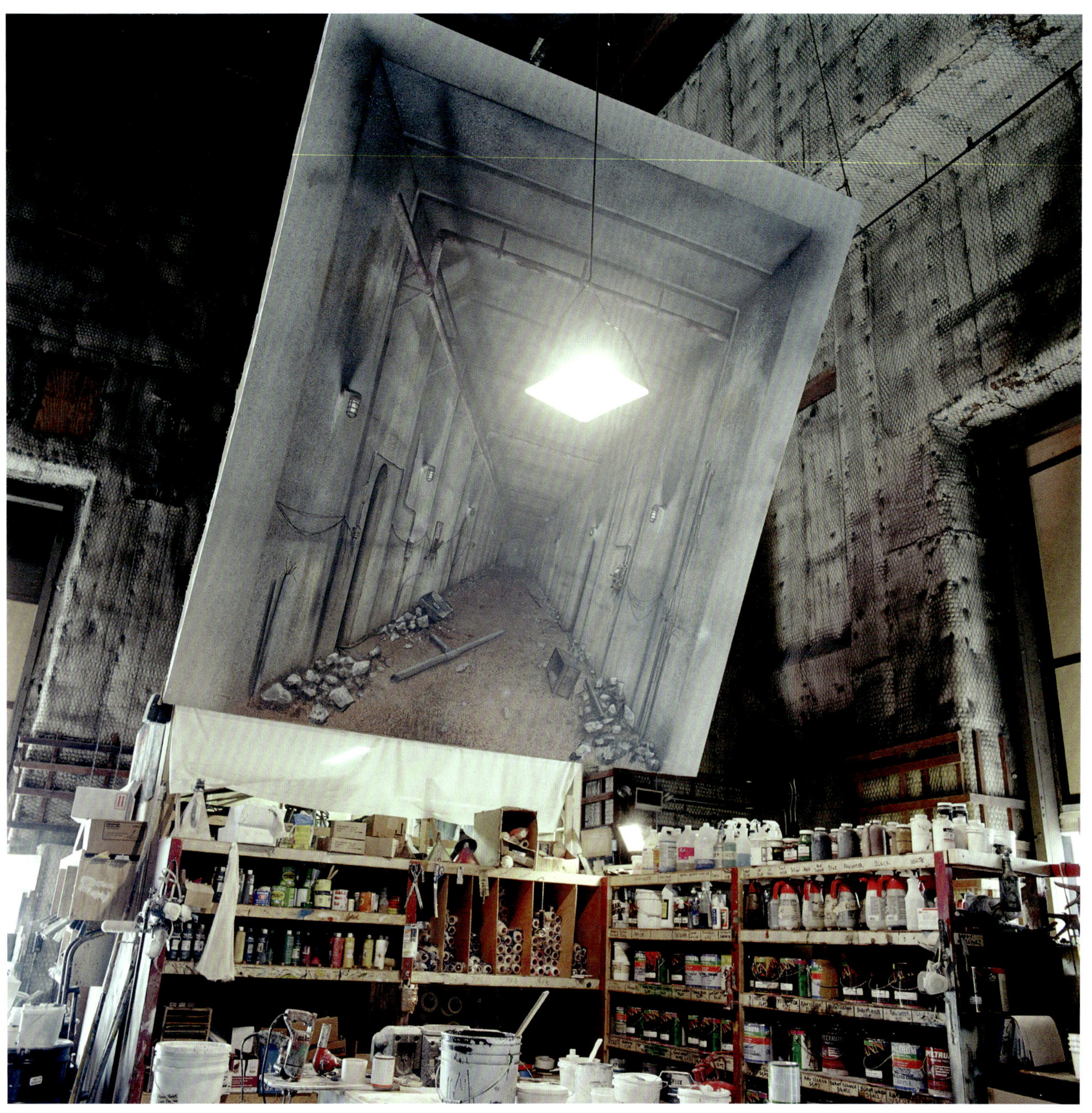

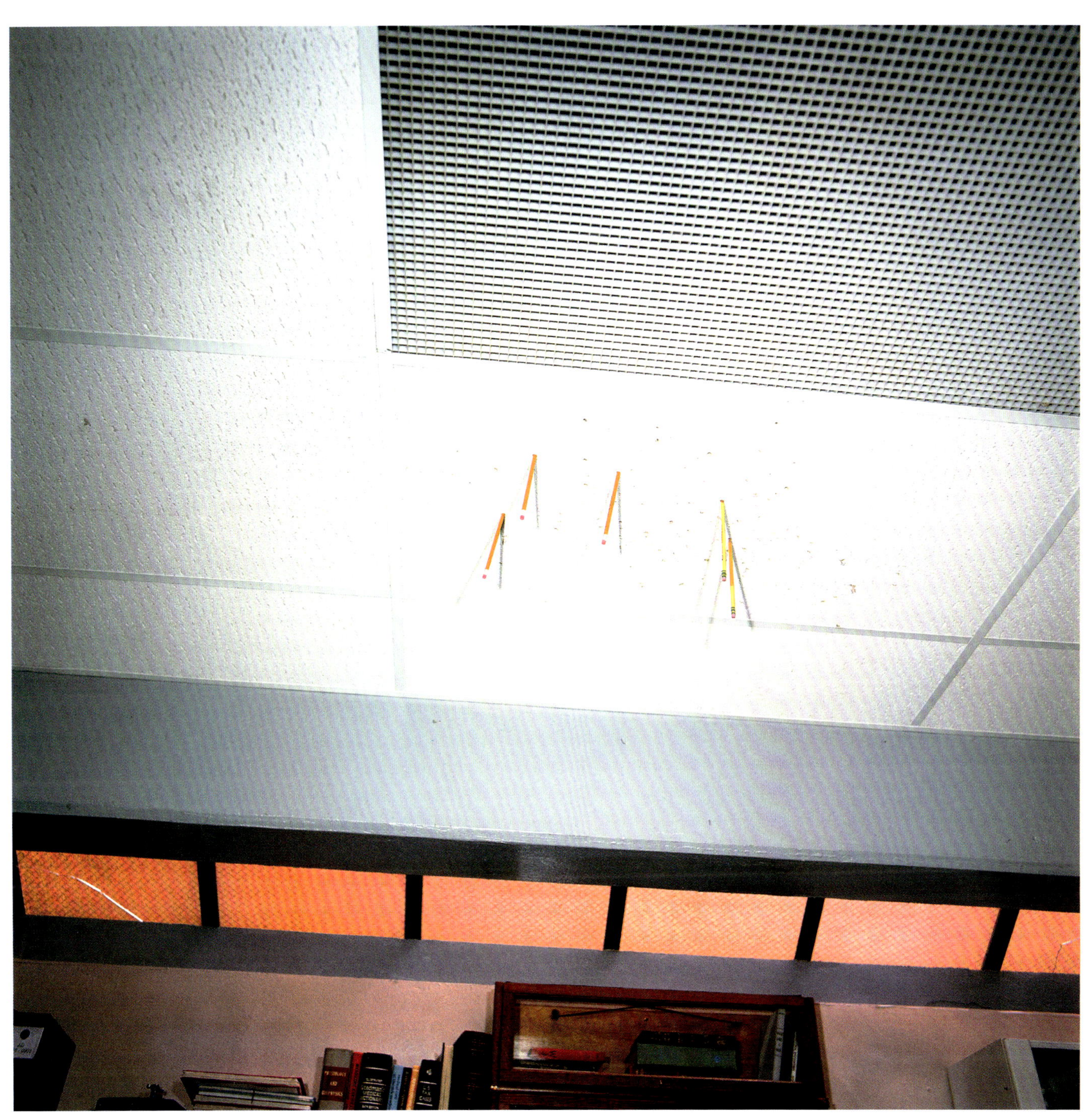

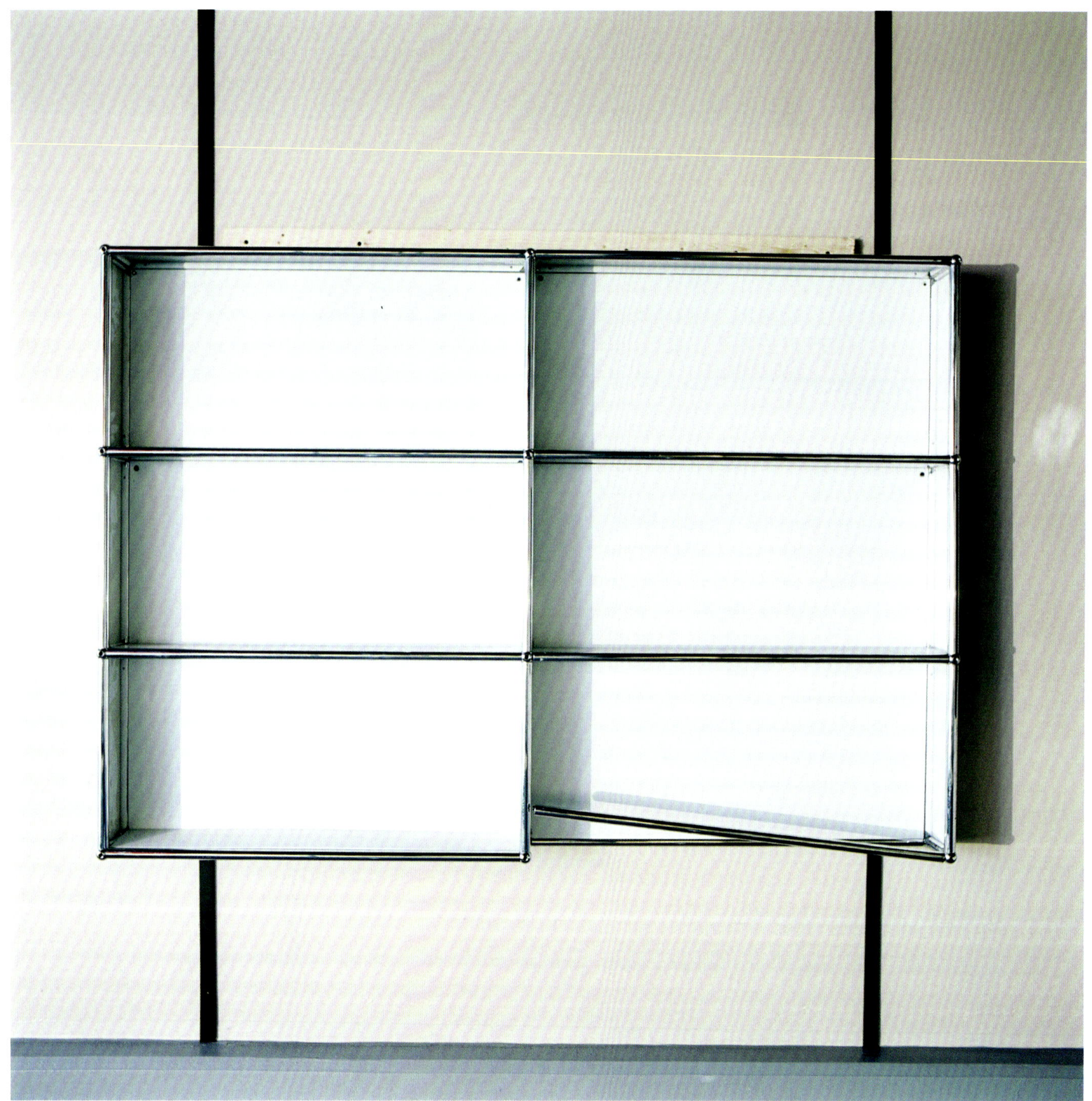

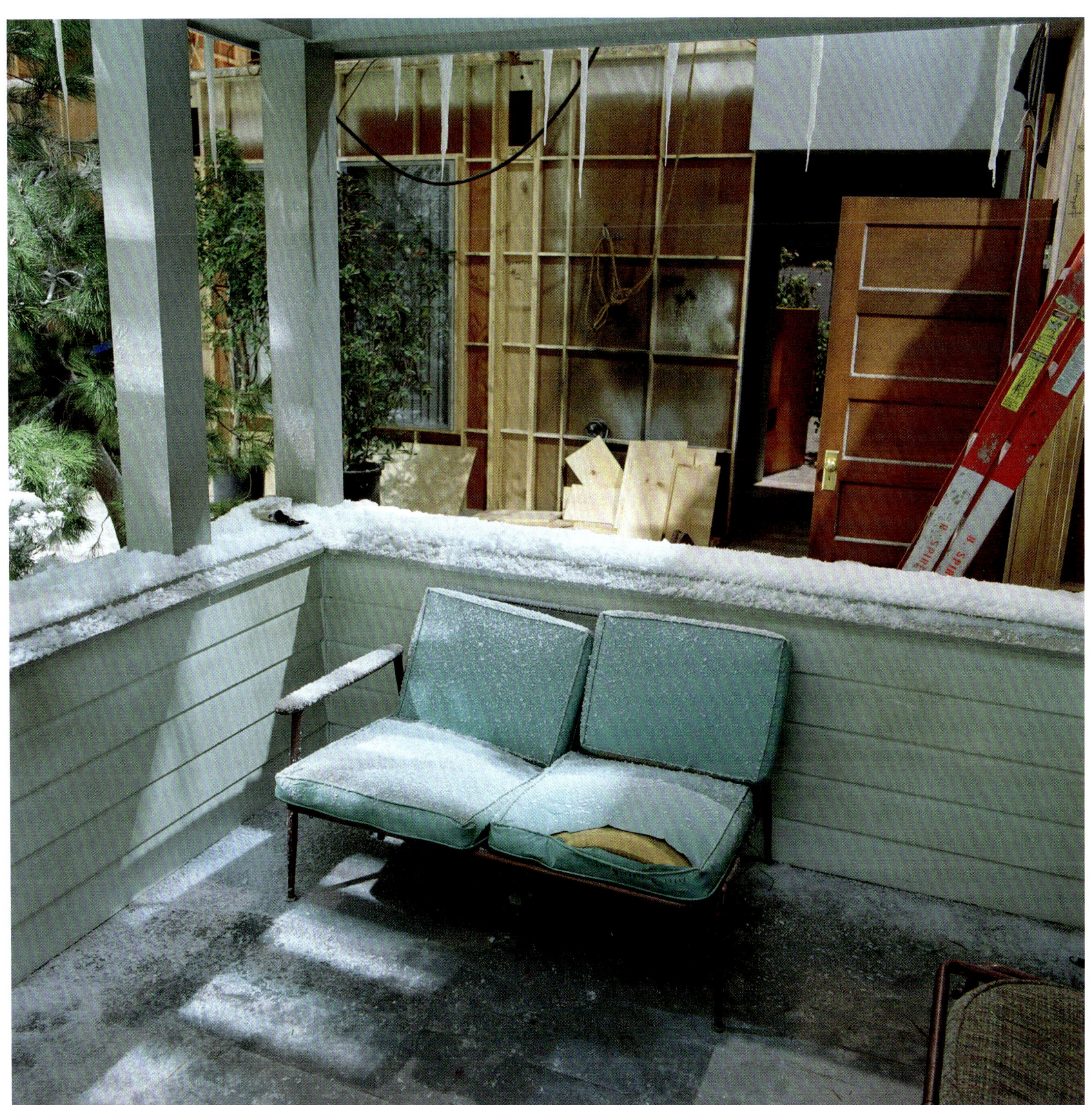

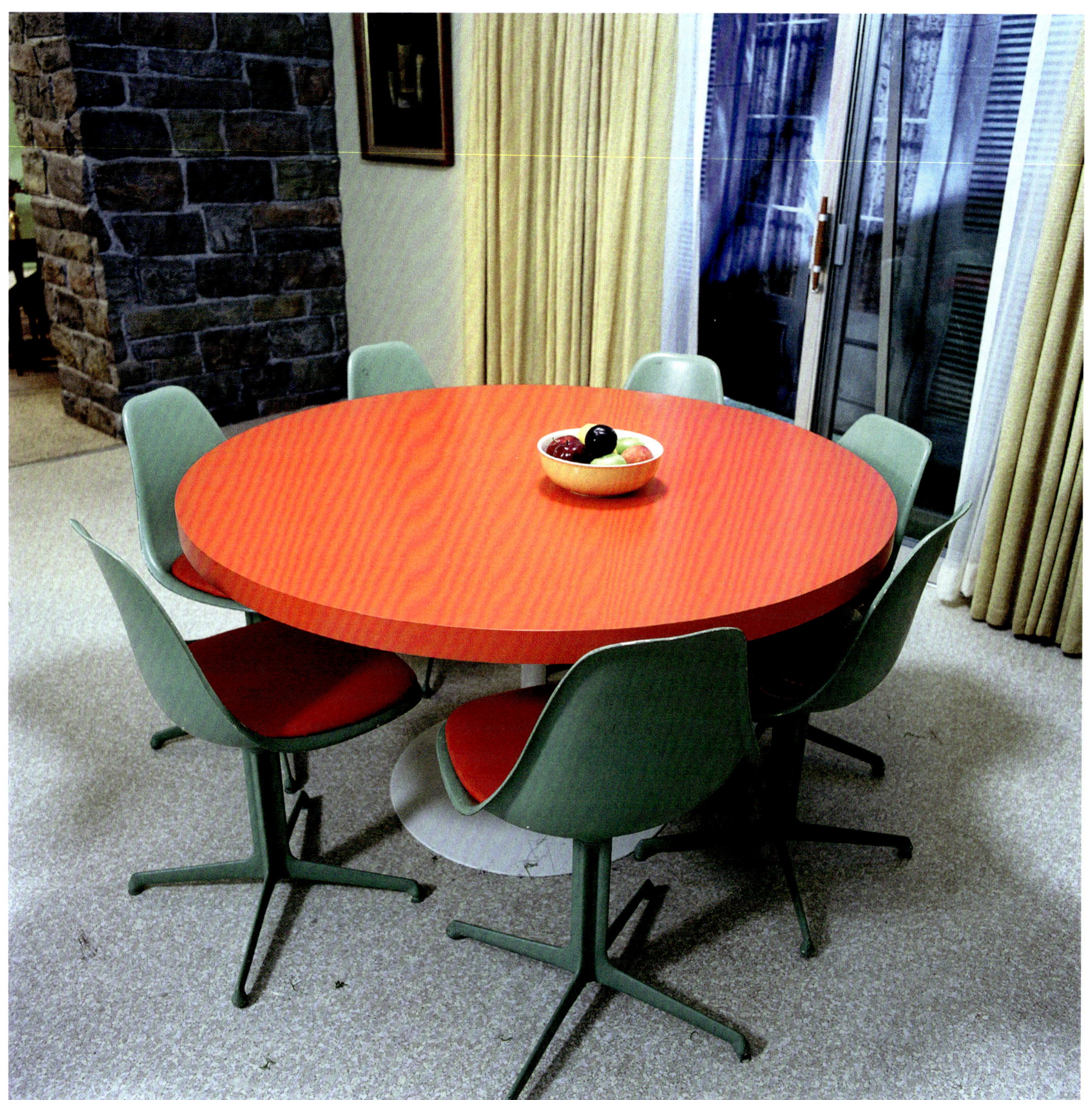

All photographs from the series *X-Files*, Fox Studios, Los Angeles, 2002

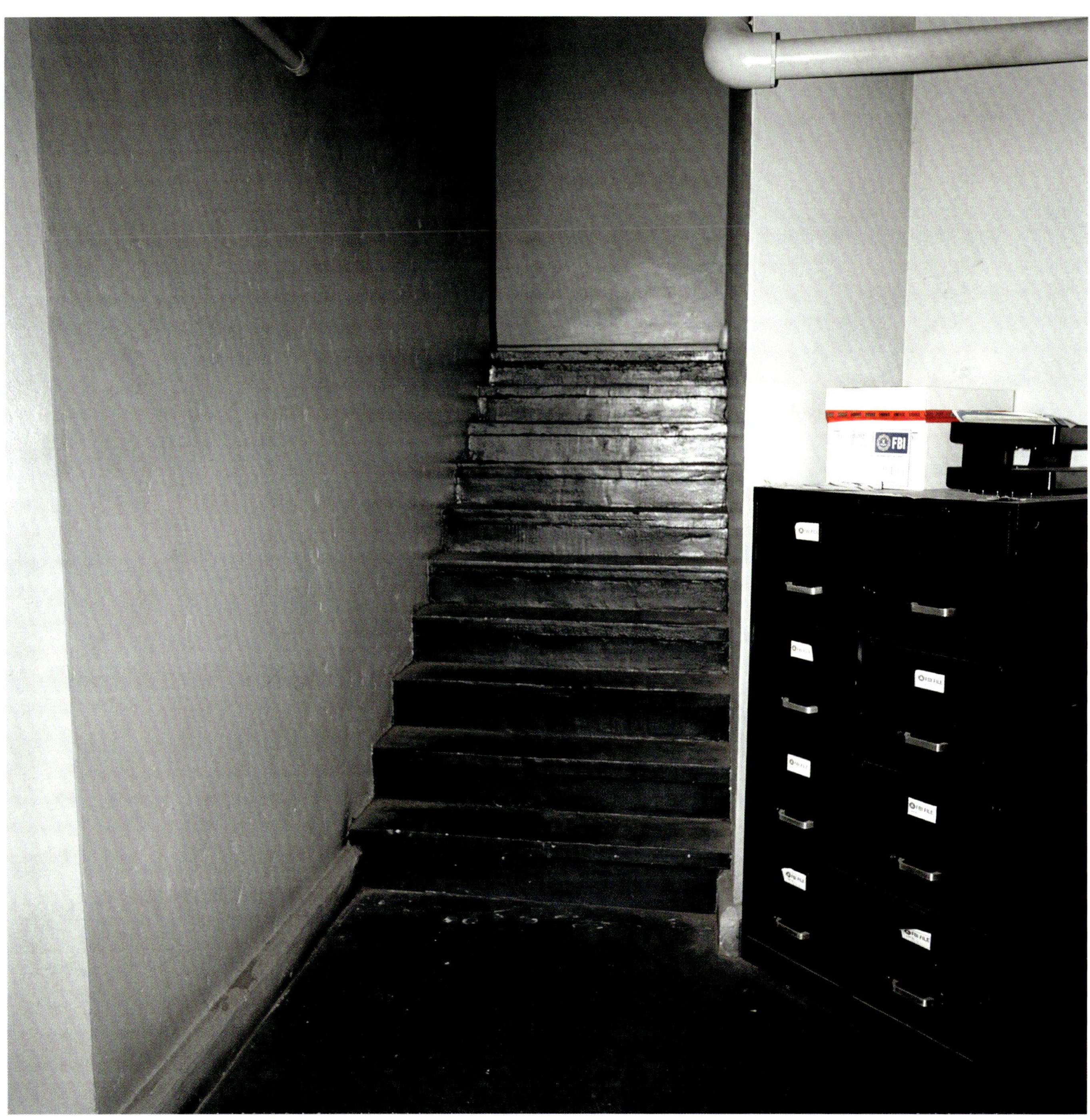

Sarah Charlesworth
Academy of Secrets

Brad Phillips

Sarah Charlesworth should be here now to see how the witchy power of images has cursed America. She might know what to do about it.

Born in New Jersey in 1947, Charlesworth died, far too young, of a brain aneurysm in Connecticut at the age of sixty-six. Among the many contributions she left behind is *Academy of Secrets* (1989). In this series, Charlesworth excised images from educational and art history books—spoons, clocks, antlers, hearts, lotus flowers—photographed them on a white board, and intensified the colors in the darkroom. Stripped of context, floating in saturated fields of pigment, these objects become empty talismans, begging to be assigned meaning.

Charlesworth was a central figure in that loosely knit group of artists that came to be known as the Pictures Generation. Her influences included Joseph Kosuth and Douglas Huebler, whose 1973 artist book *Secrets*—a gripping compilation of nearly two thousand anonymously written secrets—made an impression. She appreciated the rigor of those artists but challenged the Conceptual art movement's academic stuffiness by treating images, not language, as the primary sites where meaning, authority, and ideology are produced. At a time when American culture was increasingly governed by mass media, Charlesworth understood that photographs were not to be trusted. They were not documents neutrally reproducing reality but components of a system through which narratives of power and victimhood are manufactured and circulated. She emphasized beauty in an art world drowning in wall texts, index cards, and instructions. The "secret," for Charlesworth, is not buried inside the image; it emerges in the act of looking—in the viewer's need to stabilize what resists explanation.

One of art's most profound qualities is its ability to describe things for which language can be utterly inadequate. That feeling in your stomach as a child when you briefly lost your mother in the grocery store, a broken heart, a frightening diagnosis. Impossible to write accurately, but somehow an Edvard Munch painting or a crushed car by John Chamberlain says it perfectly. This is clearly magical, and *magic* was a word Charlesworth used often. In her test Polaroids, she makes it clear that artists and illusionists share similar powers. Who else can freeze flowers in midair, or liberate a pair of eyes from its face?

Seeking to understand what photography *does* instead of what photography *shows*, she used her camera, her X-Acto knives, and her impeccable sense of composition to explore the spooky power of an image to convey discrete, often contradictory meanings while masquerading as objective truth.

Charlesworth didn't provide artist statements or explanations because, like any good magician, she knew the audience completed the work. She understood that pictures can affect viewers in powerful ways, and that wall texts and press releases can just as powerfully deflate that experience. It's no accident that the Buddha appears throughout her art. Like him, Charlesworth was fascinated by the way our minds continuously invent the world. In *Academy of Secrets*, she invites us to observe not images but our consciousness at work, forever searching for meaning, and forever complicit in its creation.

Brad Phillips is an artist and writer in New York.

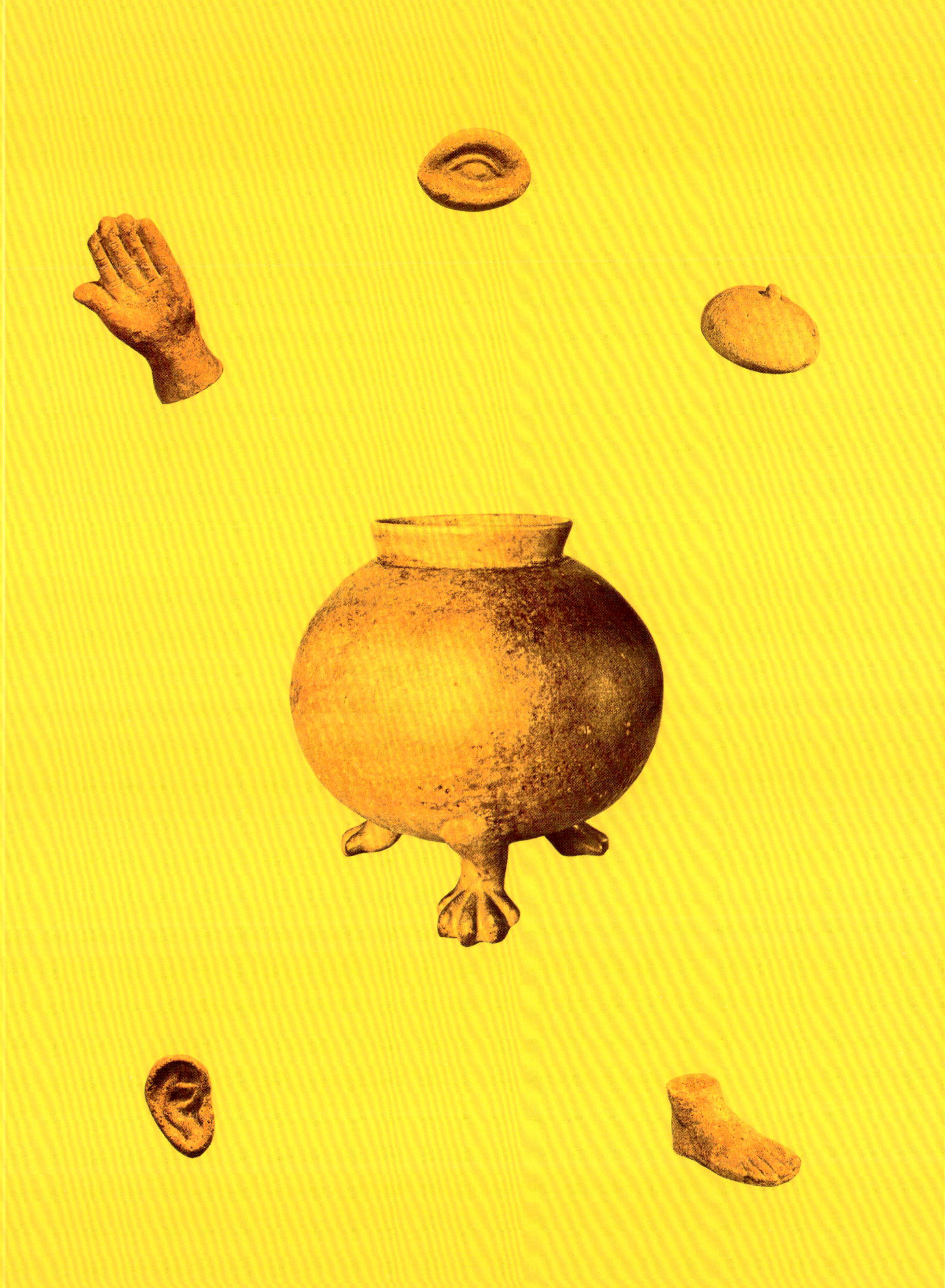

Page 95:
Self Portrait, 1989.
Cibachrome print with lacquered wood frame

Opposite:
Of Myself, 1989.
Cibachrome print with lacquered wood frame

This page:
Paste-up (Flowers), ca. 1989. Collage on board

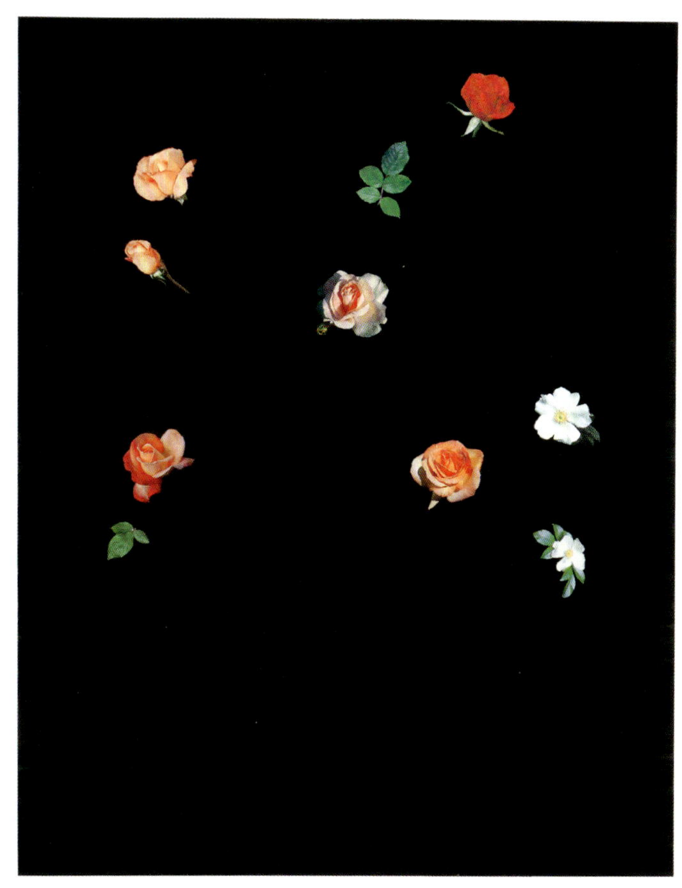

This page:
Paste-up (Eyes), ca. 1989.
Collage on board

Opposite:
Animation, 1989.
Cibachrome print with
lacquered wood frame

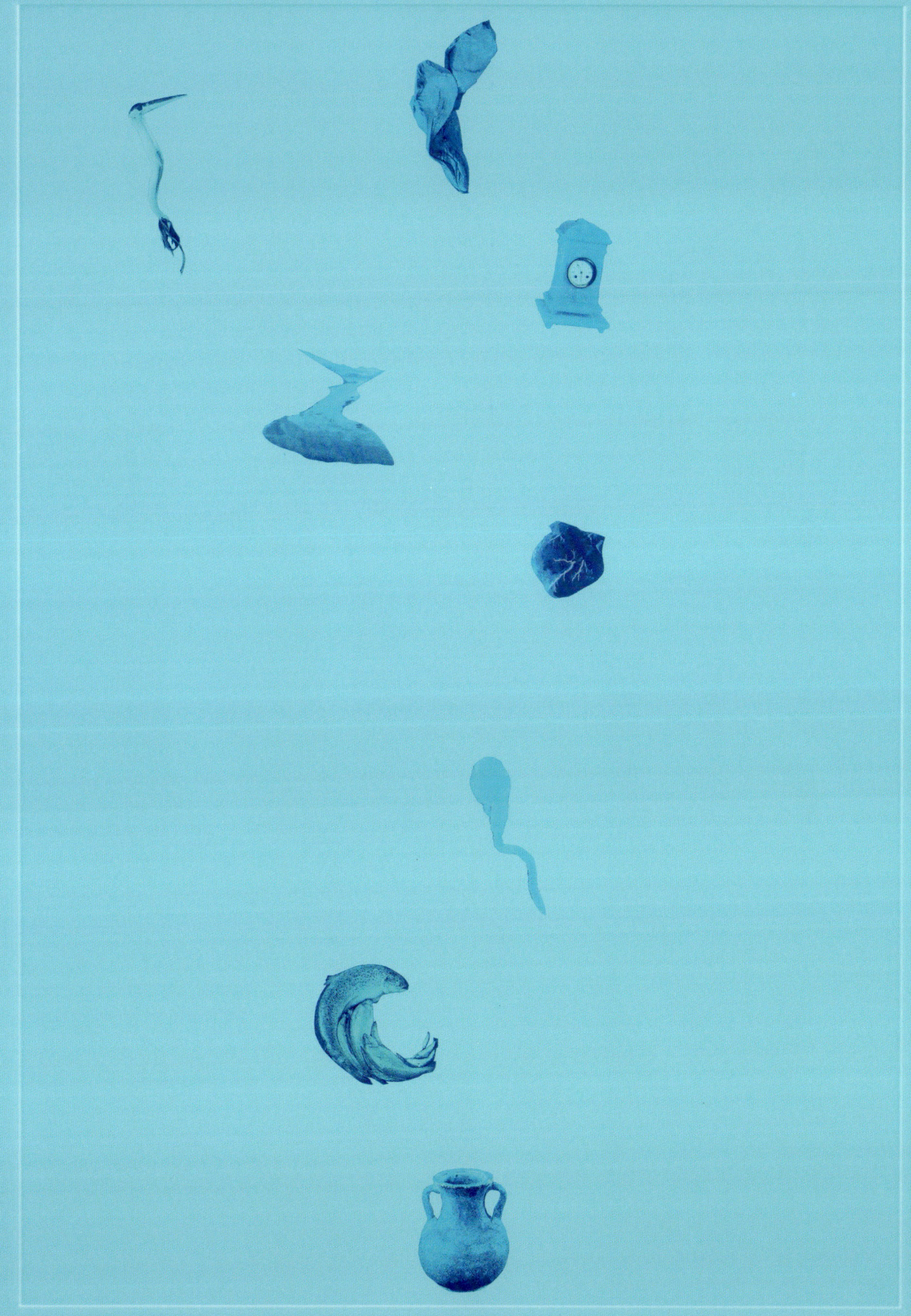

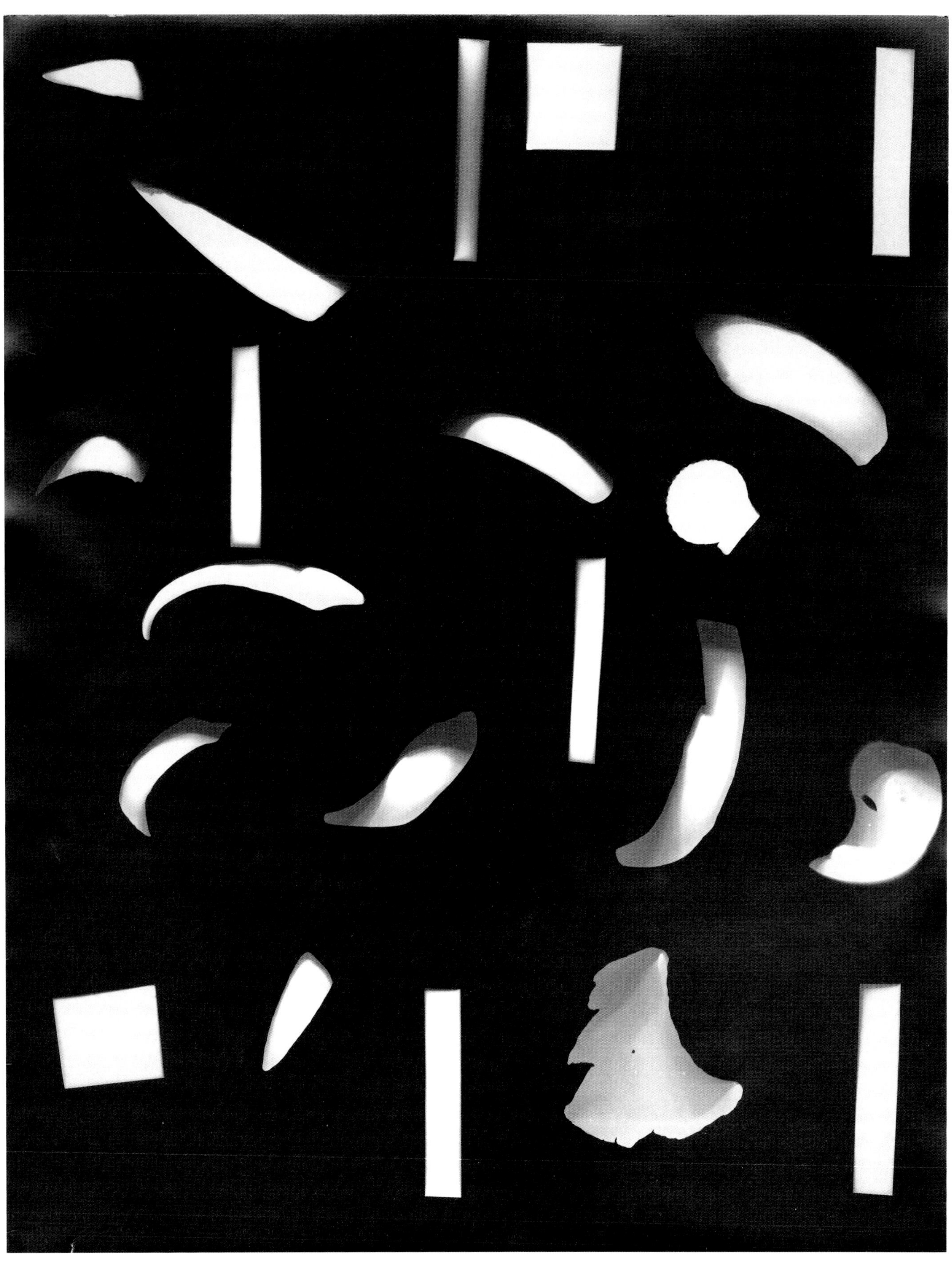

Opposite:
Test print (Photogram),
ca. 1970s.
Gelatin-silver print

This page:
Test print (Natural History Museum), ca. 1969.
Gelatin-silver print

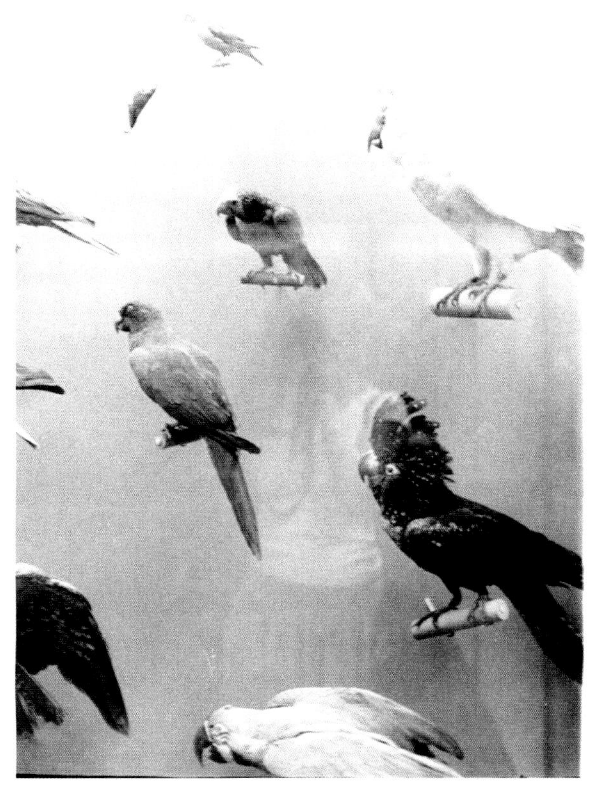

This page:
***Test frame (Flower)*,**
ca. 2004. Polaroid

Opposite:
***Reference print (Telekinesis)*,**
ca. 1992–93.
Chromogenic print

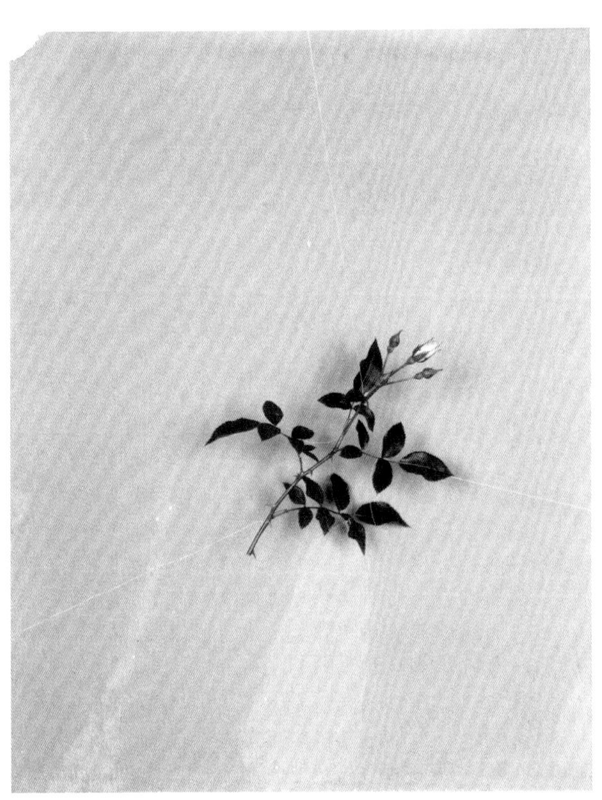

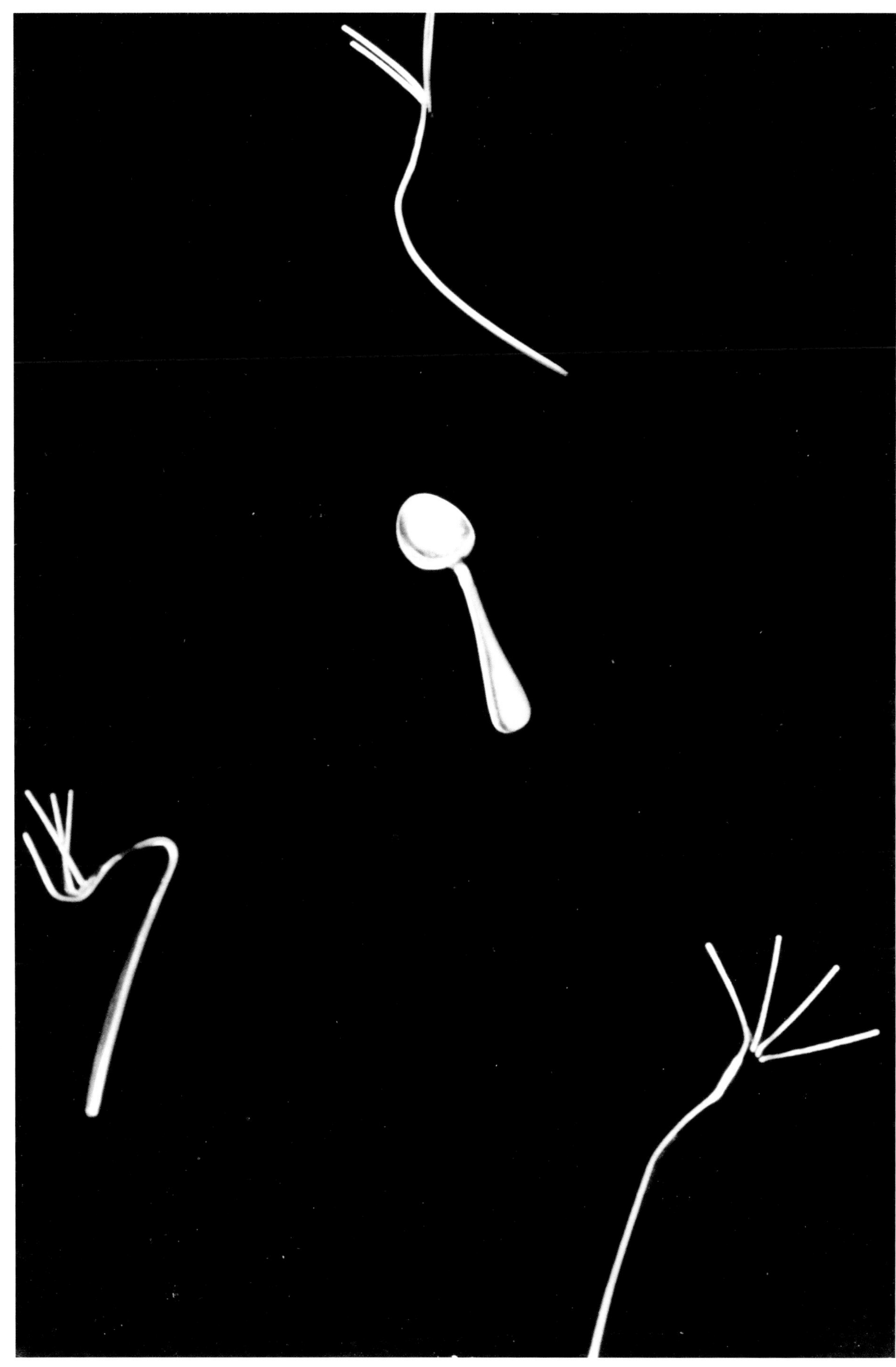

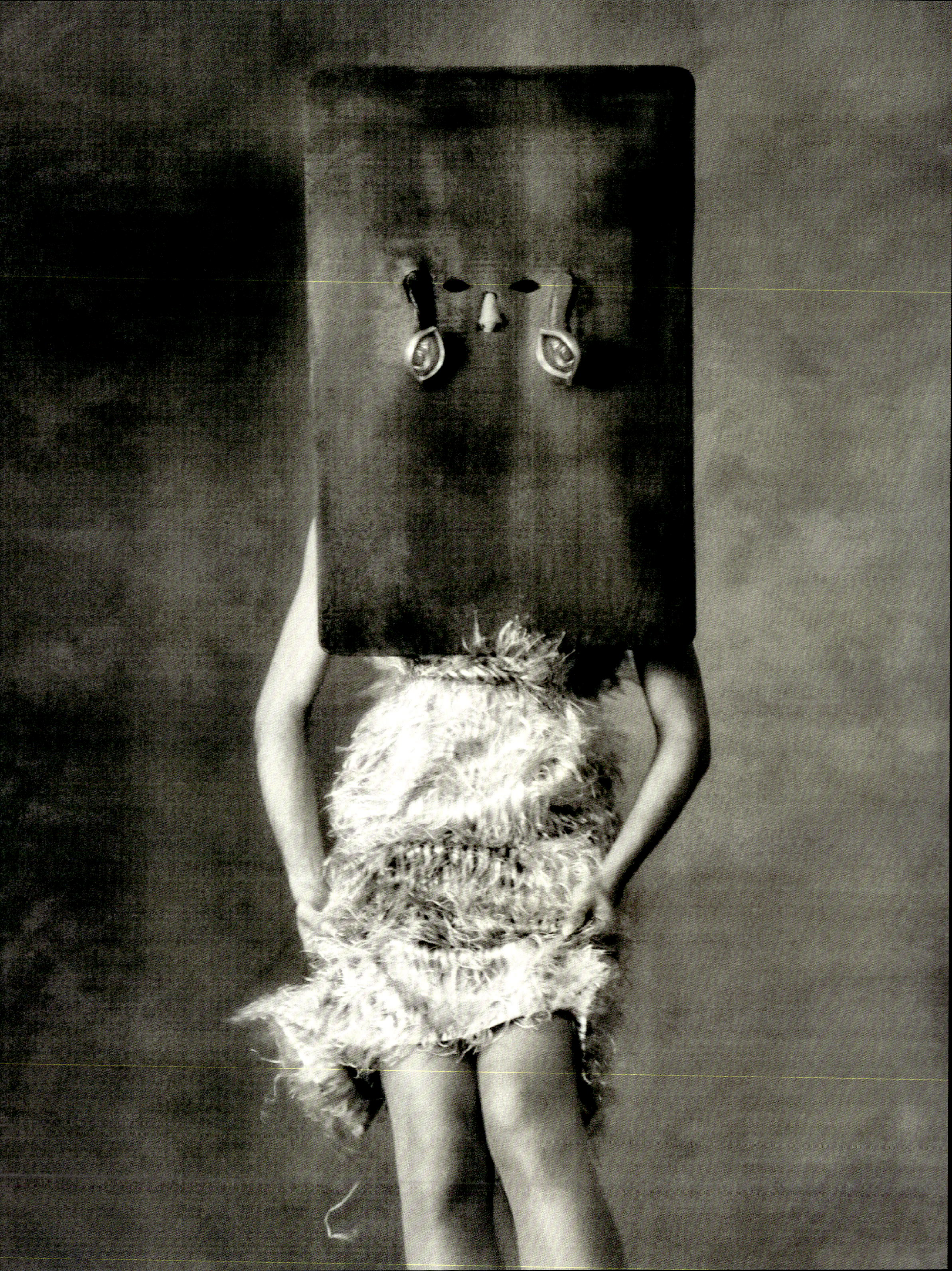

Szilveszter Makó

With his distinct theatricality and closely guarded process, the artist conjures his own private world. It's become a public obsession.

Chiara Bardelli Nonino

Inside the Box

Page 104:
Raya Martigny, for *Acne Paper*, 2025

This page:
Marina Abramović, for *M: La Revista de Milenio*, 2026

Opposite:
For *Hodakova*, 2024

> I've read that Goethe, Hans Christian Andersen, and Lewis Carroll were managers of their own miniature theaters. There must have been many other such playhouses in the world. We study the history and literature of the period, but we know nothing about these plays that were being performed for an audience of one.
> —Charles Simic, *Dime-Store Alchemy: The Art of Joseph Cornell*, 1992

SZILVESZTER MAKÓ WANTS TO BE IN CONTROL. Order appeals to him, but only if self-imposed. "I once had a breakdown on a shoot because it was so structured," he recalled. "There were three blackboards behind me, covered in printed references. Every detail was laid out, haunting me. I told them: 'You chose the wrong photographer.' They were extreme control freaks, and that was the problem—*I* am the control freak. You cannot have two. It becomes murderous."

His protectiveness extends to the postproduction process: Not even his closest collaborators know exactly how his images are made in the darkroom. Interviews unfold only through slow, heavily filtered written exchanges.

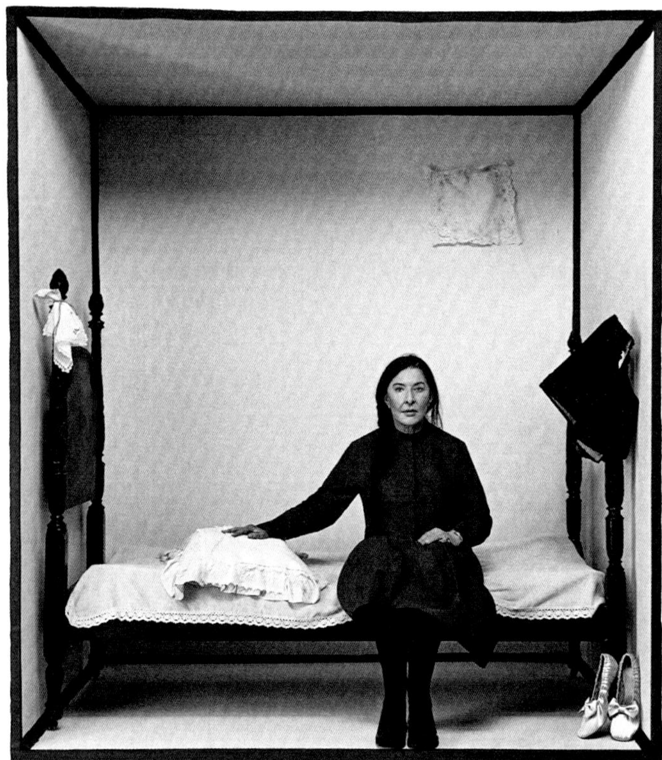

Perhaps not surprisingly, Makó doesn't subscribe to the label of *photographer*—not entirely, at least. He might just as well be the manager of his own miniature theater, putting up shows for an audience of one. He takes pictures mainly to satisfy his own eye, he said. Should others be moved, wonderful; should they not, the performance would remain untouched.

Makó's mystique is intensified by a knot of contradictions. The young Hungarian artist claims to resist the culture of "fast images, fast production, fast consumption," yet each of his photoshoots becomes a social media sensation. He once wanted to be a painter but found the medium too slow; photography keeps pace with his mind, which moves quickly, restlessly. He told me he unsettles people, yet he is a favorite among A-list celebrities—arguably the most easily unsettled demographic. He constructs fantasies but insists that whatever stands before his lens must actually be there: no Photoshop, no CGI, no AI.

"I often think in opposites," he said. "I enjoy holding tension between severity and play." It seems that this underlying tension is the key to Makó's poetics: He manages to move seamlessly from one world to the next, one day on set with Elle Fanning; the next with New York City's First Lady, Rama Duwaji; then collaborations with brands such as Maison Margiela, Dior, and Ami Paris. Understanding Makó means accepting the friction at the heart of his work, screening his images for hidden clues, and tracing them back to their point of origin.

"My childhood and adolescence were strict, yes, but never without play. I found a game inside every rule."

Now based in Milan, a city he admires for its restrained, melancholic elegance, Makó was born in northeastern Hungary and grew up in Lillafüred, a small town nestled at the foot of the Bükk Mountains. If you google it, it looks like something out of a fairy tale: a Grand Hotel rising like a storybook castle, a waterfall spilling into a pristine lake, and woods that look like theatrical props.

For two formative years, Makó attended a Waldorf school, an experience that made a deep impression. He sewed his own clothes, knitted basketball nets, planted seeds, studied herbal medicine, and cared for animals. It was an education grounded in slowness and tactility, an early training in constructing worlds from the ground up.

The scenery may have bordered on the idyllic, but his household operated on firmer ground. Makó was raised by his

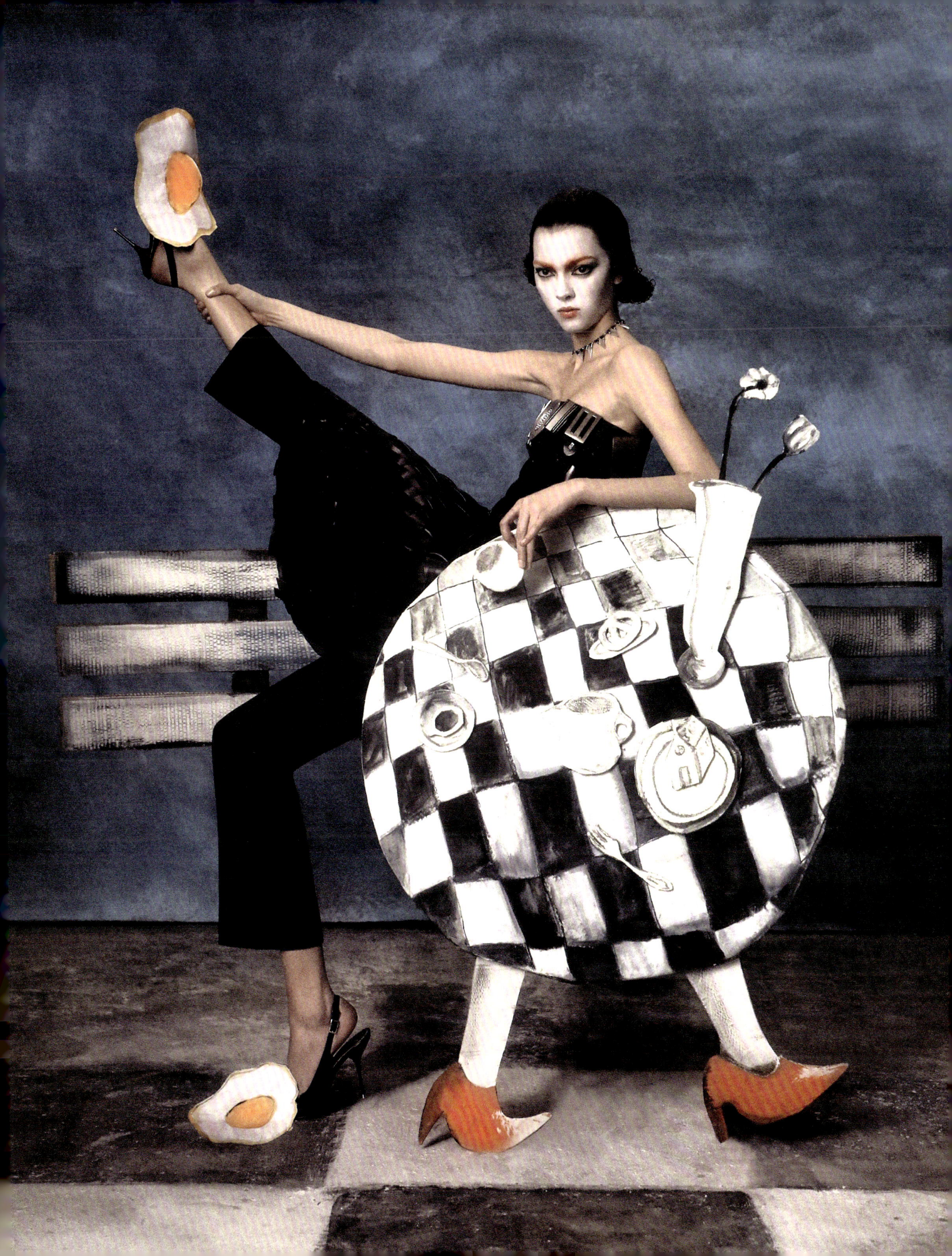

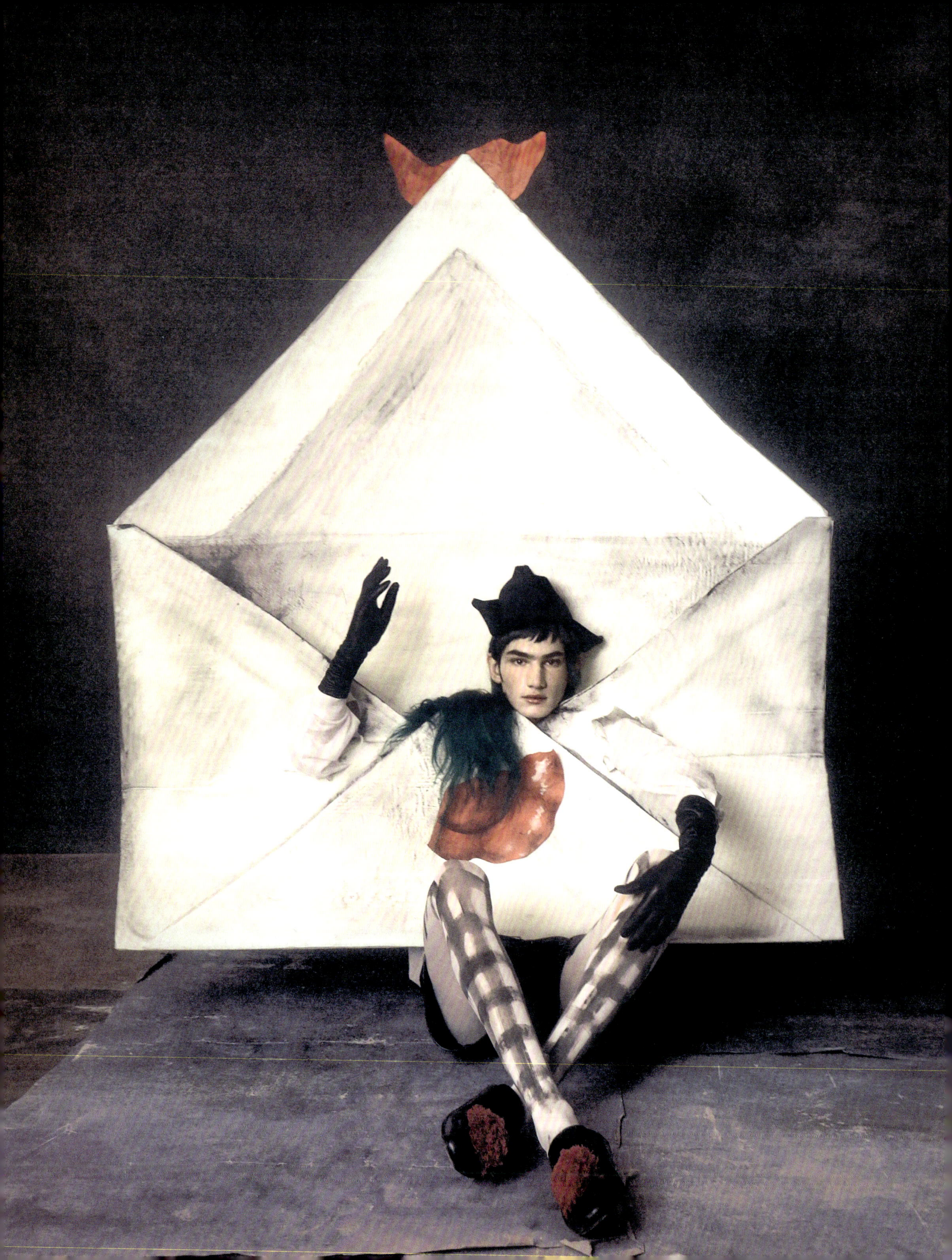

Opposite:
For *Hero Magazine*, 2023

This page:
For Maison Margiela, 2022

conservative, postcommunist grandparents, a generation forged in coal dust and factory rhythms. "I grew up inside a structure built on discipline, tradition, and rules," he said. "That framework is still deeply embedded in me, and I prefer it that way. It runs through the work whether I allow it or not."

For Makó, boundaries are not a metaphor but a method: He is a master of thinking inside the box. "There is this Hungarian saying, you either work from A to Z or A to B," he told me. "I work from A to B. It is remarkable what you can produce within a restricted parameter." The box is a recurring theme throughout his work. It is a playhouse, a safe space where imagination can roam free under watchful control: "My childhood and adolescence were strict, yes, but never without play. I found a game inside every rule." His portrait of the performance artist Marina Abramović—at ease on a small Victorian bed squeezed into a hermetic white cube, ballet slippers propped up on a wooden leg—perfectly conveys the willful intensity of her defenselessness, her un-Makó-esque art of *surrendering* control.

Makó says he exists somewhere on the autism spectrum, suggesting that what others might perceive as compulsions are, for him, simply the mechanics of daily functioning. He is detail-oriented to a degree that borders on obsession. Recently, his team noted that he brings the same lipstick to every shoot, the only shade that on his set can be used as blush—a small signal that everything is precisely as it should be.

When discussing his influences, the artist repeatedly invokes the same nineteenth-century Hungarian ballad, "Ágnes asszony"

His sets and props are visibly handmade, textured, bearing the trace of touch.

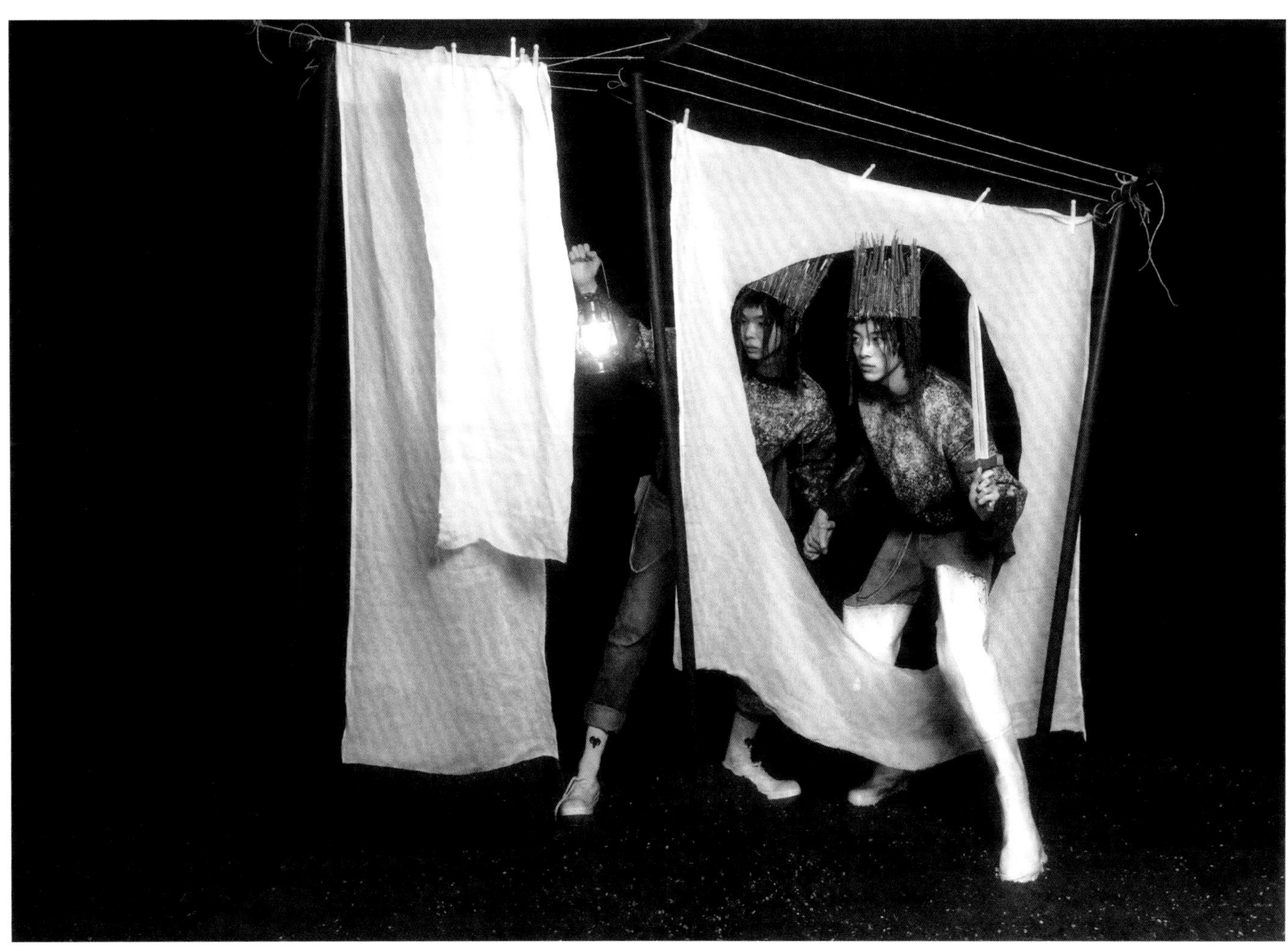

This page:
For *WWD*, 2025

Opposite:
Gwendoline Christie, for *Vogue Czechoslovakia*, 2024

by János Arany. The poem is set in a rural village where a woman is seen washing bedsheets in the river. They are stained with blood: She murdered her husband in his sleep the night before. From that day forward, she returns to the river over and over again, scrubbing at a stain that will not disappear. It is a story of madness embedded in the mundane—of repetition, of imagined stains, of performing the same gesture with the same objects until reality itself begins to fray.

In a sense, this is precisely what Makó does with his props. He reuses, recycles, and reimagines them until they break, until they have exhausted all their potential. He finds waste "the most irregular," an adjective that comes up often when he describes his worldview. "It's a kind of slow fashion; it builds a language," he said. "I'm not interested in producing something new for the sake of it, and I don't think photographing the same objects or concepts over and over again makes the work any less effective."

A cardboard box barely large enough to contain a body; a cardboard box disproportionately larger than one. Red-and-white checkered bedsheets. Several house-shaped headpieces. A Pinocchio nose. Pointed hats. A cardboard sword. These are just some of the things that recur again and again in Makó's photographs.

It matters to him that his sets and props are visibly handmade, textured, bearing the trace of touch, perhaps echoing his early training as a painter. They share the same muted, grainy surface he seeks in his photographs: a simplified, slightly degraded version of the everyday. In an era marked by digital fatigue, this emphatically handcrafted quality allows his photographs to stand apart, like children's drawings come to life. He wants his pictures to be "dancing on the edge of being too much." His images pull you in with beauty, then invite you to make up stories about what you see.

Makó often describes his mindset as "brutalist," which may partly explain his decision to live and work in Milan. When he speaks about his inner architecture, though, the style morphs into something more intricate. He imagines "lots of little rooms," each distinct, each filled with carefully gathered trinkets. Every object is collected and stored, separate yet connected in a sort of organized chaos; from the outside he thinks it would probably look very eclectic. "If it connects to other people," he mused, "then I'm very grateful, but it's highly unlikely." But there are private rooms inside everyone. Makó simply chooses to render his visible—probably his only unkept secret.

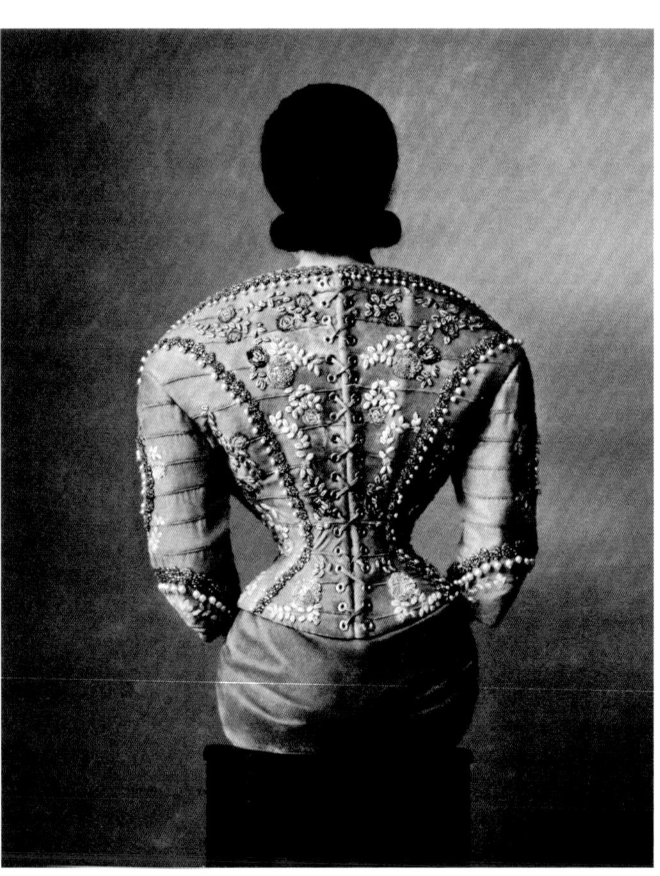

Chiara Bardelli Nonino is a writer and editor based in Milan.

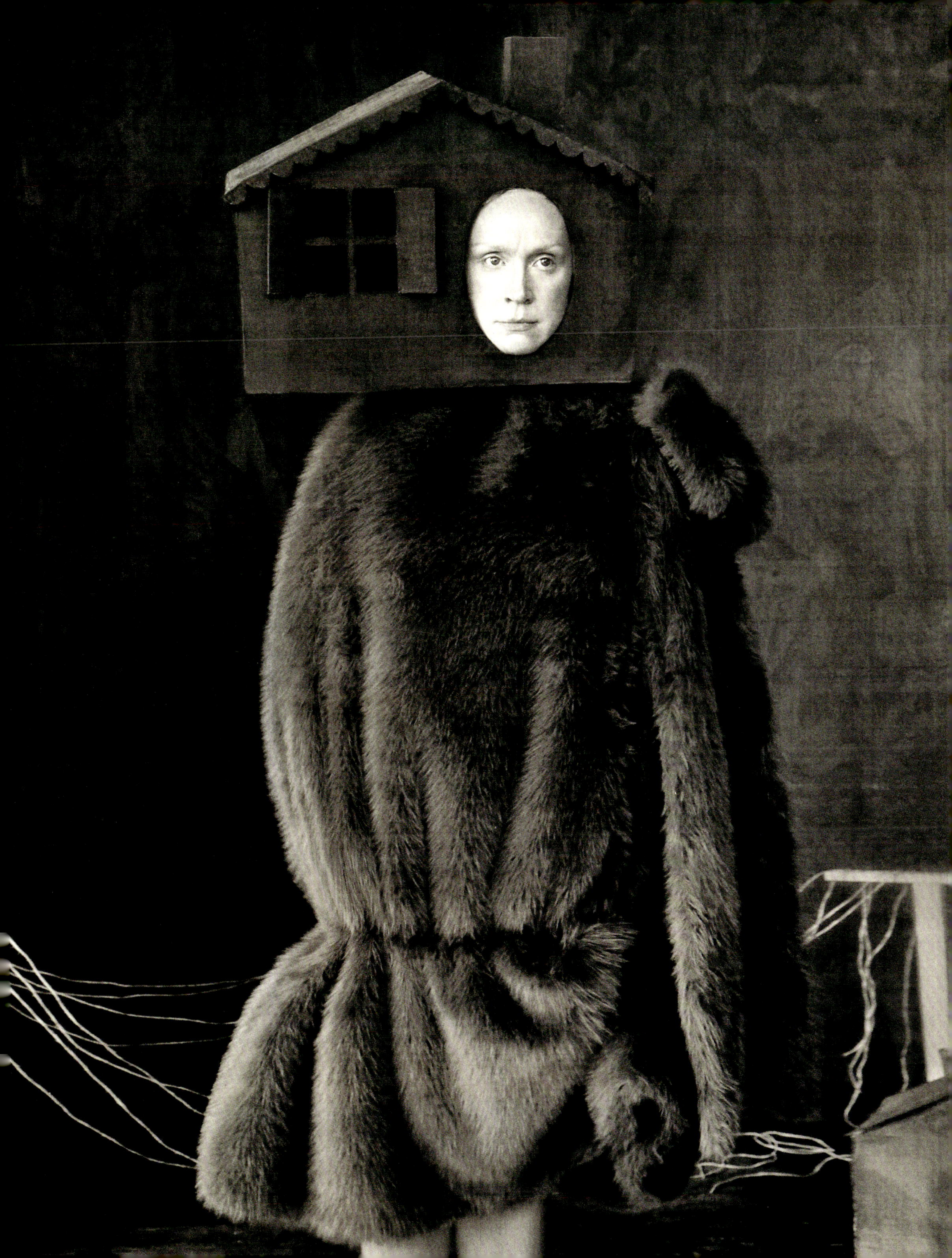

Private

A series of elaborate, mass-market whodunits reimagined detective work as an aesthetic experience, showing how easily evidence blurs into artifice.

David Campany

Eyes

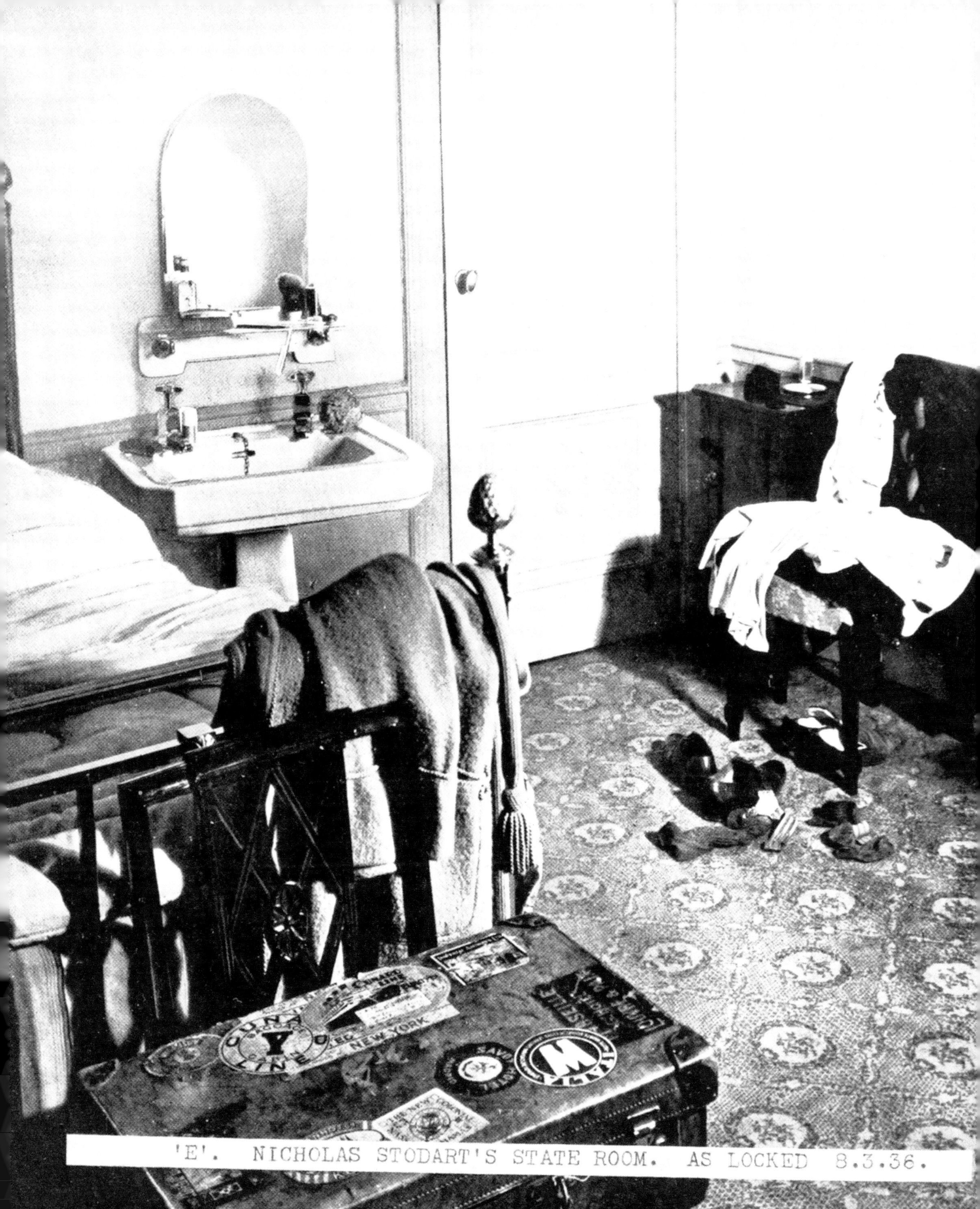

'E'. NICHOLAS STODART'S STATE ROOM. AS LOCKED 8.3.36.

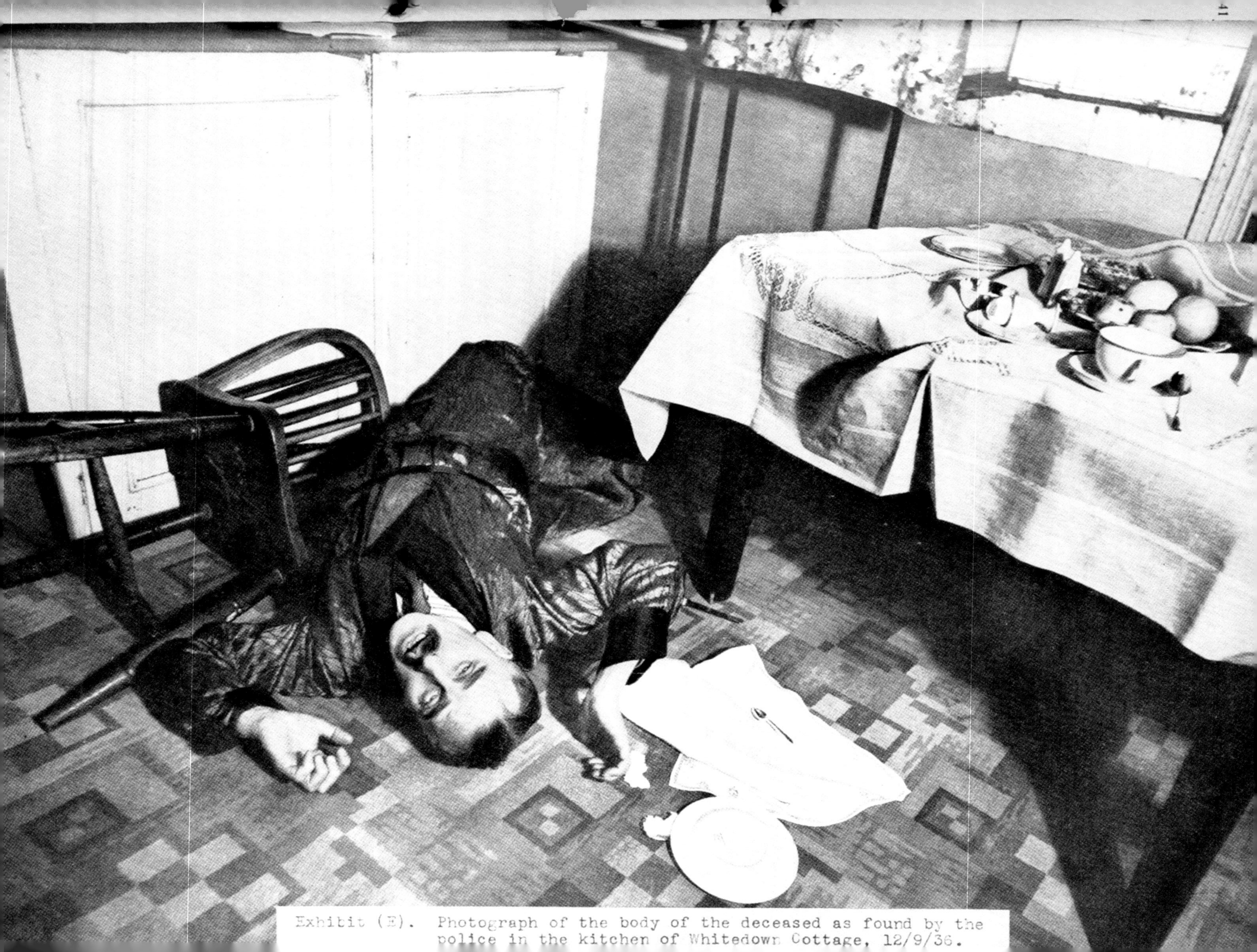

Exhibit (E). Photograph of the body of the deceased as found by the police in the kitchen of Whitedown Cottage, 12/9/36.

WHAT COMES TO MIND WHEN YOU THINK OF A detective? A loner, doggedly solving crimes with cold logic and brilliant intuition? Such figures have long been familiar in novels, cartoon strips, and cinema, almost to the point of cliché. There is no narrative more archetypal than the whodunit, with a secret to be discovered and, in the process, human character revealed. Indeed, the genre is so well-worn that what has really mattered for the better part of a century are the innovations in the form. Think of the almost metaphysical games played with plot structure in the potboilers of Agatha Christie and Raymond Chandler, the camerawork entirely from the detective's point of view in Robert Montgomery's 1947 noir film *Lady in the Lake*, or the shuffling of linear time in Christopher Nolan's 2000 puzzle movie *Memento*.

One of the most innovative takes on the detective genre was a series of four publications in the 1930s that took the form of police files. The British writer Dennis Wheatley and the budding art historian J. G. Links devised fictional crimes to be presented as not stories but dossiers of evidence of the kind a detective might accumulate in the course of an investigation: facsimiles of typed and handwritten letters, newspaper cuttings, telegrams, witness statements, receipts, travel tickets—all bound in brown folders tied with red ribbon. The reader would sift through the material and draw their own conclusions before unsealing the answer at the back. *Murder off Miami* (1936), *Who Killed Robert Prentice?* (1937), *The Malinsay Massacre* (1938), and *Herewith the Clues* (1939) were labor-intensive marvels of publishing, making use of many different printing methods and papers as well as physical artifacts such as samples of real human hair, patches of bloodstained fabric, and extinguished matches. This would be impressive enough in a limited-edition publication,

Unless noted, all images from *Who Killed Robert Prentice?*, 1937

This page, left: *Murder off Miami*, 1936

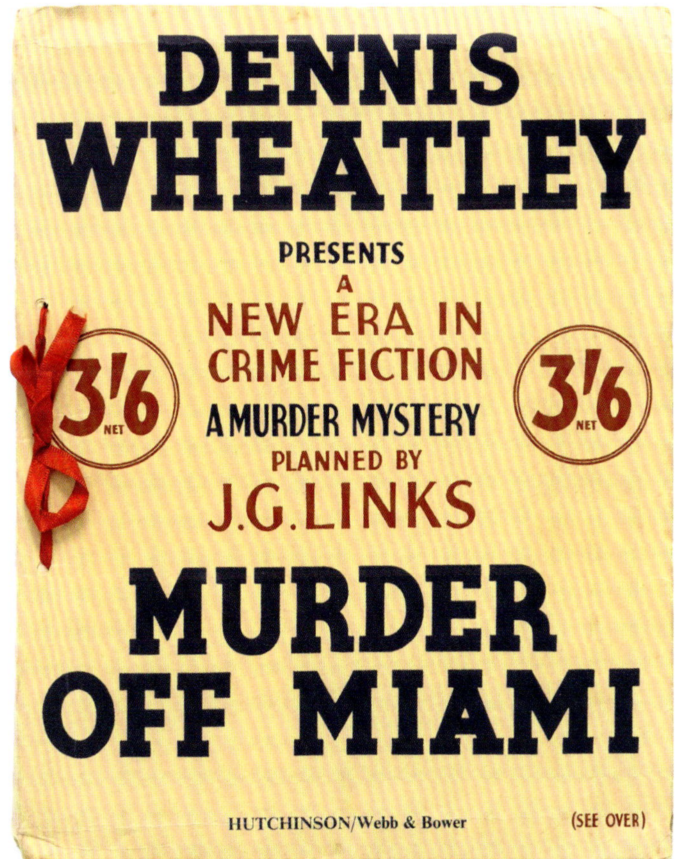

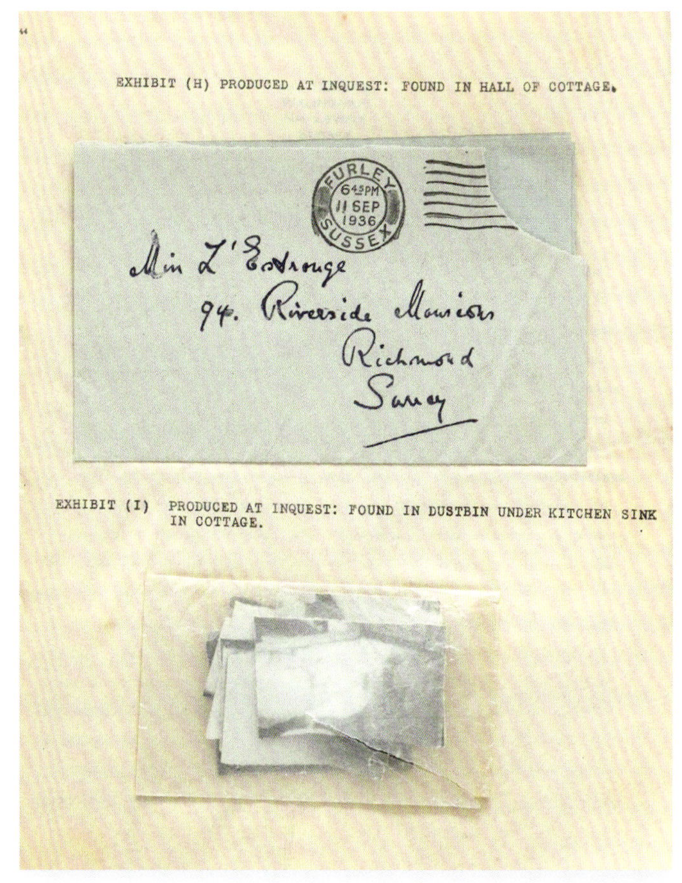

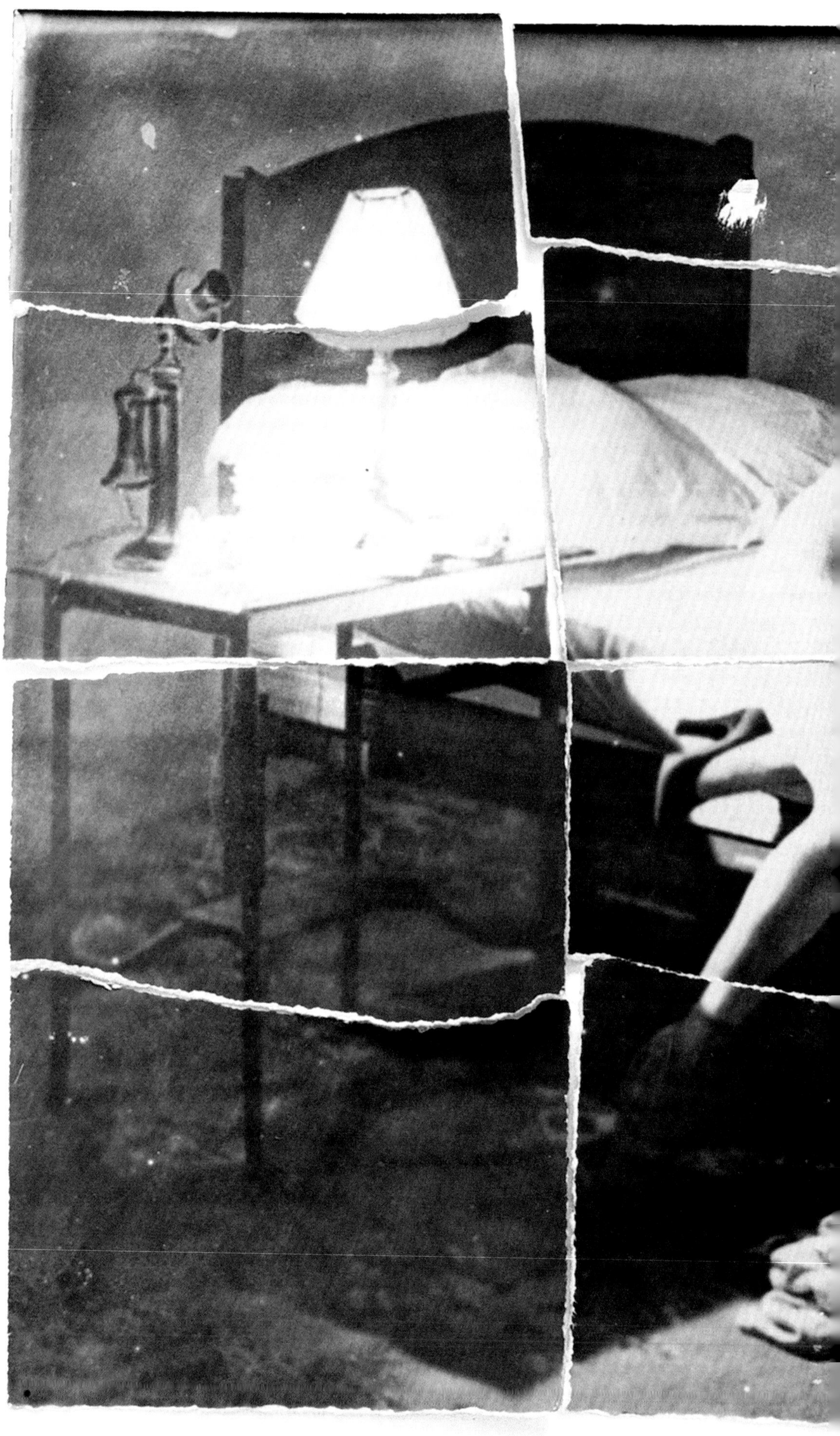

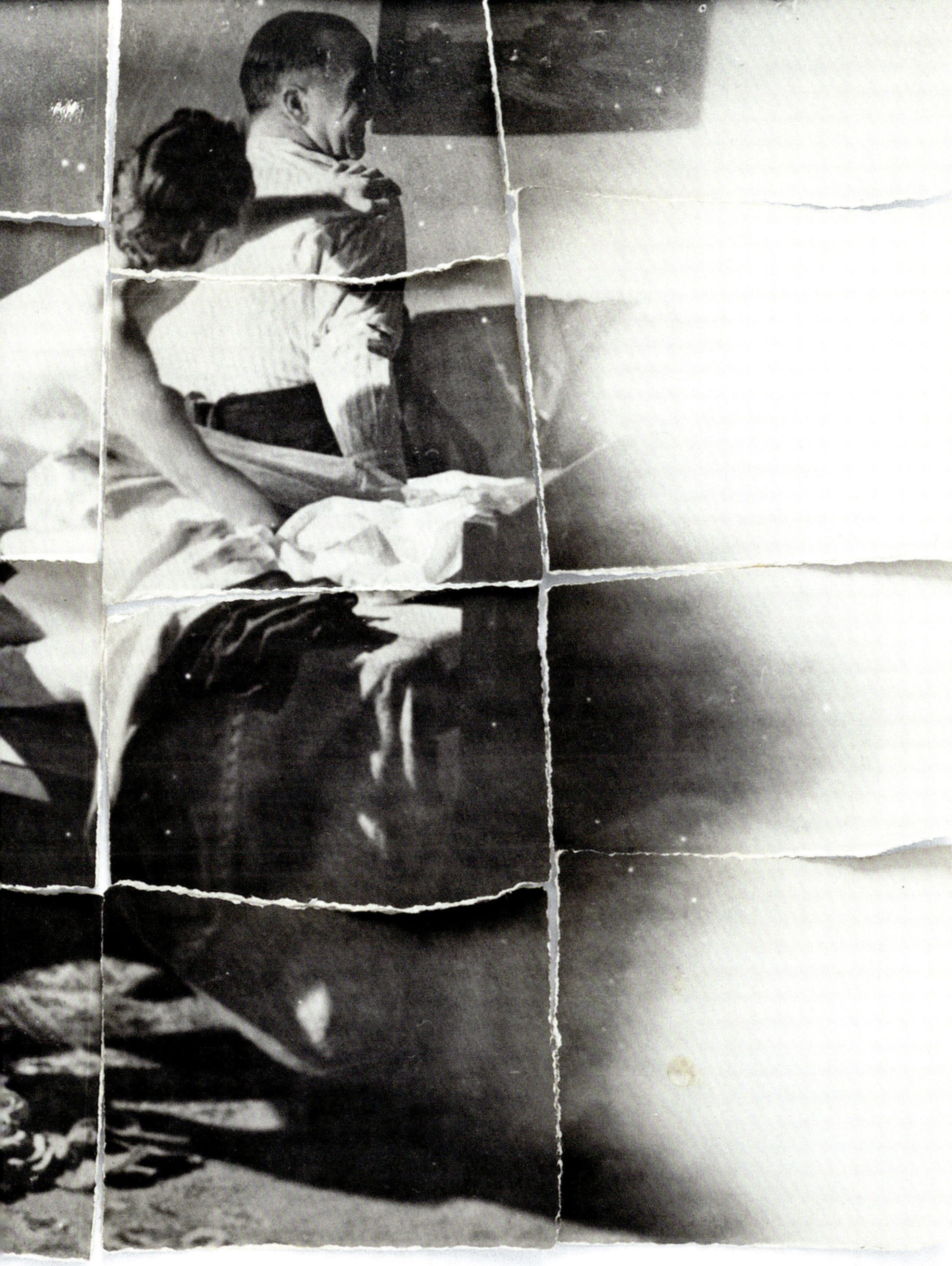

Marcel Duchamp, ***The Bride Stripped Bare by her Bachelors, Even (The Green Box)*, 1934**

but these books sold in the hundreds of thousands in Europe and the United States.

As technical feats, the Wheatley-Links publications were unparalleled in popular publishing, and the closest comparison is from the most extreme edge of the avant-garde. Marcel Duchamp's *The Bride Stripped Bare by Her Bachelors, Even (The Green Box)*, from 1934, produced in an edition of three hundred, contains facsimile fragments of notes and photographs the artist made while conceiving and fabricating his arcane sculptural work *The Bride Stripped Bare by Her Bachelors, Even (The Large Glass)* (1915–23). Duchamp was encouraging art lovers to behave more like detectives than connoisseurs, coming to know the secrets of *The Large Glass* through enigmatic clues. The Wheatley-Links books were doing the opposite, turning the world of police detection into a distinct aesthetic experience and, in the process, encouraging an awareness that evidence is not so far from artifice, and easy to fake.

These publications were unparalleled in popular publishing, and the closest comparison is from the most extreme edge of the avant-garde.

The series' most remarkable moment comes in *Who Killed Robert Prentice?* Glued to a page is a little glassine pocket containing the torn-up fragments of a photograph. The image is not a halftone reproduction but an actual darkroom print. Pieced together, it forms a tableau of a couple dressing or undressing in a bedroom. (Clues elsewhere tell us this is an illicit affair, and that the image was captured by a hidden camera.) It is hard to imagine this photograph being printed in such huge quantities for the book, with each one then torn and packed neatly away. There must have been dozens of workers assembling these publications. We do know the profit margin was slim, and as the series progressed fewer of these expensive and time-consuming artifacts were included. Interest remained decades later, however, and in 1979 *Murder off Miami* was reissued (with fragments of hair provided by nuns from convents across Europe!). The other titles soon followed.

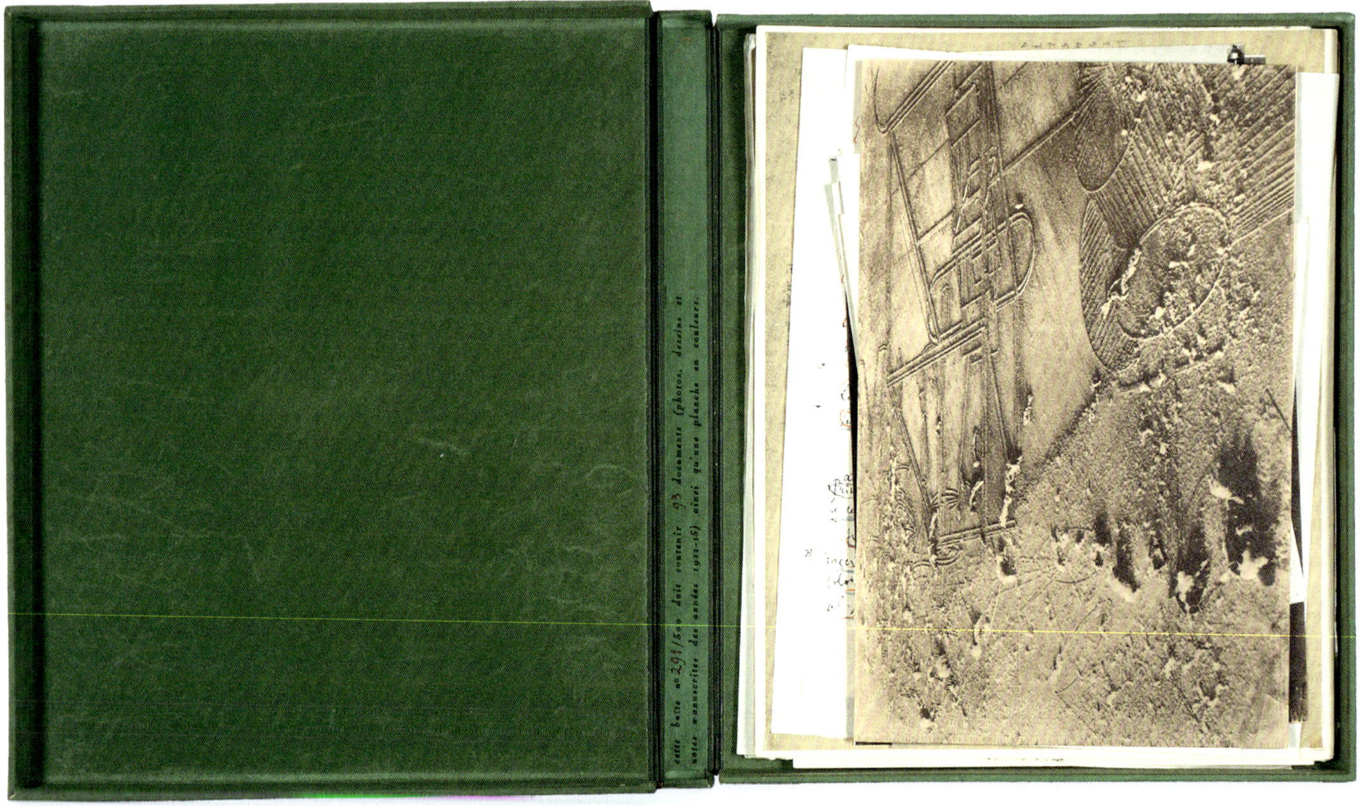

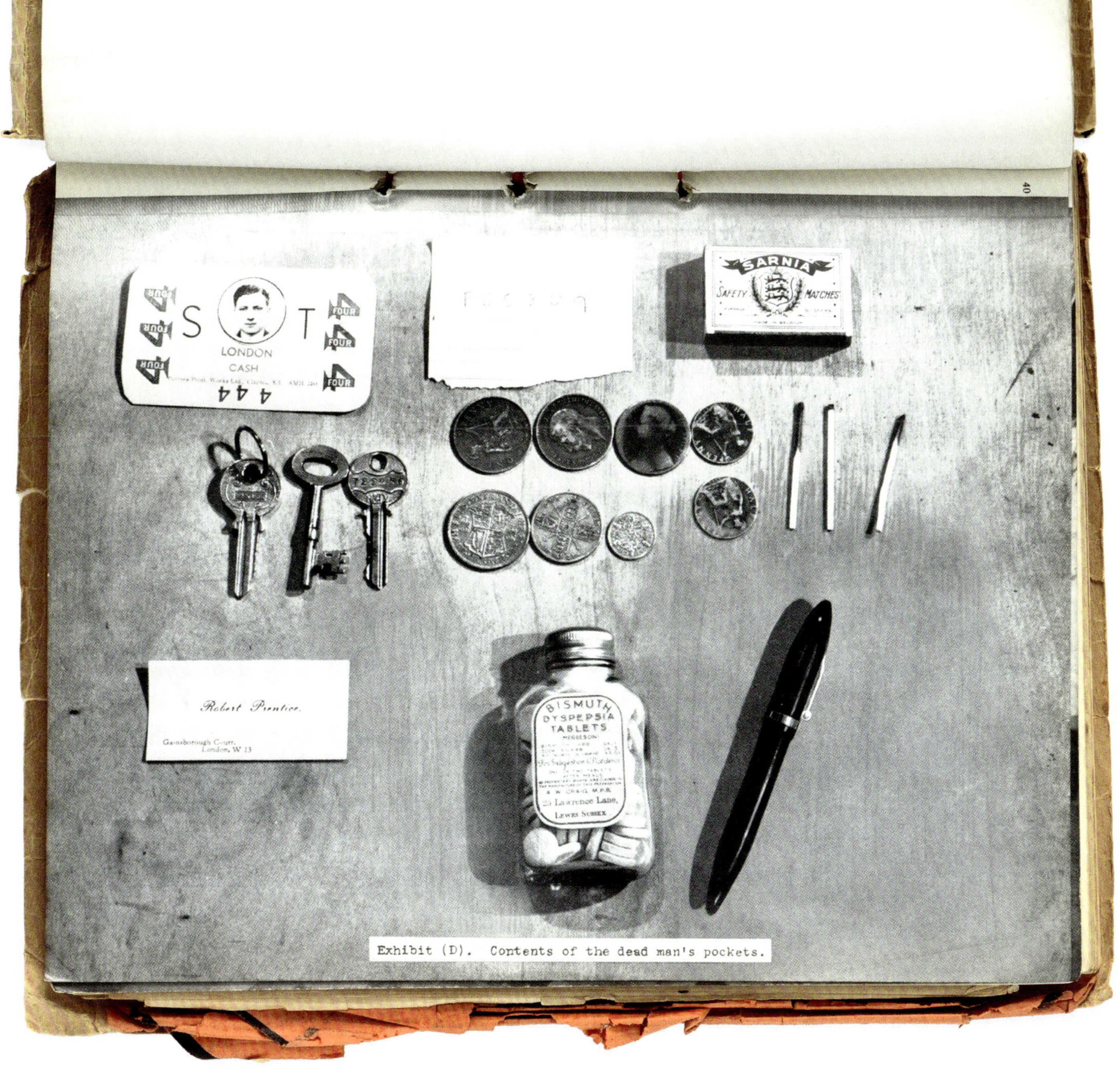

The use of multiple printing techniques and inclusion of real or facsimile documents have been important aspects of ambitious photobook craft for some time now. Rhiannon Adam's *Big Fence/Pitcairn Island* (2022), a disturbing account of sexual abuse in an isolated community, mixes poetic documentary photography with reproductions of archival material. Other photographers have known directly of the Wheatley-Links books. You can see their influence on Christian Patterson's landmark *Redheaded Peckerwood* (2010): His imaginative retelling of a real-life couple on a murder spree mixes his own photography with reproductions of archival-looking documents that may be fact, fiction, or somewhere in between. While there's no limit to what mixed-media photobooks can do, it's telling that, more often than not, their varied techniques are used to come at a subject or story from multiple directions, accumulating layers of uncertain information—not unlike a detective in search of an elusive secret.

David Campany is the creative director of the International Center of Photography, New York.

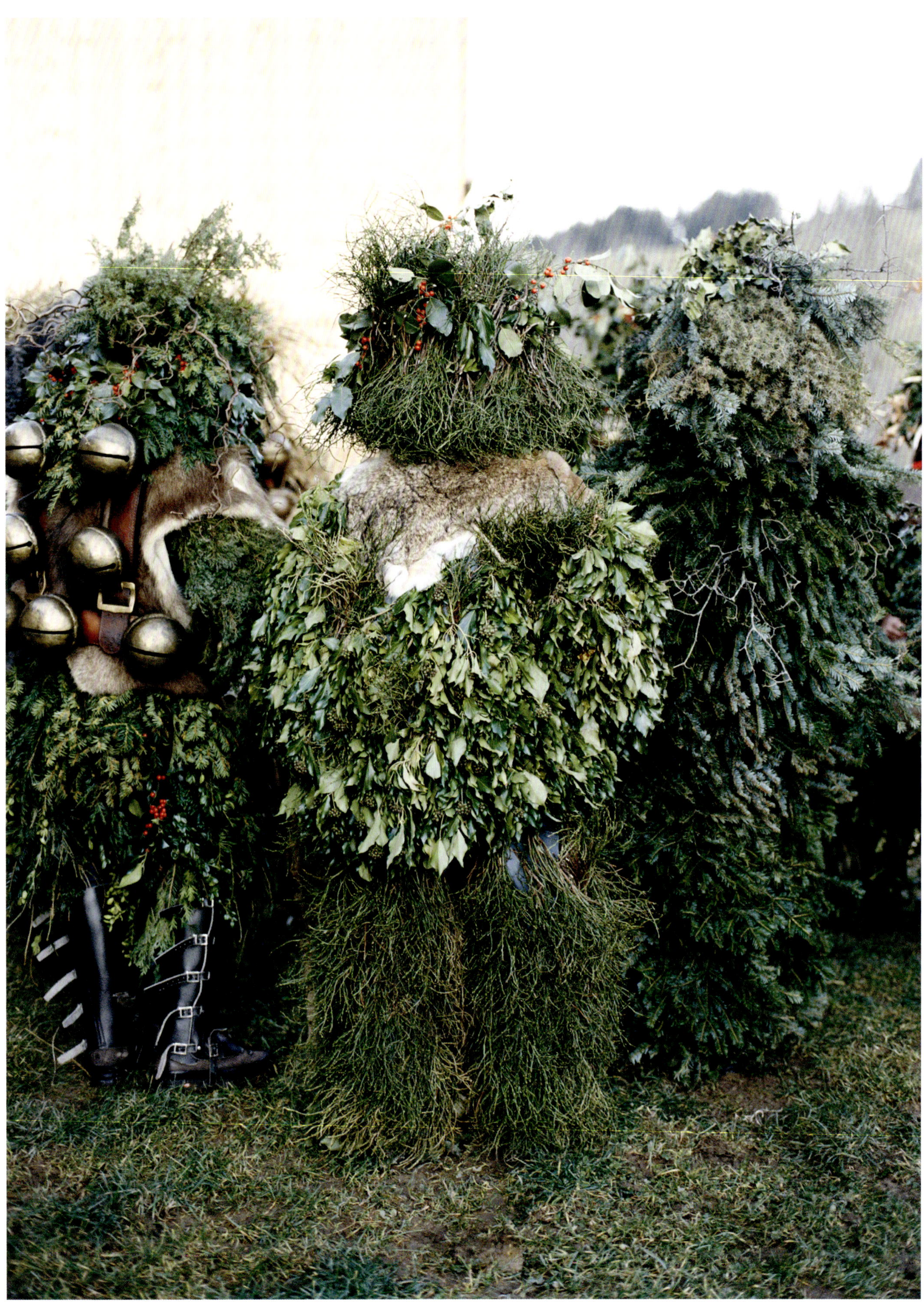

Seb Emina

Estelle Hanania *Unknown Pleasures*

Every winter in certain parts of Europe, small bands of (almost always) men get dressed up in pagan costumes and march around outdoors. Their outfits connote a nightmarish, preindustrial wilderness. Their lineage derives from old folkloric rituals. Sometimes the monsters are covered in branches and leaves. Sometimes they are soft and shaggy. They can have horns or sharp teeth, or cowbells attached to their backs. The important thing is to be scary, to frighten away evil spirits—and to offer no glimpse of the farmer, pharmacist, or insurance broker concealed beneath the mask.

After graduating from the École des Beaux-Arts, in 2006—and winning the Hyères Festival Photography Prize a month later—the French photographer Estelle Hanania traveled to Appenzell, in the Swiss Alps, to document a ritual called Silvesterchlausen, where the participating men dress as masked beings called Chläus. Besides the spectacle itself, she was interested in what it symbolized. Hanania had long been curious about the fantasy of personal metamorphosis, how it manifests in the outward paraphernalia of identity—"the way you disguise yourself to modify your initial condition of being human." Sometimes an assumed identity feels more authentic than the persona it supplants.

As Hanania's commercial career developed (she has counted Lemaire, Gucci, and Louis Vuitton among her clients), she continued to visit equivalent gatherings, from the winter masquerade in Bulgaria, where the costumes involve feathers and yak fur, to the Perchtenlaufen custom in Austria, where teams of goatlike figures get into "fights" with the audience and each other. Elsewhere, she has made series on drag queens, teenage ventriloquists, and lucha libre wrestlers. "I don't have an anthropological point of view. I'm more ethnographical," she told me. "I'm interested in questions like, Why are these people letting go like this? Why are they creating these costumes and these masks?"

For Hanania, who recently founded Myriorama, a publishing house dedicated to "self-taught, marginal, unpublished, and free art," this question of the constructed self holds a special status—she is an identical twin. "To find out who you are, and to build your own personality, is difficult when you have a kind of a mirror," she said. That line of inquiry is augmented by influences from a range of

Totem #1, 2025
Installation view, Galerie Suzanne Tarasieve, Paris. Photograph by Rebecca Fanuele

Pages 120, 123, 125: From the series *Demoniac Babble*, 2006–7

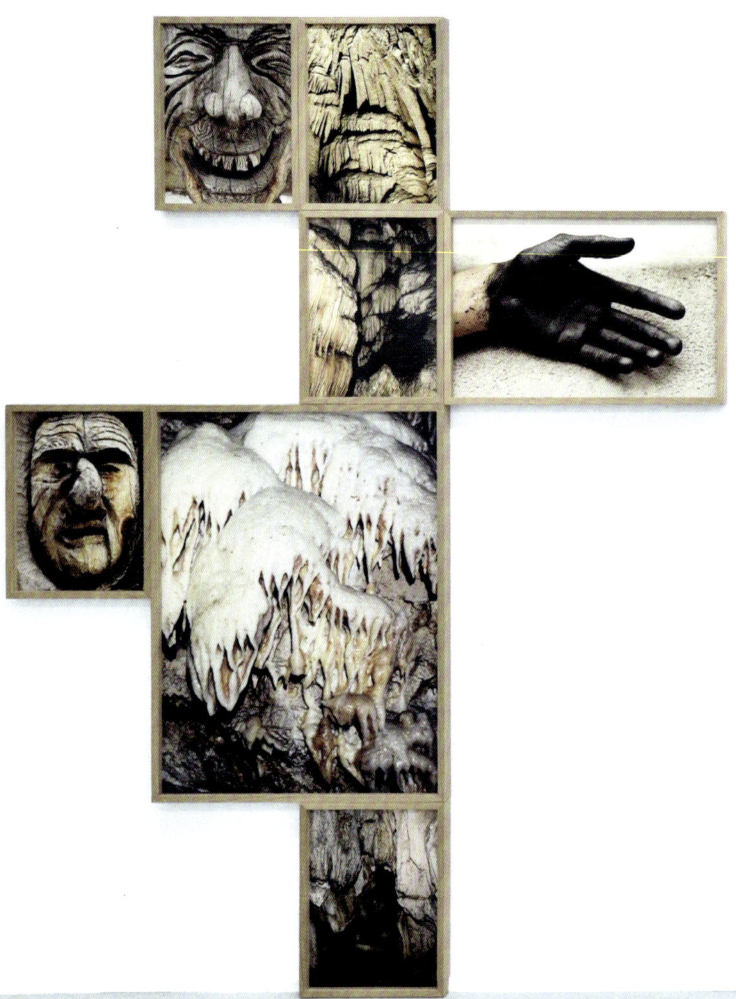

art forms, including photography (she cites Tom Wood and Abbas Kiarostami as key inspirations), film (especially the work of the Soviet director Sergei Parajanov), and visual art (from Kai Althoff to Hieronymus Bosch).

Hanania shoots in analog on a Mamiya 645 or, for slower situations, a Mamiya RZ67. She describes herself as not a particularly technical photographer, but one who knows her chosen cameras intimately. Despite its theatricality, the work is not posed; the aim is true-to-life documentation. "I love that it takes place in reality, that it's not something I invented," she said. "I'll shoot in a very up-front way. I'm not putting any effects on the image. I'm not blurring or adding color. I go along with what I have in front of me: the reality."

Perhaps it's surprising to hear these surreal traditions, whose origins tend to be hazy at best, described using a word like *reality*. But at a time when our communal sense of what's real may not even be hanging by a thread anymore, these rituals do, at least, feel unimpeachably alive. And as their geographical ubiquity demonstrates, few things are more human than marking a season by dressing up as a monster. Hanania's photographs suggest that, in certain ways, we are still living in ancient times.

Seb Emina is a writer and editor based in Paris and the creator of the arts and books newsletter *Read Me*.

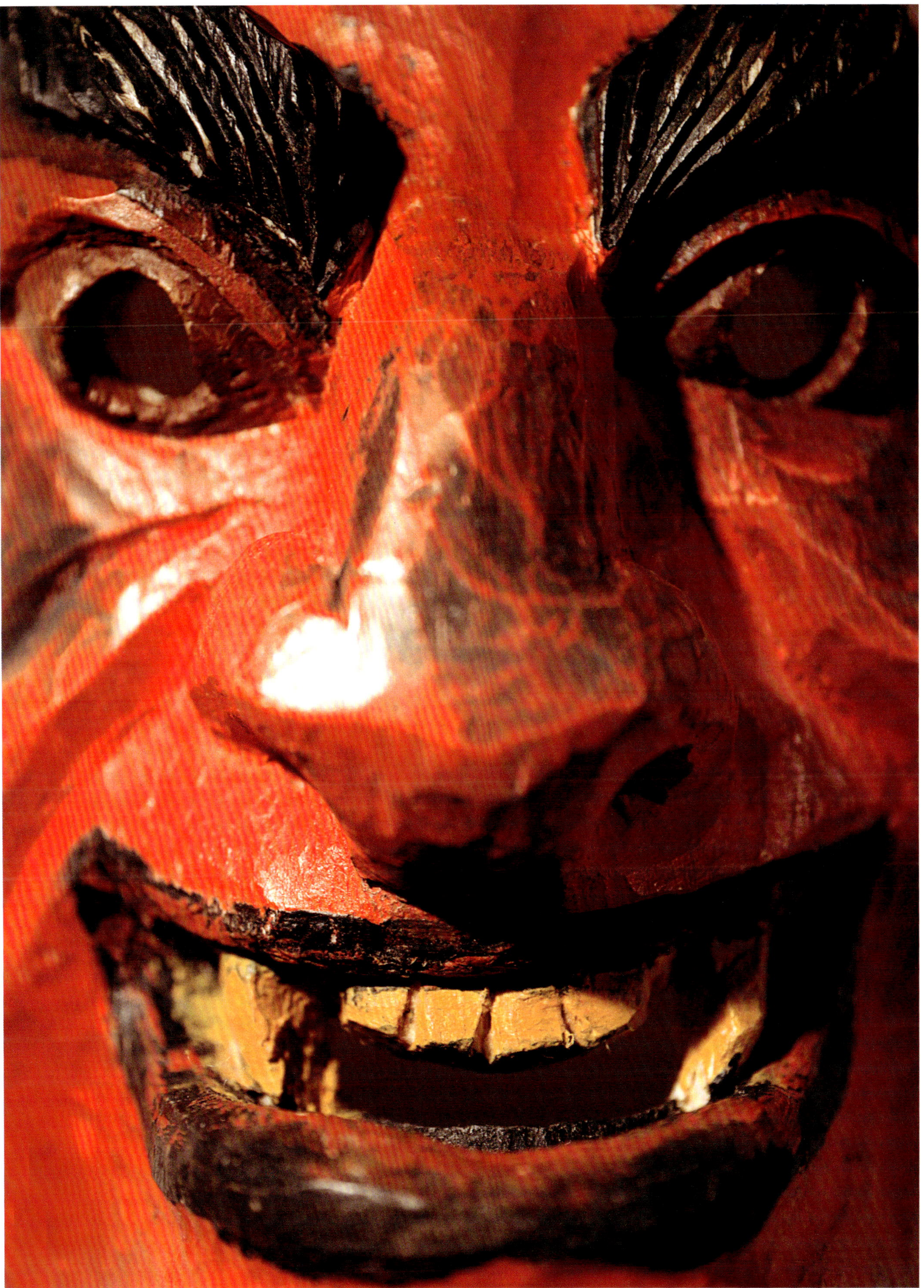

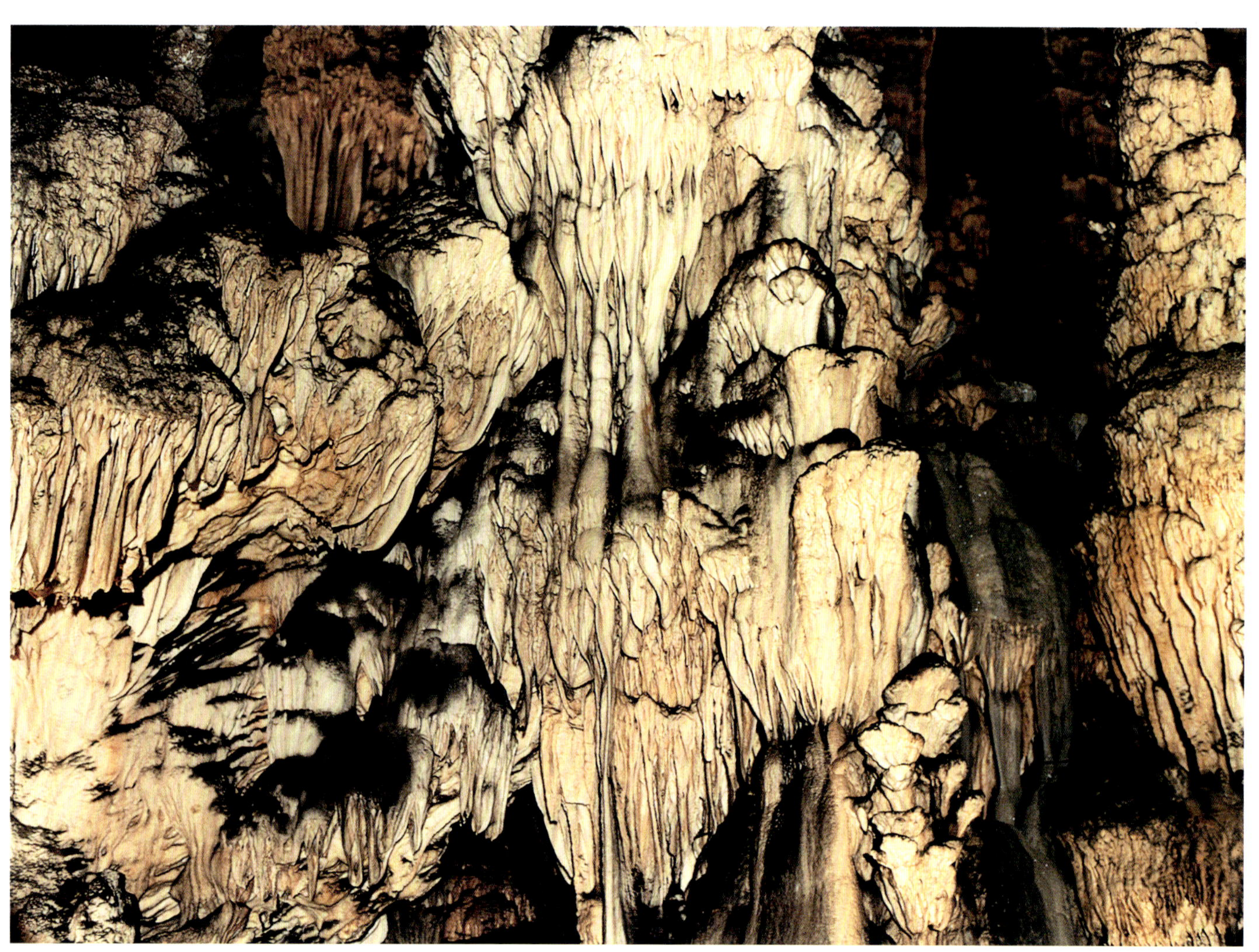

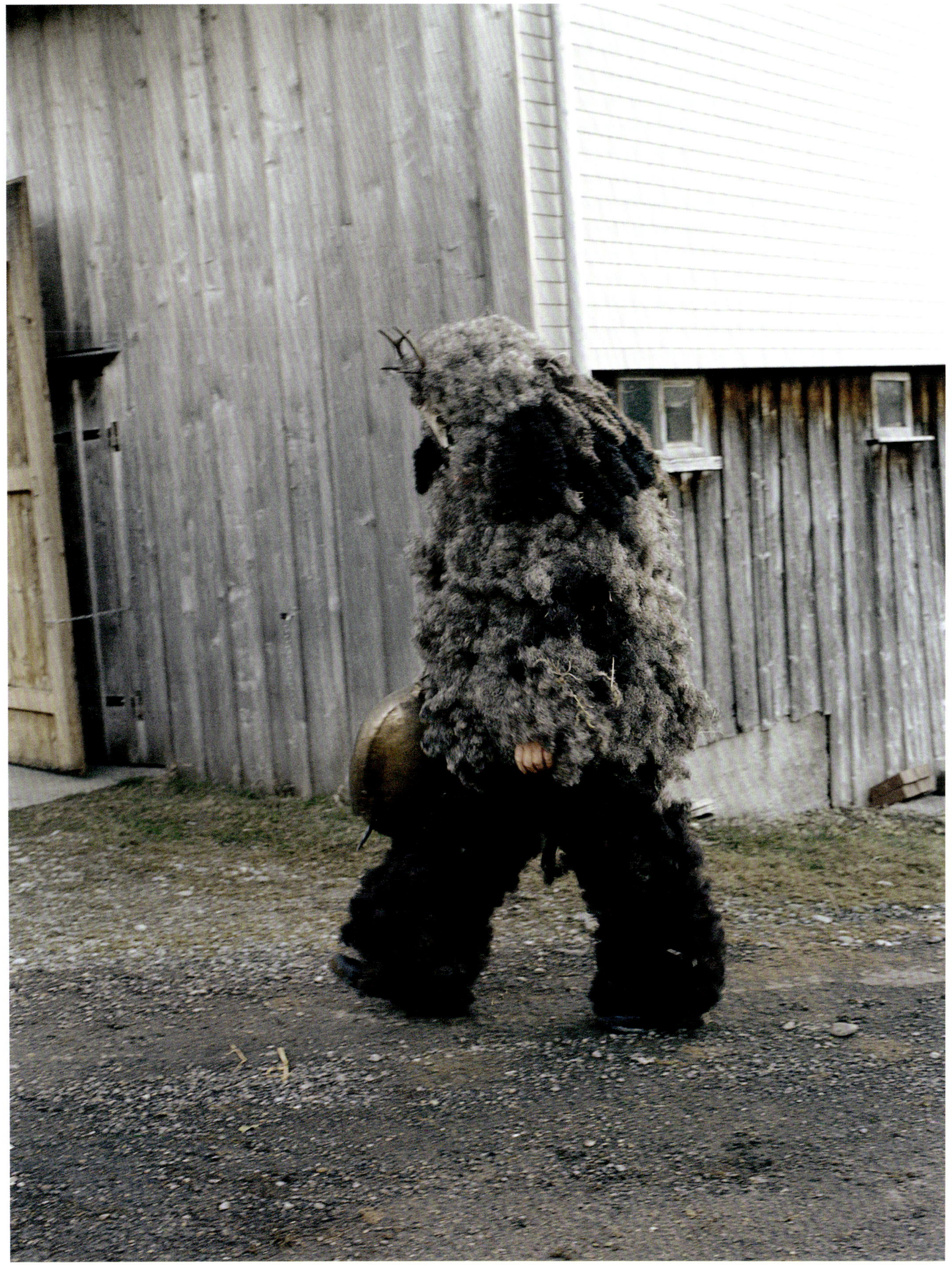

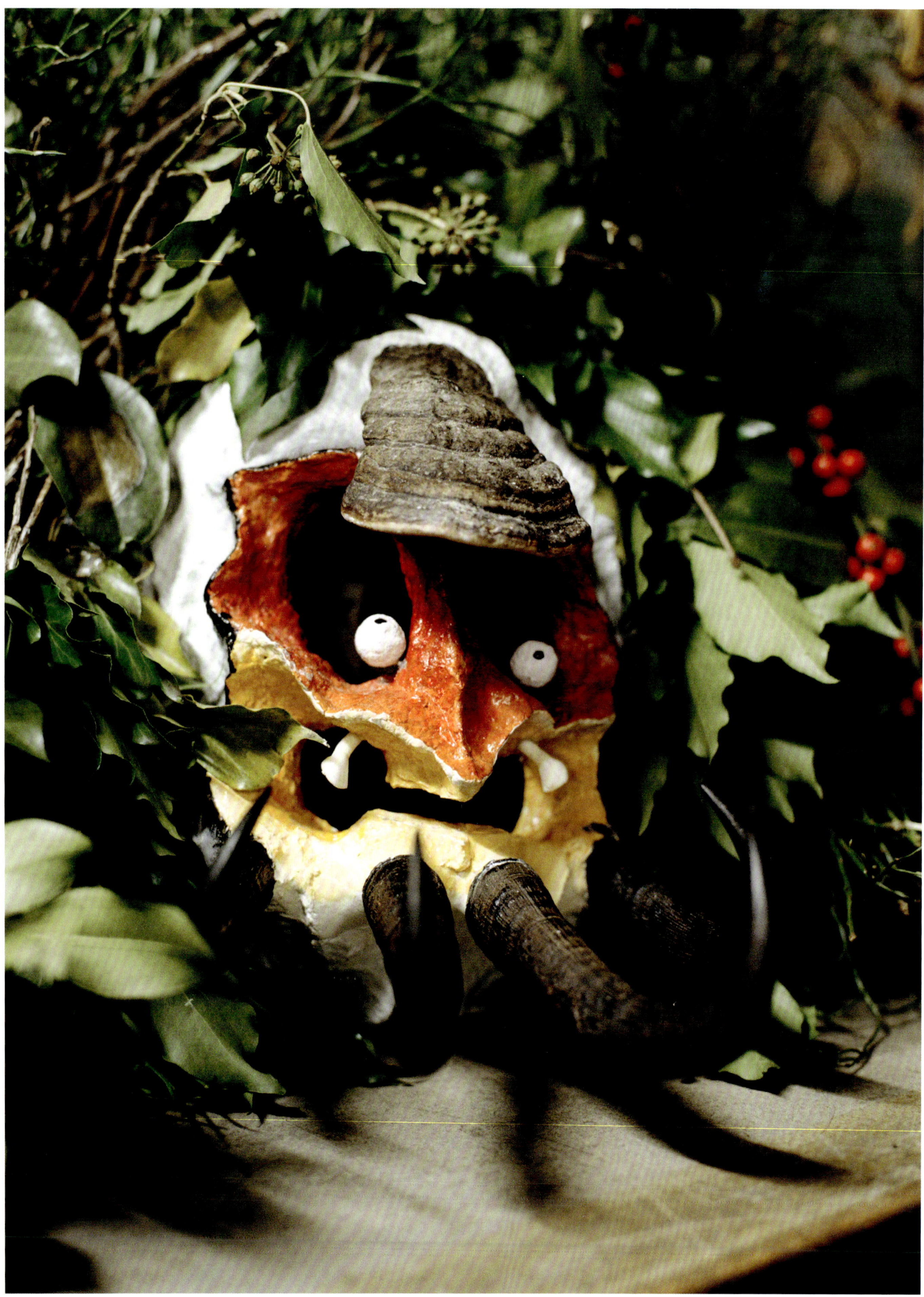

This page and 124:
From the series *Glacial Jubilé*, 2006–14

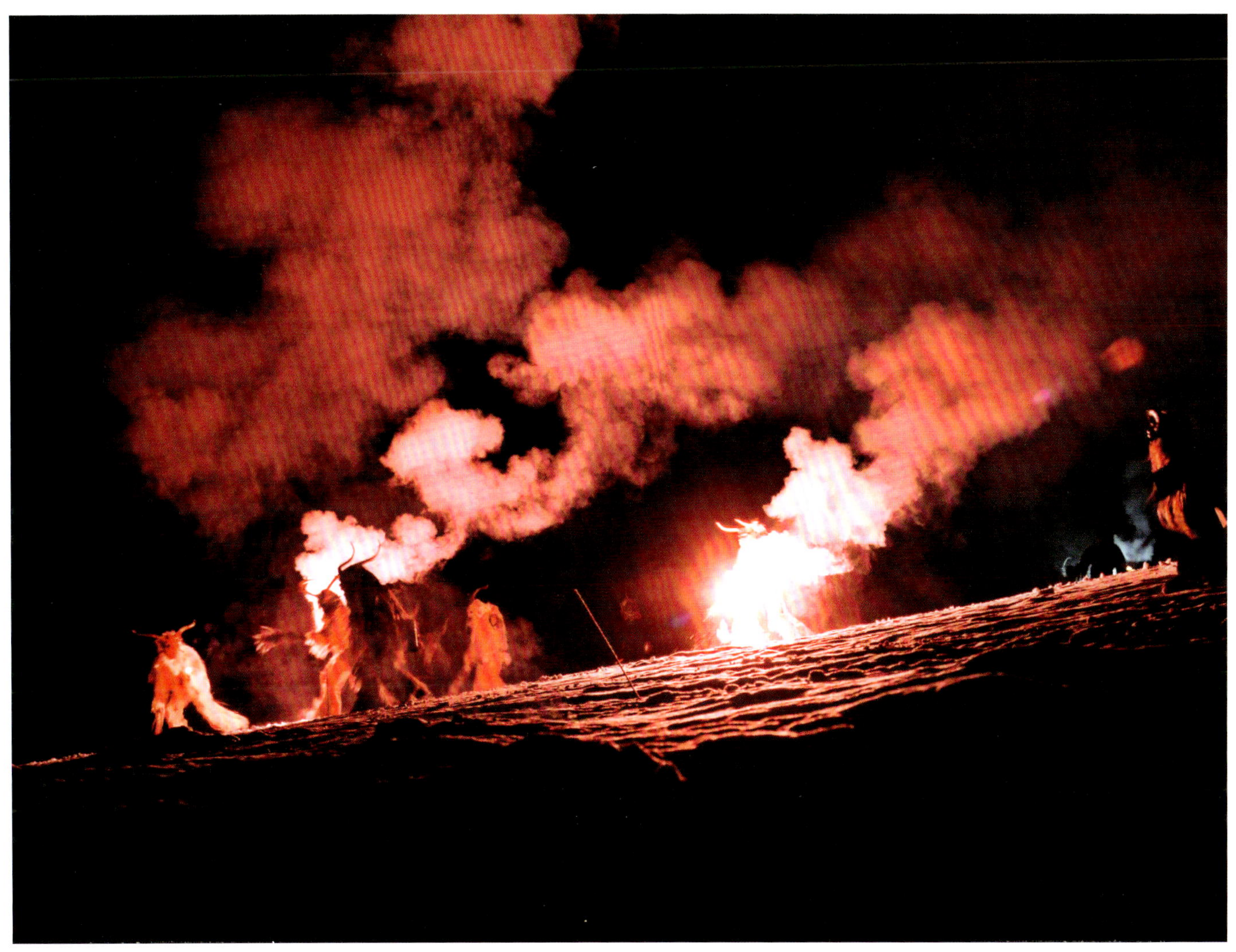

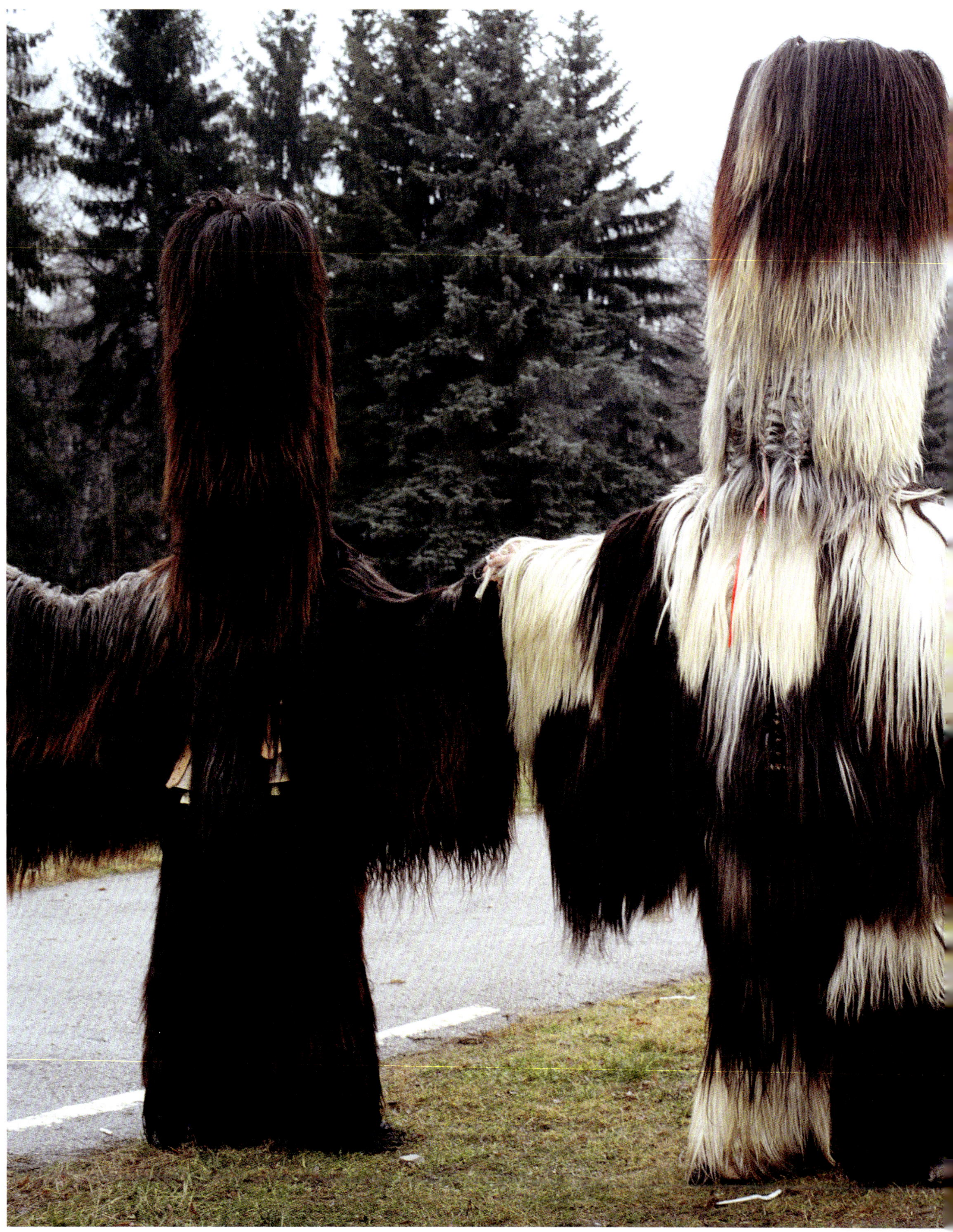

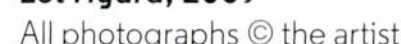

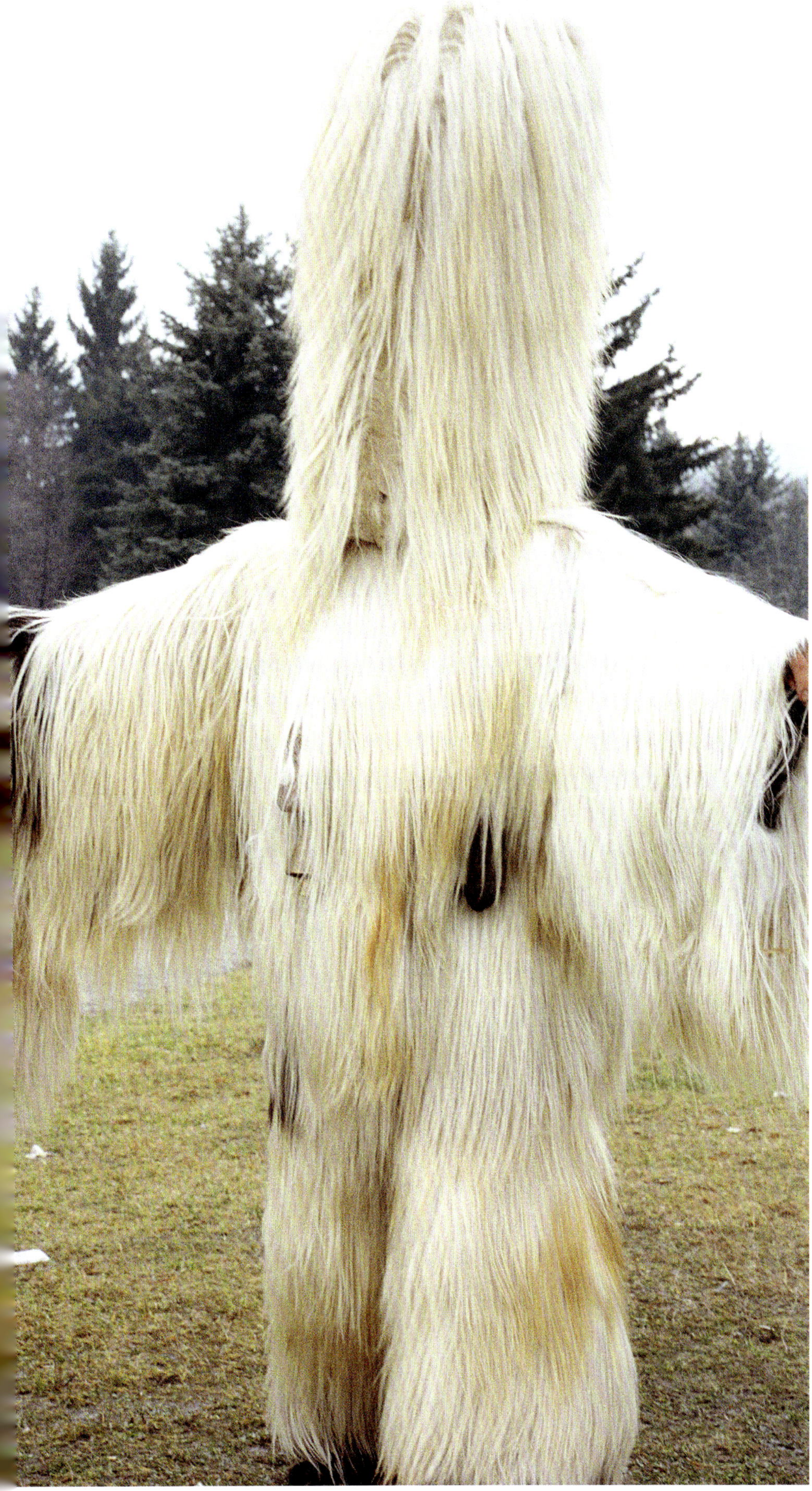

From the series *Parking Lot Hydra*, 2009

aperture

Aperture, a nonprofit organization, gratefully acknowledges the generosity of the numerous individuals, foundations, corporations, and public funders who contribute in support of our mission.

Framing the Future Capital Campaign

With deep appreciation, we thank the donors who made transformative gifts, in 2025, in support of a permanent home for Aperture:

Mark Gimbel* and Dede Welles
Dr. Bruce M. Halpryn* and Chas Riebe
Judy Glickman Lauder
Helen Nitkin*
Melissa* and James O'Shaughnessy
Thomas R. Schiff* and Mary Ellen Goeke
Jon Stryker and Slobodan Randjelović
Thompson Family Foundation

$100,000+

FotoFocus
Mark Gimbel* and Dede Welles
Horace W. Goldsmith Foundation
Agnes Gund
Dr. Bruce M. Halpryn* and Chas Riebe
Elizabeth* and William Kahane
Robert Mapplethorpe Foundation, Inc.
Robert Motherwell and Renate Ponsold
New York City Department of Cultural Affairs
Melissa* and James O'Shaughnessy
Thomas R. Schiff* and Mary Ellen Goeke
Jon Stryker and Slobodan Randjelović
Olivia Walton

$50,000–$99,999

Peter T. Barbur* and Tim Doody
Dr. Kathryn Beal
S. B. Cooper* and R. L. Besson
Documentary Arts, Inc.
George Eastman Museum
Celso M. Gonzalez-Falla*
Agnes Gund and Catherine Gund
Michael Hoeh*
Joy of Giving Something, Inc.
Cathy M. Kaplan* and Renwick D. Martin
Judy and Leonard Lauder
Vasant Nayak* and Sheela Murthy
New York City Council
Lisa Rosenblum* and Georgina Celebic
Jane Smith Turner Foundation, Inc.
The Andy Warhol Foundation for the Visual Arts

$25,000–$49,999

Anonymous (1)
Allan* and Anna Chapin
Coach
David Dechman and Michel Mercure
El Museo del Barrio
William Talbot Hillman Foundation
Ingram Content Group
Philippe Laumont*
Mark* and Elizabeth Levine
Marina and Andrew* Lewin
Leonard L. Milberg
Neuberger Berman
New York State Council on the Arts
Dr. Stephen W. Nicholas* and Ellen Sargent
Ms. Eliot Nolen of the Mary P. Oenslager Foundation Fund
Pace Gallery
Peabody Essex Museum
Yesim and Dusty Philip
Lisa* and Harry Segalas
Michael W. Sonnenfeldt, MUUS Collection
Pamela Thomas-Graham*
Casey* and Lauren Weyand
Wyeth Foundation for American Art

$10,000–$24,999

Anonymous (2)
Julie Bédard*
Bloomberg Philanthropies
Bobby Campbell Charitable Fund
Kate Cordsen* and Denis O'Leary
Susan and Thomas Dunn
Gucci
Terry Hermanson
Florian Koenigsberger
Leica Camera USA
Anne Levy Charitable Trust
Mailman Foundation, Inc.
Nion McEvoy and Leslie Berriman
James McKinney
Richard and Ronay Menschel
Ministry of Culture of the Czech Republic
MPB
Norton Museum of Art
Marnie S. Pillsbury
Theodore and Mary Jo Shen
Diane Sherman
Anne Stark
Charlotte and Scott Tracy

$5,000–$9,999

Katie Adams
Sarah Arison
Lisa Marie Baker
Rebecca Balyasny
Tina Barney
Joan Berkowitz
Maria Brisbane
Thomas and Megan Brodsky
Susie Casdin
Nina Cheney
Anne Cohen
G. Andrea and Manola Danese
Nicole Drapkin and Marc Schaffer
Furthermore: A program of the J. M. Kaplan Fund
Larry Gagosian
Rob Giampietro* and Susan Cernek
Howard Greenberg
Mrs. John (Susan) Gutfreund
Béryl and Rex Hamilton
The Hyde and Watson Foundation
Nina and Adrian Jones
Lohrfink Foundation
Alison and Tim Lord
Jessica Marinaccio
The Ordover Family Foundation
Claudia and Gunnar Overstrom
Grace Jones Richardson Trust
The Herb Ritts Foundation
Judy Sandler and Skip Klein
Sciame Construction
Drs. Marsha and Stephen Silberstein
Susanna Singer
William and Catherine Sweeney Singer
Ellen and Lawrence Sosnow
Shira P. White
Kelly Williams

$1,000–$4,999

Alexandra Ackerman and David Stern
Margo Alexander
John Alschuler and Diana Diamond
Anonymous (4)
Bob Bach
Rosebud Baker
Dawoud Bey*
Claudina Bonetti
Pascal Caillon
Héctor Méndez Caratini
Chirag Chotalia
Christie's
Deborah Crowley
David Zwirner
Jeffrey Davies
Judy Ditner
Sharon and John Dye
Aaron Ealy
Katama and Jay Eastman
Maryam Eisler
Dr. John E. Ellis
Daniel Emerson
Dana Emmott
Hany Farag and Sherry Reese
Christine and John Fitzgibbons
Dawn and Chris Fleischner
Pietro Fontana
Christian Gapp
Susan Gilbert
Hannah Gottlieb-Graham
Laura and Eric Gould
Stephen Greenberg
Terry Greenberg
Jeff Gutterman
Jessica Handelman
Newell Harbin
Chloe Heins
Susan Hermanson
Allison and Keyes Hill-Edgar
Jeffrey and Diane Hirsch
Julie and Will Hobert
Polly and Alastair Hunt
Steven and Robin Hurwitz
Joie Jager-Hyman
Darlene Kaplan and Steve Zuckerman
Jodie Kelley and Scott Sinder
Rania Al Khalifa
Marci Klein
Mary Lapides
Bonnie Lautenberg
Nora Lavori
Georgia Lee
Joshua Lewin and Kaavya Viswanathan
Dana Lightsey and Peter Harris
Dr. Jennifer Mascarenhas
Scott Mead
Susan Meiselas
Sarah and Adam Meister
Robyn F. Mewshaw and Ben A. Indek
Justin Miller
Wesley and Katherine Mitchell
Dr. Kenneth Montague* and Sarah Aranha
Jeanne Moutoussamy-Ashe
Peyton Muldoon
Patricia A. Murphy
New York City Tourism Foundation
Peter Norton and Gwendolyn Adams Norton
Philipp Nüernberger and Maren Trautwein
Deirdre O'Neil and Shawn Colo
Lauren Panzo
William R. Peelle Jr.
Stephanie and John Perenchio
Julia Pershan and Jon Cohen
David Z. Pinsky
Mark Quinlan
Donna Redel
Jordan Reyes
Rakia Reynolds
Yancey Richardson
Heidi and Richard Rieger
Sara and Mario Rodriguez
Jennifer Rogers
Gabriele Rossi
Paul Sack and Shirley Davis
Sargent's Daughters
Amy Savin
Michael Sbabo and John Myung
James Seder
Susan and Robert Semmens
Brett Shapiro
Martha and Matthew Sharp
Harriette Silverberg-Natkins
Leslie Simitch
Tabitha Soren
Alexandra Stones
William Glenn Street
Christine Symchych and James McNulty
Tammy Dowley-Blackman Group, LLC
Kathryn Telingator
Paula Gately Tillman, In Memory of LeRoy E. Hoffberger
Lara Trafelet
Elizabeth Chai Vasarhelyi
Jurek Wajdowicz
Susan S. and Kenneth L. Wallach Foundation
Artur Walther
Ronald and Vicki Weiner
Linda Wisnewski
Alice Sachs Zimet

Listings include donations from January 1 through December 31, 2025.

* Aperture trustee or trustee emeritus as of December 31, 2025.

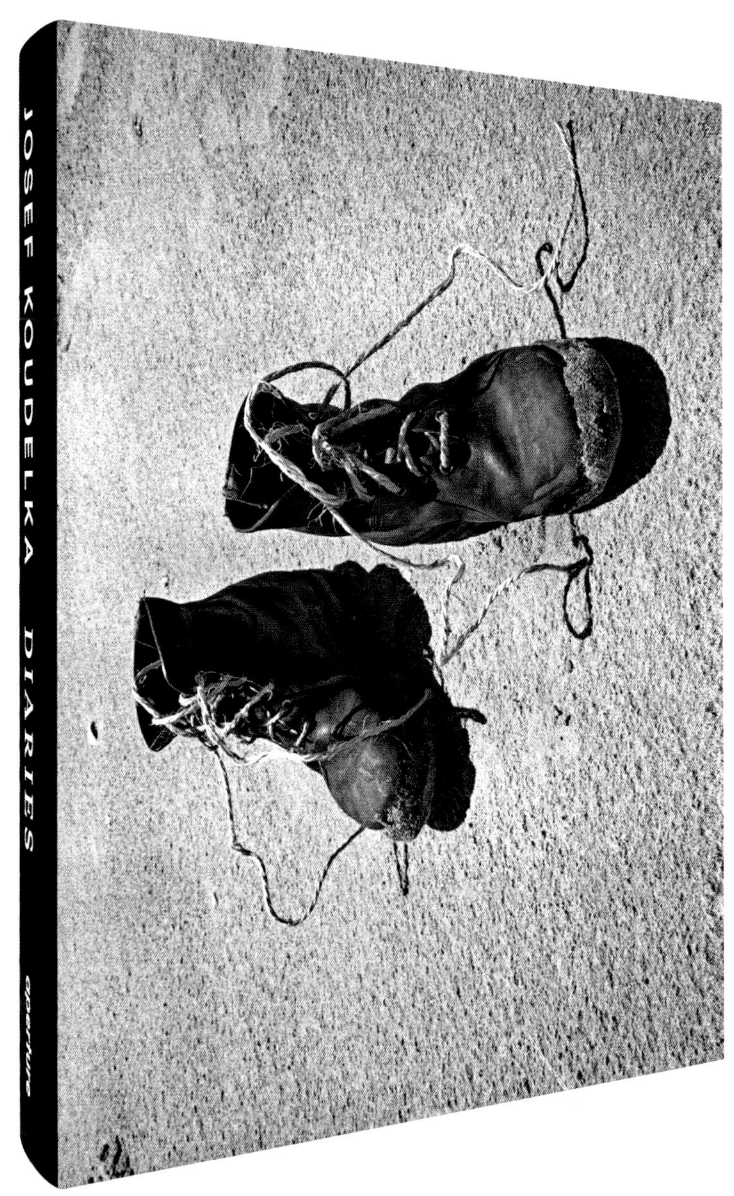

Available Now

Josef Koudelka's *Diaries*

Distilled from sixty-nine journals kept over the course of fifty-plus years, *Diaries* offers a rare look inside the mind and artistic process of the renowned and iconoclastic Czech photographer.

aperture.org/koudelka-diaries

aperture

The PhotoBook Review

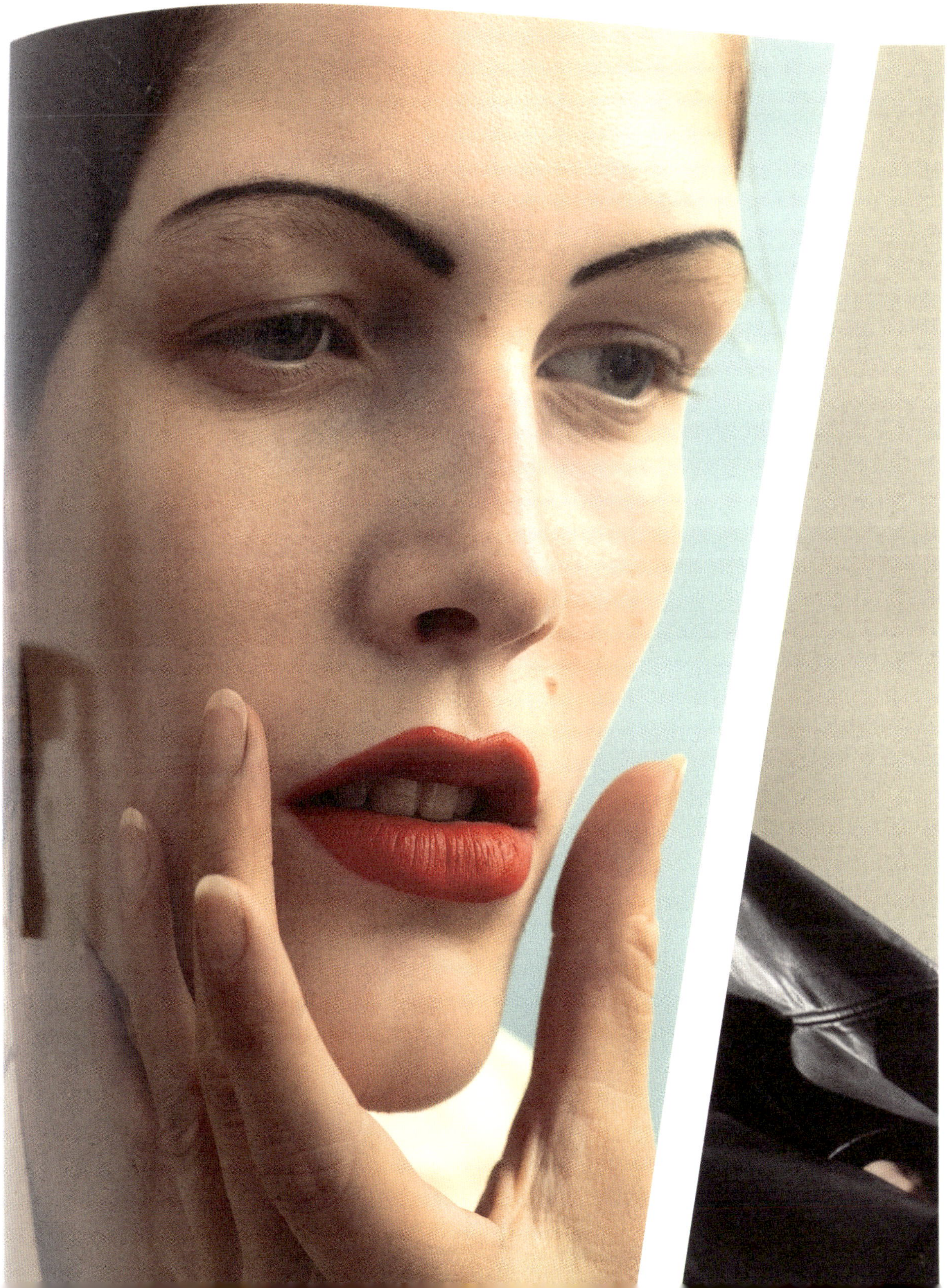

Smells Like Print

Aaron Schuman speaks with TBW's Paul Schiek about the highs and lows of bookmaking.

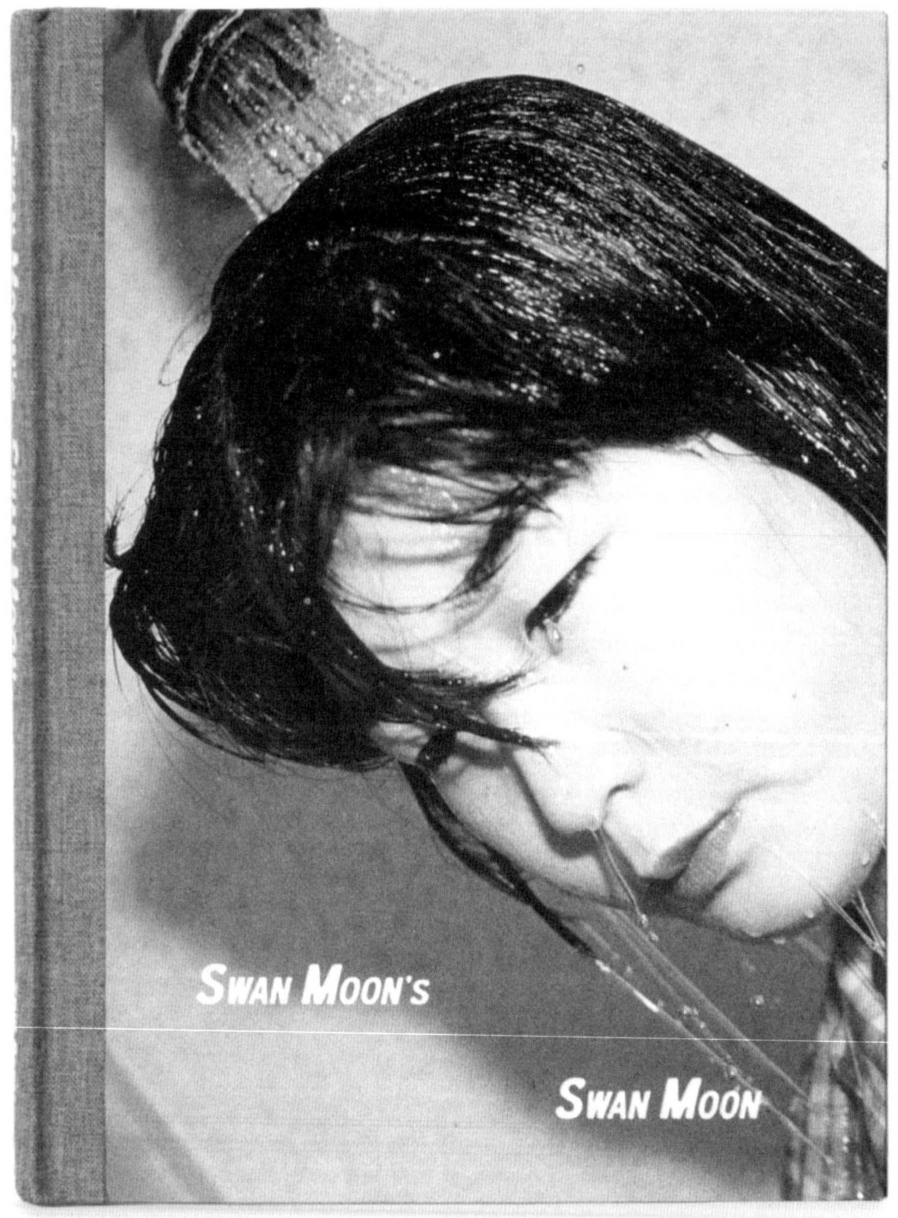

"We are almost extinct," begins the rollicking, Kerouac-esque manifesto on the About Us page of the TBW Books website. That couldn't be further from the truth. Since its founding by Paul Schiek, in 2006, in Oakland, California, TBW has become a pillar of photobook publishing in the United States, known for artist-shaped titles that balance traditional craftsmanship with a flair for experimentation and risk that betrays Schiek's DIY roots.

Aaron Schuman: **How did you initially get into photography?**

Paul Schiek: I know it seems like a pretty common answer among artists and designers these days, but I found my way into photography through punk and skateboarding. I was born and raised in Wisconsin, and had very little access to culture so was seeking it out as much as possible as a teenager.

AS: **Is punk culture what eventually drew you to Oakland?**

PS: I was in my twenties and didn't have any art education. But by the grace of whatever, I ended up at CCA [California College of the Arts], which had an amazing photography program, with Jim Goldberg and Larry Sultan teaching there. I just fell into this cradle where people were willing to nurture me.

AS: **When you applied to CCA, what did you show them to get in?**

PS: I still have my portfolio. I just mounted about fifteen pictures onto cardboard—a few punk band photos, and then seven or eight "artsy" self-portraits of me standing on a fire hydrant in the middle of the night or whatever. Also, I would paint old furniture, kind of like Keith Haring, and took pictures of that in front of a white sheet. I was just winging it, but somehow I got in. Eventually, I landed in a couple of photography classes that changed the whole course of my life—specifically Image, Context, and Sequence with Jim Goldberg. We looked at books nonstop.

AS: **When did you start to think about publishing your own books?**

PS: Toward the end of school, I was making all this point-and-shoot, heavy flash, black-and-white work. Back then, there was a process at CCA where you'd submit your name to the three on-campus galleries, and they'd give you a date for your grad show. Everyone would produce a postcard to promote their show. I was fascinated by these postcards and started thinking about how each card was like the page in a book. So I went to Jim and Larry and said, "Hey, would you be okay if I don't do an exhibition but instead funnel all my resources into these postcards, and make a book out of them? The book will be my gallery."

I just went to what I knew from the DIY punk scene, which was publish it yourself. Everyone in my class had photos of birds flying through the air, and I was like, "Fuck that—my birds have to walk." There was this kind of class element to it—walking to work, walking home—so in the back of the book I said it was published by These Birds Walk, which became TBW.

AS: **How did TBW then begin to publish other photographers' books?**

PS: I wanted to make more of my own books, so I started this book series that was kind of like a pyramid scheme. I'd say to the public, "I'm going to publish four books over the course of the coming year, which you can buy in advance, so send me the money now." The first series included my own book, my friend Mike Brodie's, and then I asked Jim Goldberg if he'd do one—which he was a little bit reluctant about, but he saw my enthusiasm and threw me a bone—and then Ari Marcopoulos, who I'd met when he visited one of our classes at CCA. Once I had Jim and Ari on board, I knew people would buy the series.

Opposite:
Swan Moon, *Swan Moon's Swan Moon* (2025)

Page 133:
Blommers & Schumm, *More* (Roma, 2025)

This page:
Cover and spread from TR Ericsson, *Nicotine* (2024)

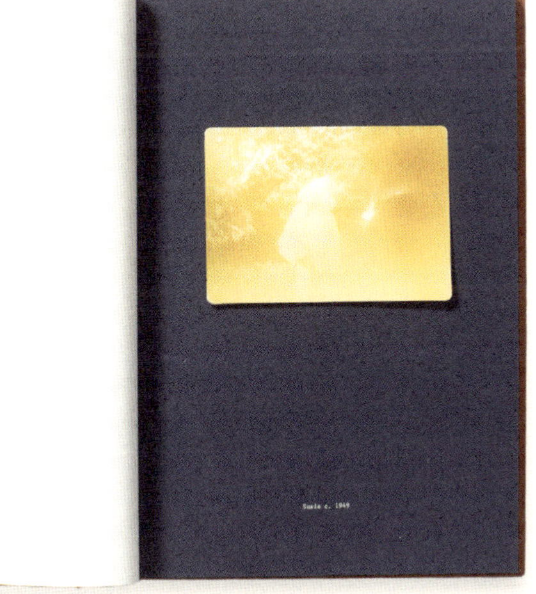

AS: **How involved were you in the editing and design of these books?**

PS: With TBW, I'm basically the editor, sequencer, and designer of all the books. In Jim's class, he drove home the importance of sequencing. We talked a lot about how weaker individual images can drive and support and strengthen other images, how and why to use text, and so on. So, eventually, experimenting and playing with sequencing and design became my artistic practice almost exclusively.

AS: **When you work on a book, do you simply ask photographers to hand over all their material and then make your own thing out of it? Or is there more of a dialogue?**

PS: It varies. Sometimes I have free rein, sometimes I try to take a back seat.

AS: **What's an example of when things didn't quite go to plan with one of your early books?**

PS: Back then, I didn't even know the difference between RGB and CMYK, and with postcard printing there wasn't any proofing. I was working with Katy Grannan on a project, which was a big deal for me at the time, and when her postcards came back, channels C and K had printed, but M and Y hadn't. The postcards were supposed to be black-and-white, but they all came out looking blue. I remember picking them up and being like, "Whoa, Katy, you're not going to believe it! Your images look so fucking cool—like a Blue Note record!" And she said, "But they're supposed to be black-and-white." And I was like, "Yeah, I know. But they look awesome like this! Let's go with it." Needless to say, that didn't happen.

AS: **So today, when a project arrives on your desk, what's your starting point?**

"I just went to what I knew from the DIY punk scene, which was publish it yourself."

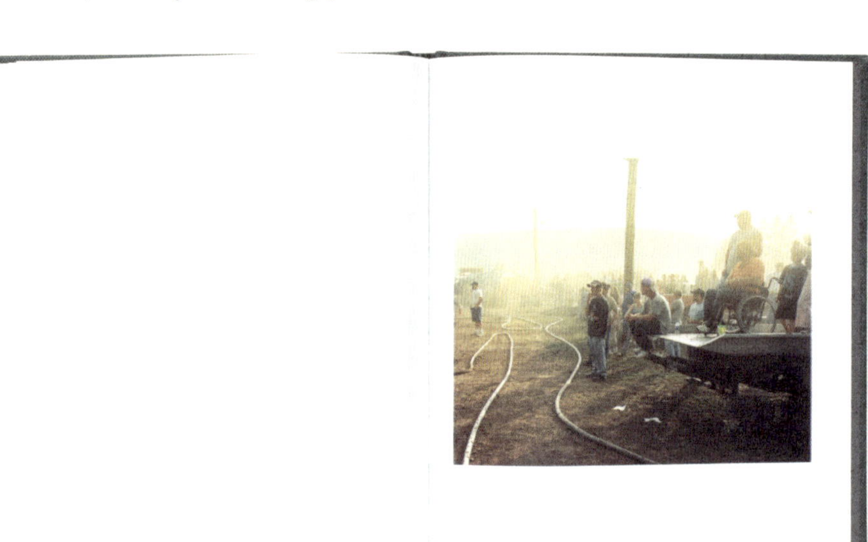

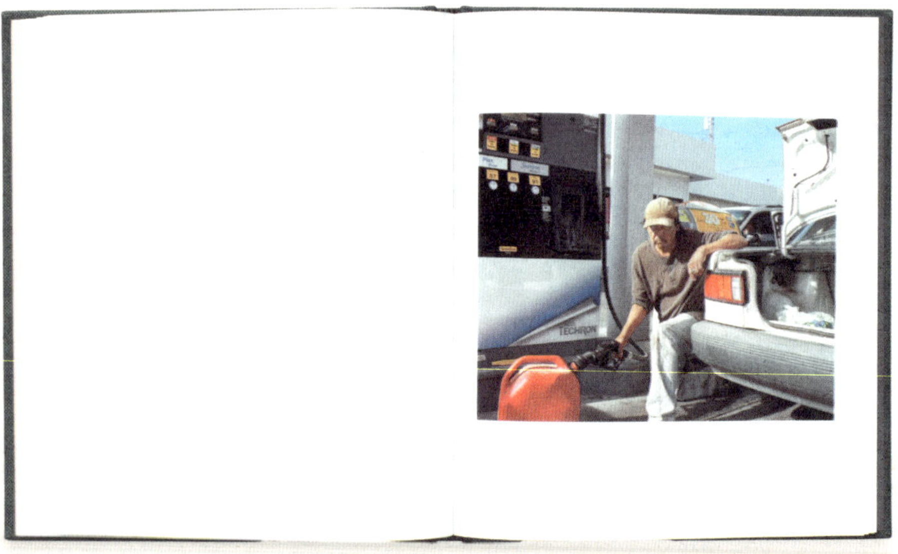

Curran Hatleberg, *Lost Coast* (2025)

PS: Firstly, I ask myself two fundamental questions: Is this something I'm interested in, and can I bring something to this project to make it better as a photobook? Secondly, I think about physicality—how can the book feel, act, unfold.

AS: **Is there an example of a book you've produced that fully embraces the idea of the book as an object?**

PS: I think *Nicotine* (2024) by TR Ericsson. TR made these artworks by printing old family photographs onto screens, then passed nicotine through the screens onto paper, making a printed physical object that smells like and is essentially created from nicotine and cigarette smoke. The challenge for me then became how to translate that into a book.

AS: **You recently published *Swan Moon's Swan Moon* (2025), which also seems to take advantage of design in some clever ways. How did that book come about?**

PS: I moved to Mexico four years ago and started hosting workshops with guest artists. Swan happened to be a participant. One day, she showed everyone about fifteen photos that she'd taken of her friends in LA in the 1990s. She and her friends were in this mod scene, and they'd dress up in thrift store clothes and try to make kind of noir films using amateur cameras. This totally made sense to me in terms of how I'd made pictures in the punk scene back in the day, so I just loved the spirit of it. I picked out six of them, pulled her aside privately, and said, "If you were to give me access to your archive, I guarantee that you have a whole book in there."

AS: **What did you discover once you dove into her archive?**

PS: Well, the book was definitely there. I was pulling out overexposed photos of flowers, or a light leak from the LA sun on a desolate beach, or a mistake in her camera where one portrait was properly oriented and the next one was upside down. Then I asked if she could make me a playlist to listen to while editing, so I could get into the vibe of her mod scene. We had lots of conversations about the people in the book, how she knew them, her memories of the scene and making the photos. Also, I just loved Swan as a

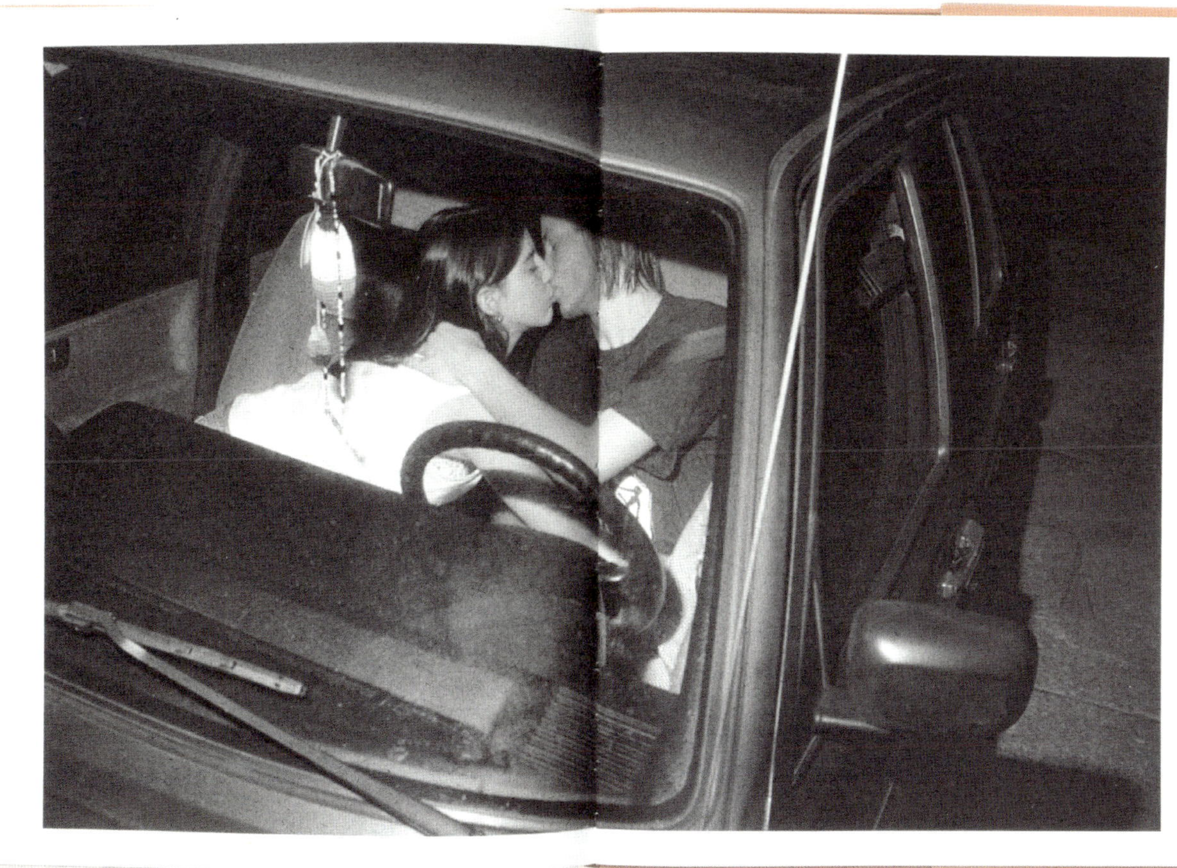

Peggy Nolan, *Juggling Is Easy* (2023)

person—she was so quiet and chill and kind. The intimacy of making a book with an artist is like a mini-marriage. You have to deal with finances, heartbreak, loss, and success. You have to stay up late arguing over typefaces.

AS: **Looking forward, how would you like TBW to evolve?**

PS: In two years, I'll be celebrating the twenty-fifth anniversary of publishing under the TBW name, so I've been doing a lot of soul-searching. I have five employees, and a lot of relationships with artists who rely on TBW to get their work out there. I don't want for things to just lose steam or get watered down. Ultimately, what I'm interested in doing is making books that contribute something which hasn't been spoken before to the canon of photography books. Whether it's for the next two years or twenty years, I feel strongly committed to continuing to publish work by overlooked and underrepresented artists. I want to push that further, because I think that is where our community and world at large need to be going. For example, Peggy Nolan is an incredible artist and human being whose work went completely unnoticed until we put out her book *Juggling Is Easy* (2023). Both the responsibility and power to be able to do that as a small publisher makes me genuinely excited. It's still punk in a way.

Aaron Schuman is a writer and photographer based in the United Kingdom.

Los Angeles Story

In Culver City, Arcana keeps the flame of indie bookselling alive.

Noa Lin

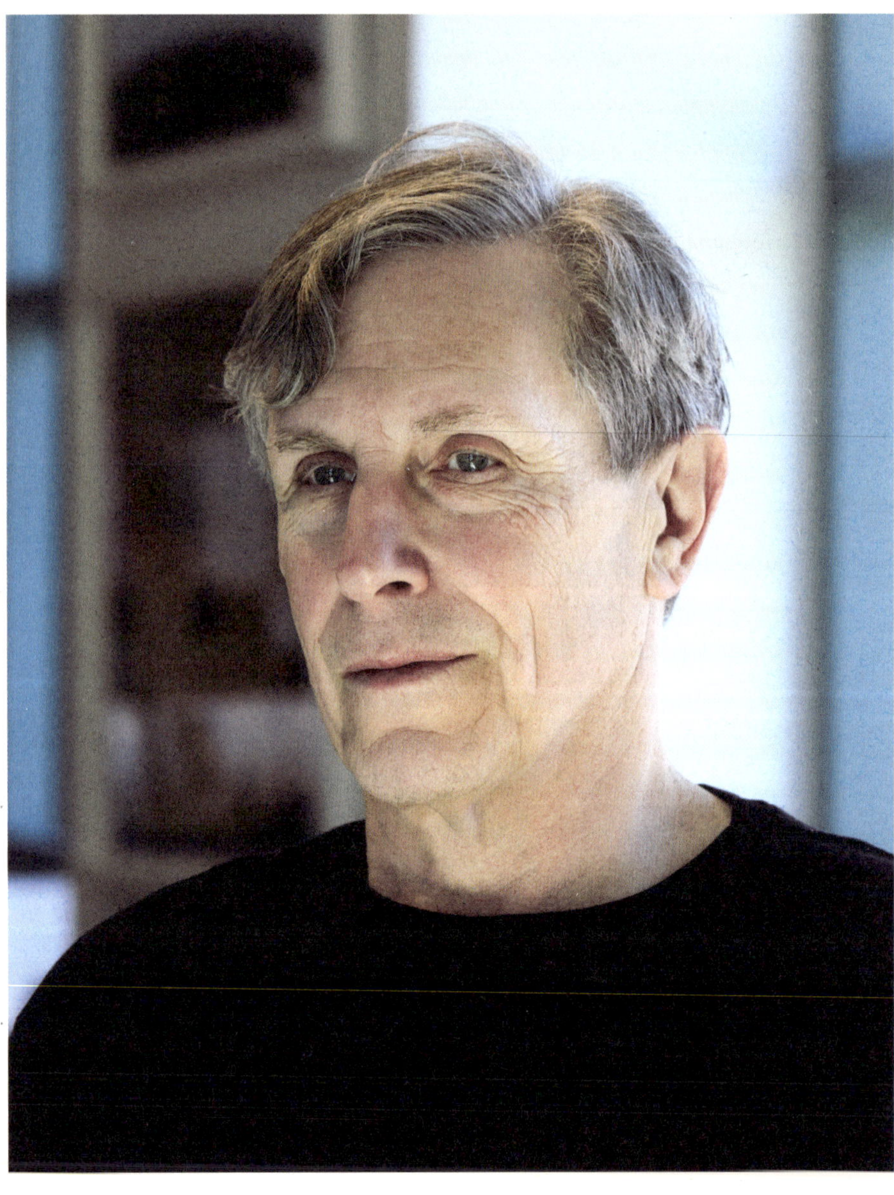

"We probably have the most comprehensive selection of photography books in the United States," said Lee Kaplan, owner and founder of Arcana: Books on the Arts. "Certainly west of New York."

I'm inclined to believe him. Located in the Helms Design District, the multi-building site of a former factory bakery in Culver City, California, Arcana doesn't feel like your typical independent bookstore—simply due to the scale. Rambling across 4,500 airy square feet, Arcana is the largest bookstore solely focused on art and design that I've set foot in. In an era of unbridled Amazonification, Arcana's expansive and eclectic inventory affirms a statement that Kaplan revisited often during our conversation: "Independent bookshops are not only alive, but vital."

Kaplan's own interest in books started early. As a child, he spent his summers helping to catalog his grandfather's vast collection of art and design books. In high school, he worked in record and bookstores, where a true obsession with physical media began to form. "I would get paid in books at the bookstores I worked at, and records at the record stores," he said. "Over time, I started building up a record and book collection when I was rather young. I just loved being around it all."

After a stint working as a book buyer, Kaplan opened the first iteration of Arcana in 1984 on Westwood Boulevard in a one-bedroom apartment. It was by appointment only. By the late 1980s, Arcana had moved to the Third Street Promenade in Santa Monica, then home to a community of other bookstores and sellers, where it would remain for more than two decades, quietly establishing itself as the premier destination for visual reference material in Los Angeles.

From the late 1980s to the early aughts, Arcana was a go-to place for Hollywood and other production industries in the city to source visual reference material. "Even in the earlier years of the internet, you couldn't really search for visual images," Kaplan said. "People didn't know what was out there. Companies and studios would come to us and say, 'Here's our visual problem, help us solve it.'" In that pre-internet age, Arcana was much more than a store—it was a place where images circulated, where visual culture was shaped and curated by the staff.

Then came the new millennium. At the 2000 Grammy Awards, Jennifer Lopez drummed up so much interest

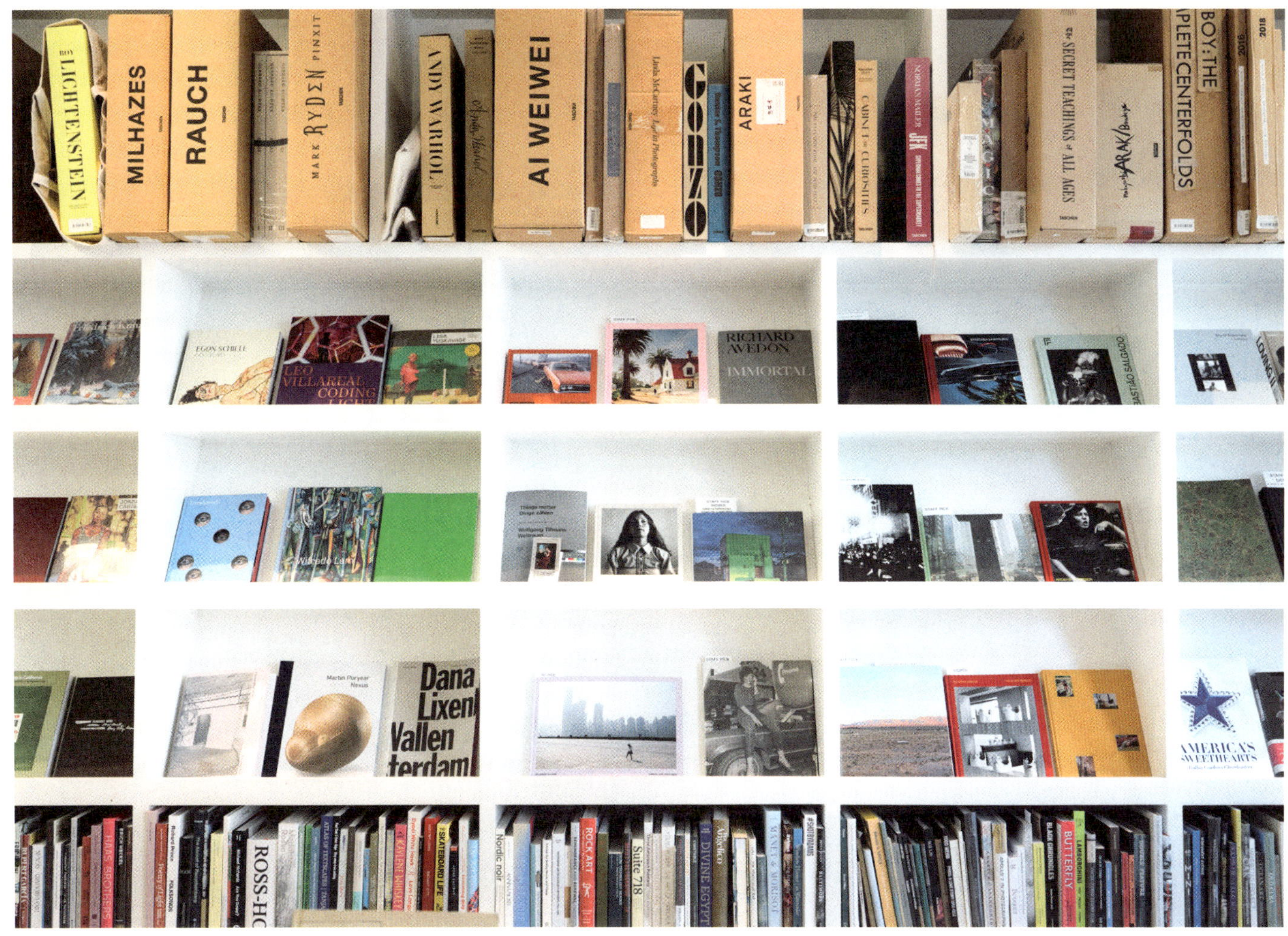

Opposite:
Lee Kaplan, January 2026

This page:
View of Arcana: Books on the Arts, Culver City, 2026

> In the age of algorithms, Arcana's appeal is its ability to impart a frisson of the unexpected.

with her green Versace dress that Silicon Valley realized the need for a dedicated image search tool: Google Images was born.

As digital image search technology became more refined and commonplace, Arcana's role in the larger ecosystem of visual culture began to shift. With studios and advertisers able to find near-infinite reference material online, Arcana's core clientele shifted away from the creative industries toward individuals. They've since built a sturdy consumer base of artists and collectors, and today, the bookshop seems to be on firmer ground than the nearby studios, as Culver City begins to lose its status as the "Heart of Screenland" due to shifting production models and insufficient tax incentives.

As shopping and search habits are codified into algorithms to show us exactly what product we might want next, Arcana's appeal is its ability to impart a frisson of the unexpected to casual art-book buyers and seasoned bibliophiles alike. During my visit, I was charmed into discovering (and eventually purchasing) a

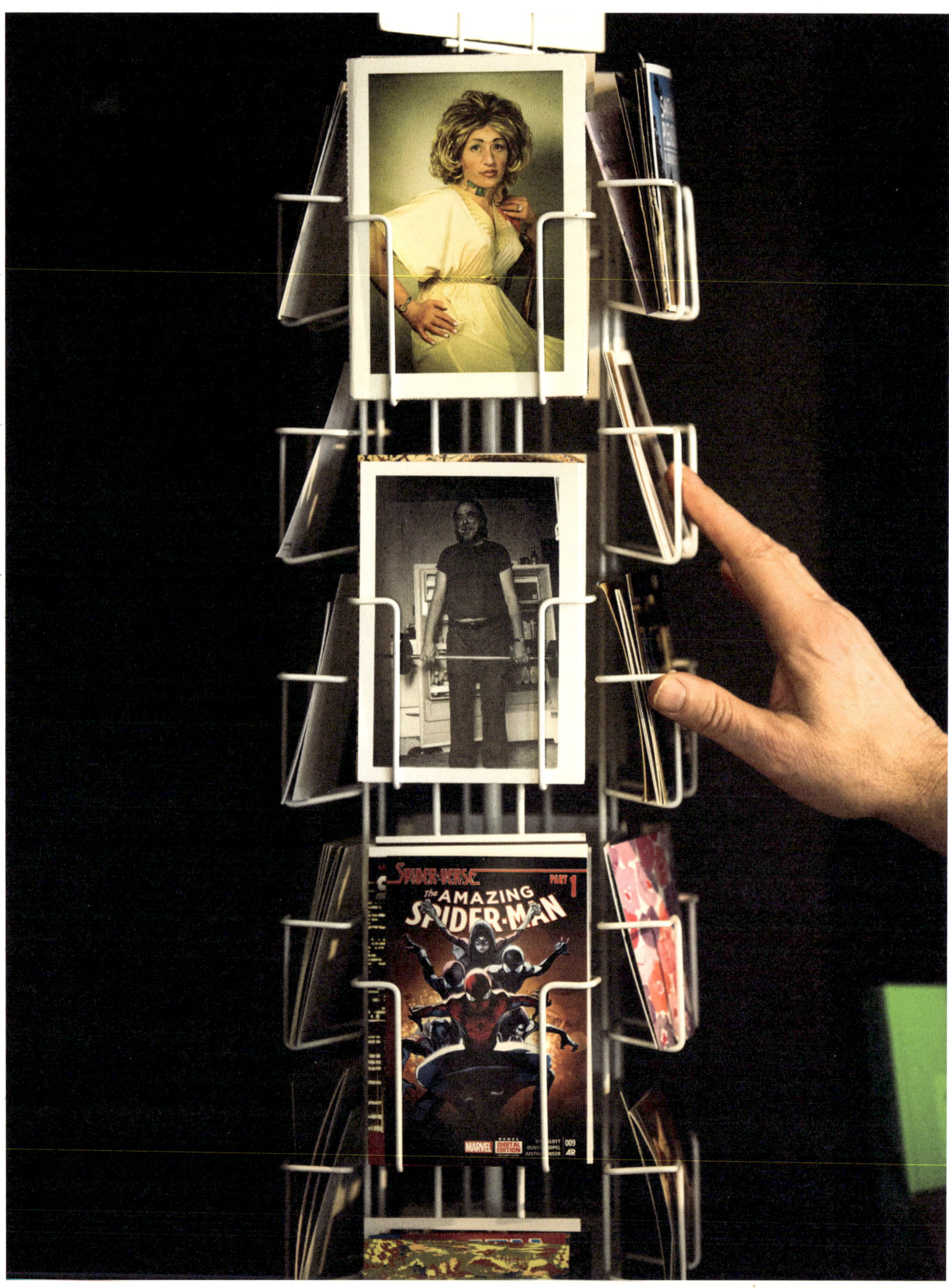
SPIDER-VERSE
PART 1
The AMAZING SPIDER-MAN
MARVEL
DIGITAL EDITION
009

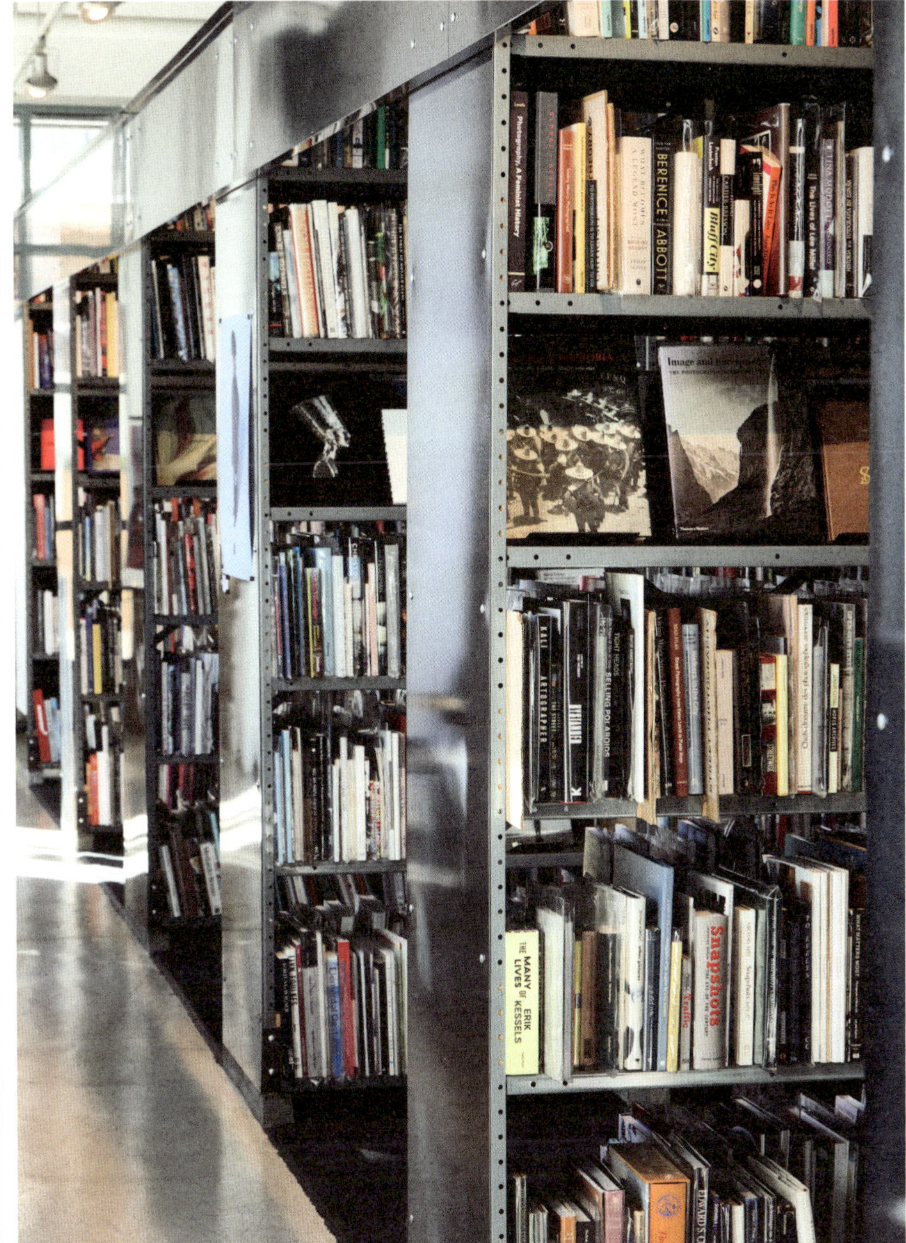

Views of Arcana: Books on the Arts, Culver City, 2026
Photographs by Michael Schmelling for *Aperture*

copy of Paul Kooiker's irreverent *Nude, Animal, Cigar* (2015). (Unfortunately Corinne Day's long out-of-print *Diary*, from 2000, was beyond my means.)

Scale can be a double-edged sword. In addition to the thousands of books on Arcana's sales floor, thousands more languish in off-site storage, waiting to be recirculated into Arcana's shelves, stacks, and vitrines. "There can never be too many books," Kaplan told me. "But there can also never be enough space." (In 2024, Arcana transferred some of its back stock to an outpost in the Reef in downtown LA, and Kaplan hopes to eventually open the space as its own store.) As a steady stream of new books enters Arcana's stock each season, more will accumulate in storage, waiting to be rediscovered, sometimes years later, this time as hidden gems or rarities.

Walking through Arcana, it becomes clear that its significance lies not only in the number of titles it holds but in the way it holds them together. This is a space where visual culture is not optimized or streamlined but allowed to accumulate, overlap, and endure.

Noa Lin is an associate editor at Aperture.

Double Dutch

For over two decades, Blommers & Schumm have blurred the line between fashion photography and performance art.

Iva Dixit

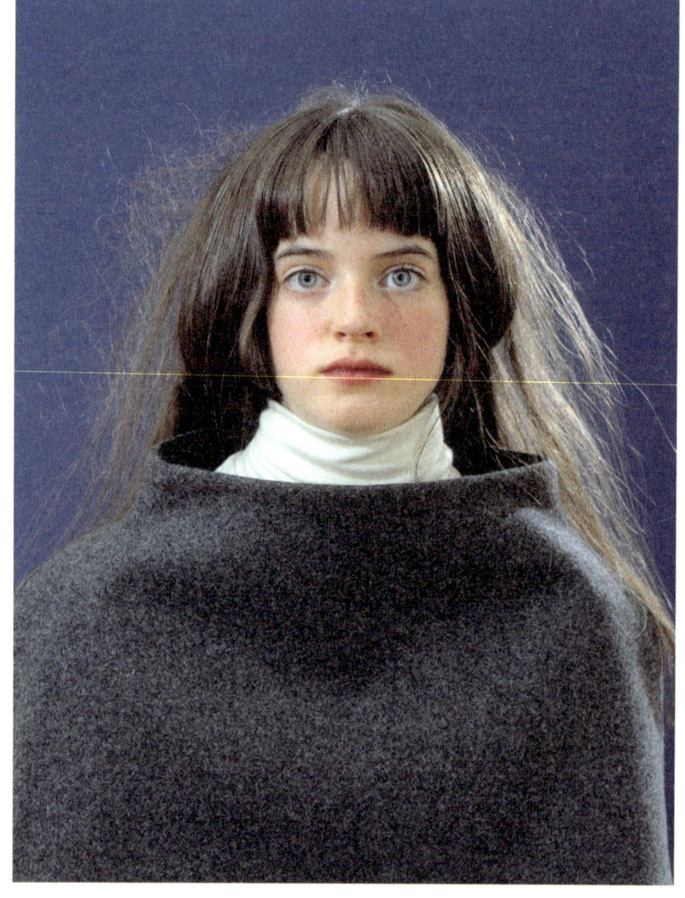

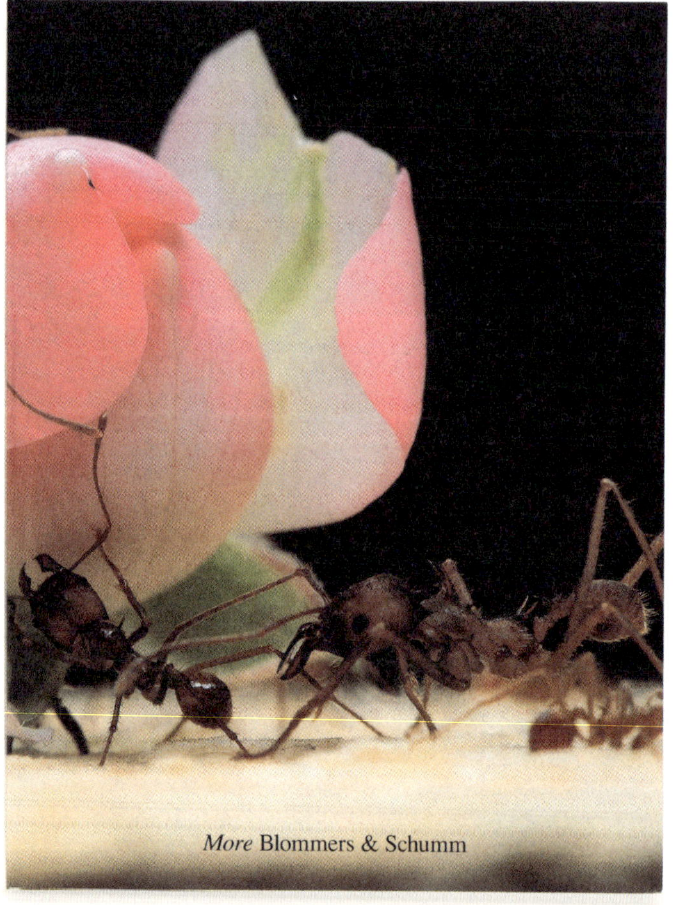

Top:
Blommers & Schumm, from the series *Class of 1998*, 1998

Bottom and opposite:
Cover and spread from *More* (2025)

From a series of ten passport-size photographs arranged neatly on a page, the faces of ten turtleneck-clad young girls stare back at the viewer. Something about them is unexplainably, implausibly *off*. The girls are arrestingly beautiful, yes, but they're all sporting hairstyles that mar that beauty instead of compounding it, leaving us unsure whether these are teenagers or hair-sprayed suburban moms from the 1980s. A Farrah Fawcett–esque flip-out fringe of pure blond frames one girl's brow, which is knit just slightly upward in an expression that could be either terror or worry or pain (or all three). On another girl, a brunette this time, a set of badly cut blunt bangs hovers over the icy blank globes of her blue eyes, which are completely devoid of any emotion. Frozen in some sort of frizzy-haired purgatory, the girls all seem to have suffered at the hands of an unknown haunting force armed only with an overzealous sense of spite and an overheated cheap blow-dryer.

But these are not ordinary unflattering photographs of unfortunate teenagers in some forgotten high school yearbook. Collectively titled *Class of 1998*, the images are professional portraits of models that

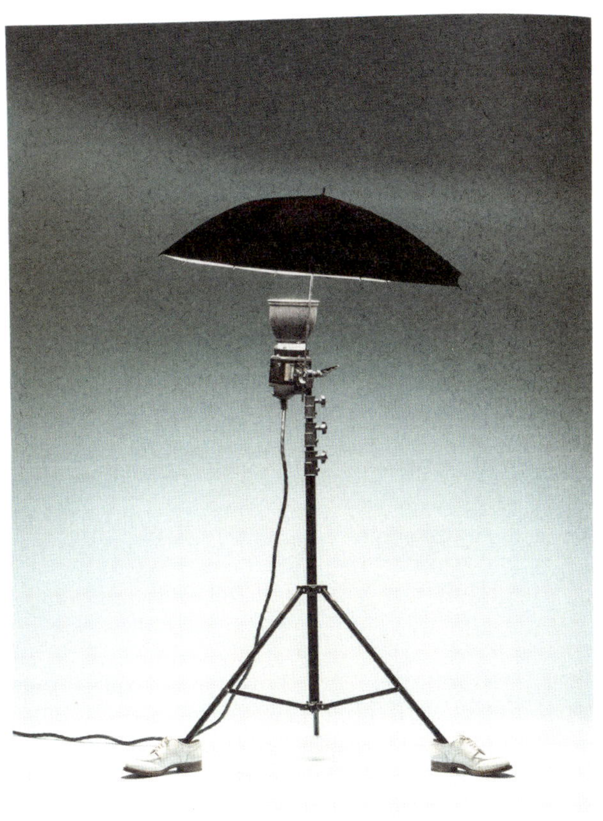

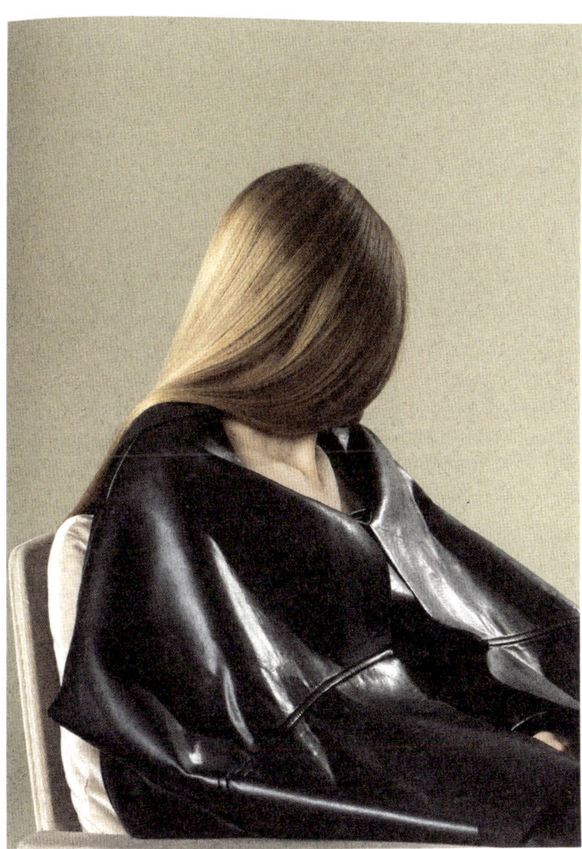

appeared in *Self Service* magazine in 1998. The girls were brand-new models recruited from an agency, their turtlenecks were by the Belgian designer Veronique Branquinho, and the photographs were taken by Anuschka Blommers and Niels Schumm, now professionally known as Blommers & Schumm. For over two decades, the Dutch duo has been blurring the line between fashion photography and performance art, making photographs that dispense entirely with all established norms of polished perfection and good taste. The portraits of the frizzy-haired models are just some of their many iconic images reproduced in ***More* (Roma, 2025; 240 pages, $63)**, a new photobook—published to coincide with *Mid-Air*, a recent survey exhibition at Foam in Amsterdam—that compiles more than twenty-five years of the pair's bizarrely playful and often freakish body of work, as seen in publications including *The Gentlewoman*, *The New York Times Magazine*, and *Purple*.

Not even inanimate objects are spared the indignity of human unease. A beige concrete hallway with a lonely light bulb suspended from the ceiling resembles the darkened hollow of a male human's crotch. What at first looks to be a thong-clad set of legs, spread apart in come-hither salaciousness, turns out to be a glowing bubble lamp. What you thought was sex is actually furniture—and you're forgiven for thinking it because, really, how can you not associate one with the other? When hit with the punch line of a Blommers & Schumm photograph, it is acceptable to feel a little embarrassed at how easily your own libidinal instincts can be pranked and played with. Every Blommers & Schumm image is a horror-comedy unto itself.

Commercial fashion photography is a genre dictated by artifice, with its own strict set of rules and regulations. What Blommers & Schumm manage to do so effortlessly is overwrite this with a more calculated artifice of their own, cranking up the strangeness, tearing apart its beloved motifs of photoshopped perfection with a kind of glee that borders on demented. On the cover of *More* is a photograph of delicate, hazy flower petals lying in gentle repose. The dreaminess of the flower is offset by sheer violence, as a trio of leafcutter ants sets about happily dismembering and harvesting it. Each ant's clawlike mandible, each ommatidium of their compound eyes, and each chitinous bristle on their hairy legs is visible and magnified in extreme high-resolution zoom as they approach the flower's corpse, appearing almost mischievously delighted with their luck. Are we attendees at a funeral for the flower, or at a party for the ants? The beauty of a Blommers & Schumm photograph is that we will never know.

Iva Dixit is a former editor at *The New York Times Magazine*.

Reviews

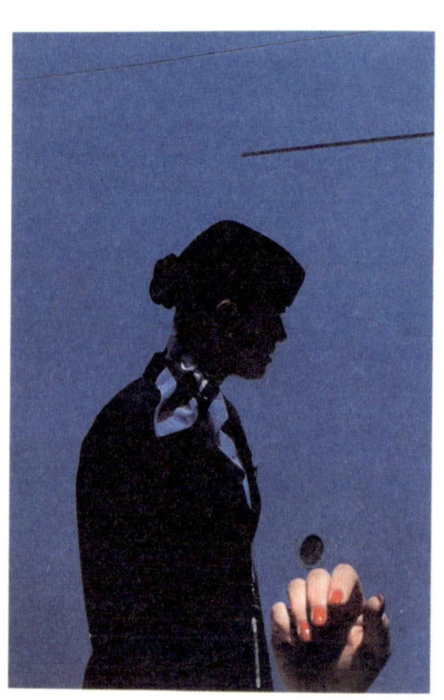

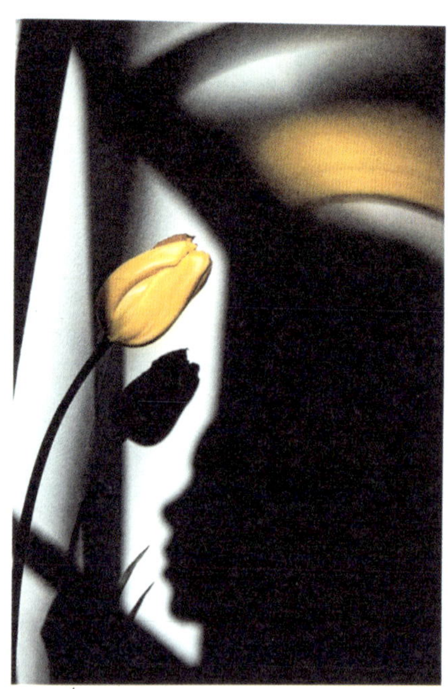

Sarah van Rij, *Atlas of Echoes* (2025)

Sarah van Rij

Sarah van Rij's ***Atlas of Echoes* (Note Note Éditions, 2025; 116 pages, $69)** delivers one dopamine hit after the other—I worried it would give me some kind of photographic hangover. Condensing seven years of photographs and surrealist-inflected collages into a brisk seventy-three images, *Atlas of Echoes* is the Dutch artist's first monograph sans her romantic and professional partner, David van der Leeuw. Van Rij here plays the jet-lagged flaneur, sprinting through cities "from San Francisco to Seoul," seemingly fueled by martinis and cigarettes, two motifs. There's little sense of time or place. Instead, she cultivates the uncanny mixture of distortion and specificity found in dreams, her eye delectating in long shadows and brief encounters, in partial self-portraits spied in espresso shots and table knives. For some, Van Rij's abstract eroticism and rhythmic, graphic style might feel too polished. The book's index includes *eyes, flower, hands, mirror, rain,* and *red*. There are no *potholes* or *rats*.

Van Rij wears her influences on her sleeve: The women's shoes are Bourdin-esque, the shadows are Friedlanderian, and the rain-slicked windows are pure

Saul Leiter. Hitchcock also looms, yet Van Rij trades sinister suspense for a kind of sunny noir (this book would be scored by Stan Getz, not Bernard Herrmann). She transforms those male, mid-century references into her own jazzily disjointed mise-en-scènes, where it's often difficult to distinguish between collaged and in-camera pictures. We're encouraged to piece together our own story and subjectivity (I kept imagining a private detective on vacation). Here, the phone's off the hook, the water is shimmering, and the shadows help you tell the time.
—**Zack Hatfield**

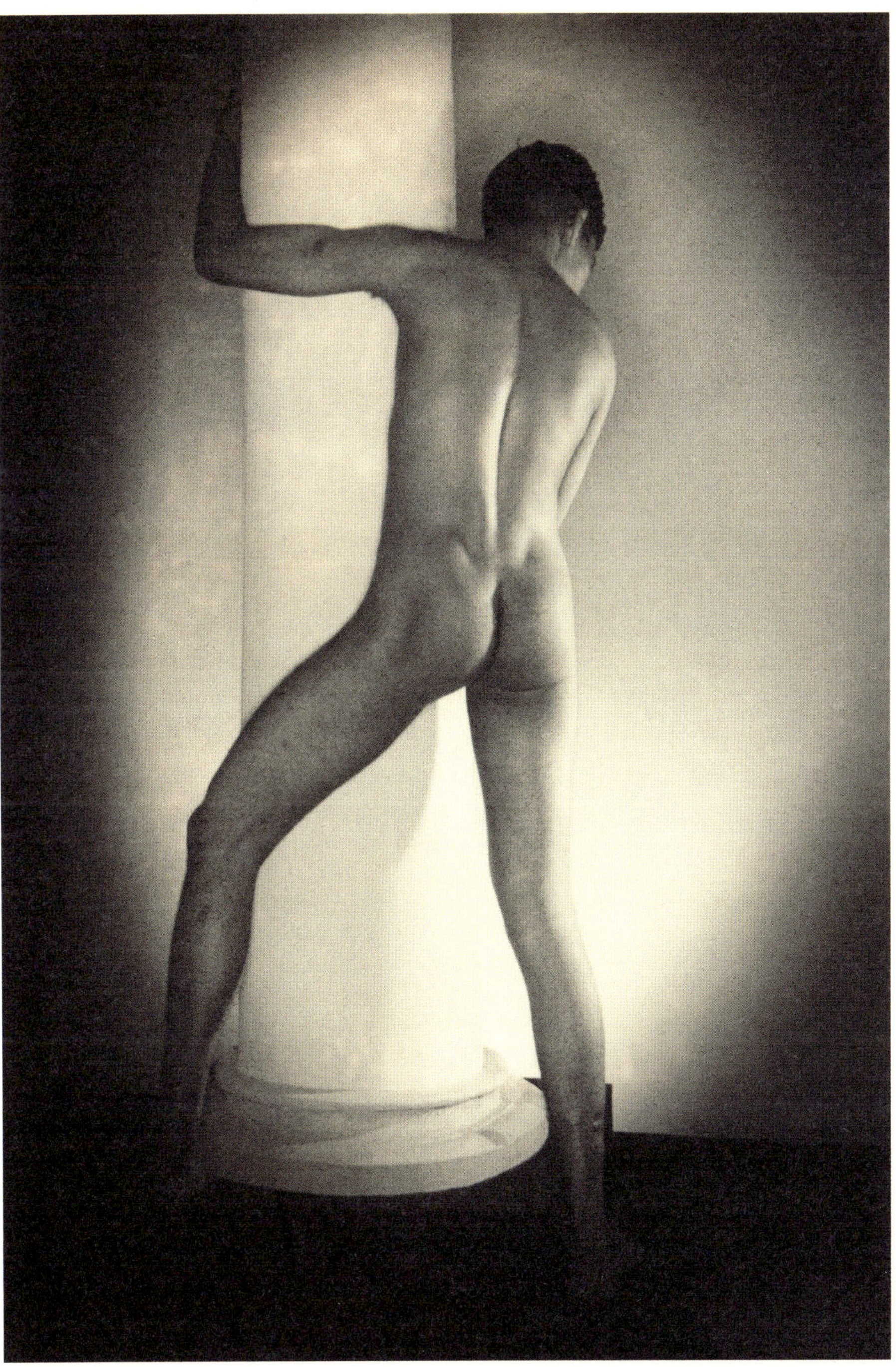

Lionel Wendt, *Untitled (Male Figure)*, ca. 1930–44
Courtesy American Art Catalogues, New York

Lionel Wendt

In an undated solarized gelatin-silver print, *In the Hands of the Cutter*, by the early twentieth-century Sri Lankan photographer Lionel Wendt, two ghostly silhouetted hands snip a roll of 35mm film whose unfurled ends dissolve into the edges of the frame. It is of and from another time and place, but hardly obsolete.

This masterful image is one of many previously unseen works in ***Lionel Wendt*** **(American Art Catalogues, 2026; 54 pages, $55)**, a new monograph highlighting Wendt's brief career (the artist died at age forty-four). Born in 1900, Wendt studied music in London before bringing his ideas for a modernist movement back home. But a straightforward reading of Wendt's place in the avant-garde is ill-advised, the curator Shanay Jhaveri points out in his accompanying essay. As a member of the elite mixed-race Burgher community and a queer man in British-controlled Ceylon, where homosexuality was outlawed, Wendt was always working from a position not easily defined.

It is this complicated perspective that caught the eye of Tyler Mitchell, who contributes a short appreciation. Tired of the "'decisive moment' patriarchs," the American photographer writes, he found in Wendt a tenderness and rich inner life that paralleled his own. Young men appear in nearly half of the photographs, some fully or partially nude, others tightly cropped. A few are posed among classical columns and statuary, borrowing from tradition but emphasizing their in-betweenness: ancient and modern, old and new. In all, brown skin appears incandescent through Wendt's painterly use of light. One can see why his portraits strike a chord with Mitchell and promise to influence other emerging artists working today. —**Frances Cathryn**

Matthew Connors

"The centre cannot hold." W. B. Yeats's famous line feels quaint in 2026, when the only consensus is that the postwar international order is now a distant relic. Saber-rattling with (of all countries) Canada once was reserved for 1990s screwball comedies animated by outlandish plotlines. Last winter at Davos, where power brokers and elites gather against a backdrop worthy of a Toblerone wrapper, Canadian Prime Minister Mark Carney soberly described "a rupture in the world order, the end of a pleasant fiction and the beginning of a harsh reality."

Matthew Connors's ***The Axe Will Survive the Master*** **(MACK, 2026; 208 pages, $75)** gathers photographs made between 2013 and 2025 that reveal how this rupture was well underway long before the United States, grappling with its imperial decline, unleashed a new era of bellicose expansionism. Unfolding as a lengthy cinematic sequence—in mostly single images, interrupted by occasional pairings—is a symphony of blues (the default hue of techie futurism), shimmering and often shattered surfaces, glitches, lasers, plumes of tear gas, and protesters running for cover. Cycles of things falling apart with motifs of sci-fi dystopia are clearly grounded, sadly, in the here and now.

Connors, who is American, has daisy-chained images from the Arab Spring, the Russian invasion of Ukraine, protests in Hong Kong, as well as scenes from Pyongyang, Los Angeles, and Havana, offering a record of limping democratic ideals in the wake of authoritarianism's tide. The book completes a political trilogy, following earlier visual tomes on Occupy Wall Street and political turmoil in Cairo. One can assume that the concept for *The Axe Will Survive the Master*, which borrows its title from the journalist Svetlana Alexievich, was completed before ICE's deadly misadventures in Minneapolis and its aftershock of Orwellian government spin. If Connors decides to chart this next chapter of democratic backsliding, his passport won't be required, though it might be confiscated.
—**Michael Famighetti**

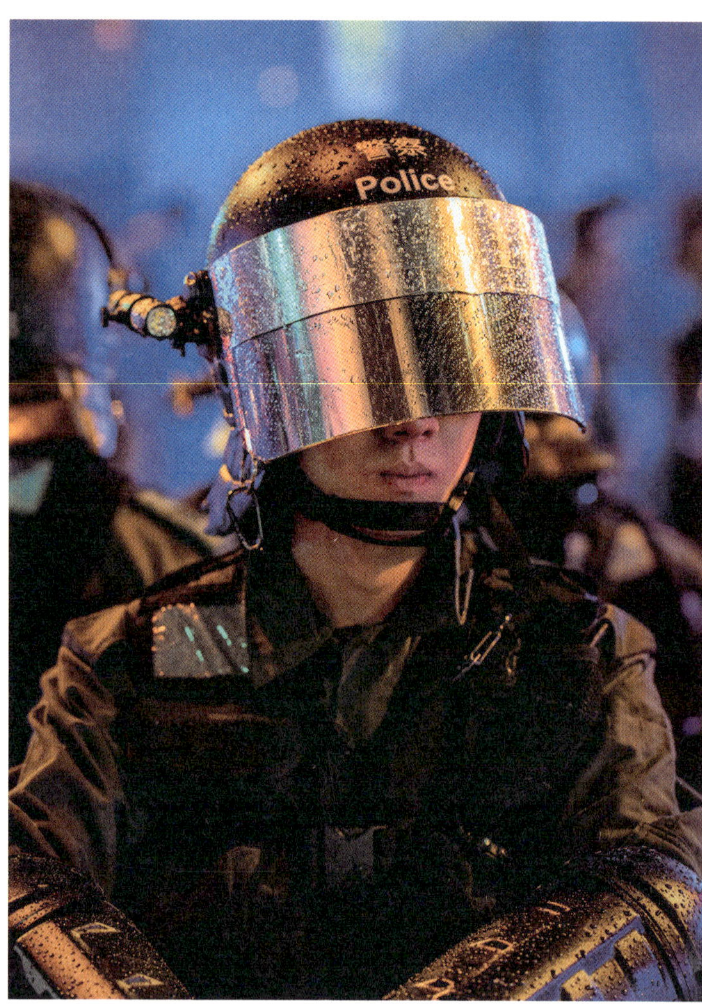

Top:
Matthew Connors, *Green Clothes, Hong Kong*, 2019, from *The Axe Will Survive the Master* (2026)

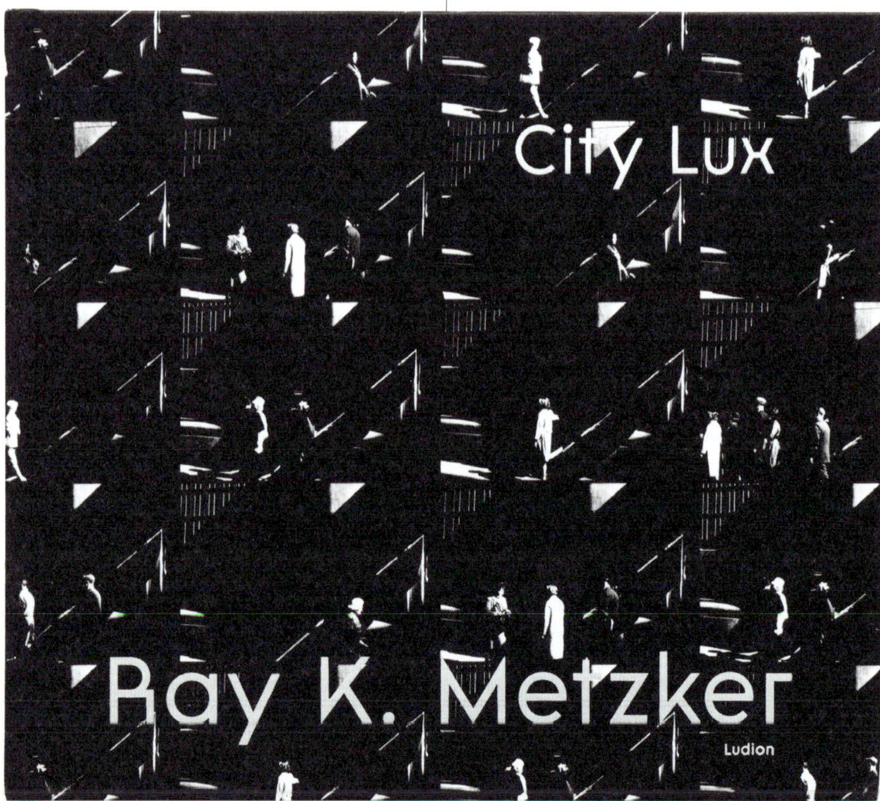

Bottom:
Ray K. Metzker, *City Lux* (2025)

Ray K. Metzker

Like Aaron Siskind and Harry Callahan, his mentors at Chicago's Institute of Design, Ray K. Metzker is one of photography's great mid-century modernists. Relentlessly experimental, technically avant-garde, Metzker was anything but a straight documentary photographer. Typically, he shattered and repeated his images until a simple cityscape exploded into jagged abstraction. But even his most pared-back pictures—a solitary walker, a silvery puddle, an open door—have a charged, cinematic quality, reminiscent of stills from a Michelangelo Antonioni film. "I really related to the light more than anything else," he told an interviewer, and as a result, his black-and-white prints are super graphic, with incandescent whites and pitch blacks of remarkable depth and clarity. In his most complex images, Metzker shuffled these elements like puzzle pieces. His results vibrate in their frames.

The catalog ***Ray K. Metzker: City Lux* (Ludion, 2025; 240 pages, $53)** expands on a 2024 exhibition at the A Foundation, in Brussels, which surveyed a career that touched down in a number of cities (Chicago, Philadelphia, Albuquerque) but rarely zeroed in on distinctive landmarks. Seen most often in multiple exposures, his urban spaces are nearly interchangeable and his figures anonymous. This may not be Jean-Luc Godard's futuristic Alphaville, but there's a sci-fi cast to a lot of Metzker's busiest images, and a sense of everything happening at once. Whether you find this exciting or unnerving, cool or overheated, the work is far from old-school, except for its roots in analog inventiveness. Because Metzker never stopped messing with time and space, his work comes across like a great jazz riff: classic but forever new.
—Vince Aletti

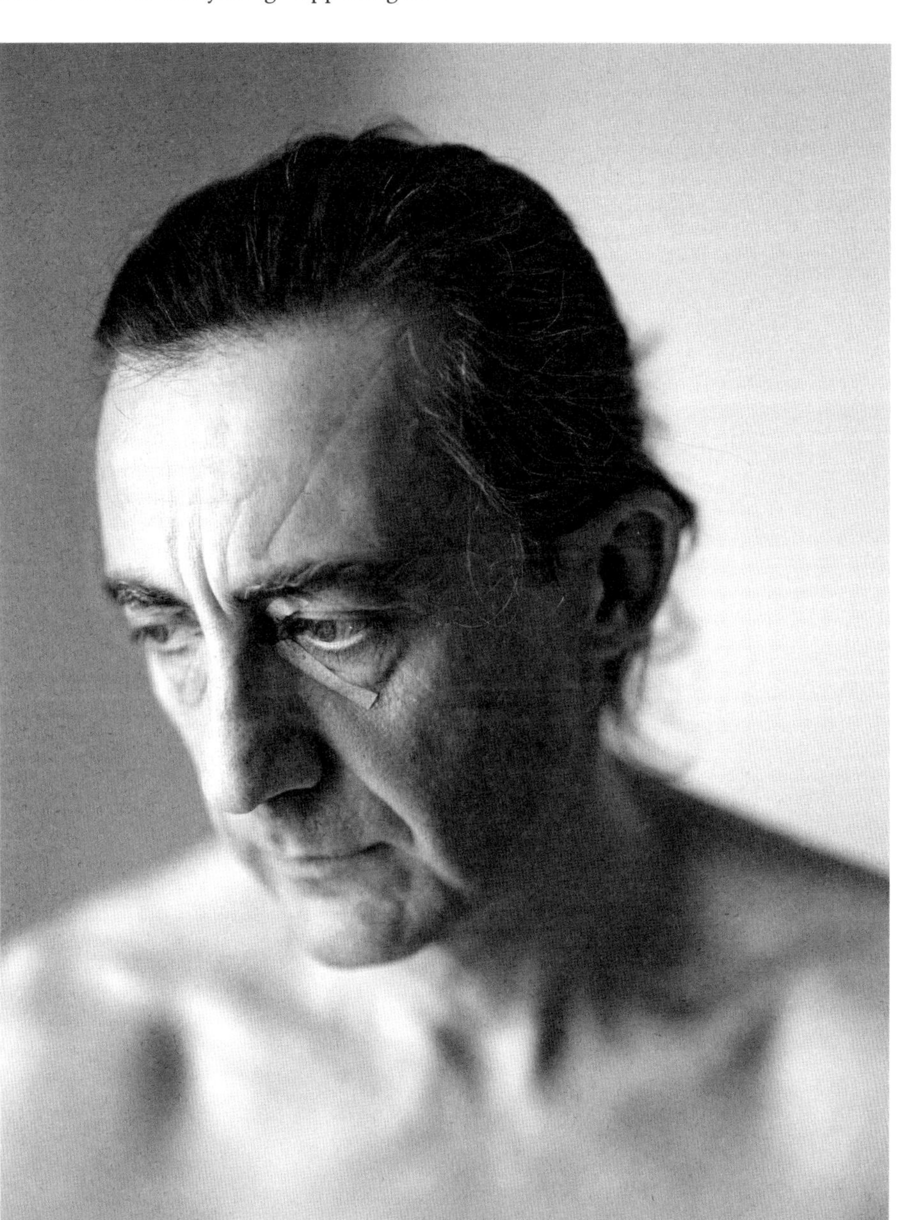

Andrea Modica, ***Italian Story*** **(2026)**

Andrea Modica

The American photographer Andrea Modica has described her latest book, ***Italian Story* (L'Artiere, 2026; 96 pages, $70)**, as "a broad narration: a record of events, a historical fiction." This implication of flexible memory is inherent in the title's Italian translation, "storia," which means both history and story. Created over four decades, these black-and-white images, taken with a large-format view camera, accordingly exist somewhere out of time, dreamlike, but not quite.

Modica's previous monographs have featured long-term projects about equine medicine, Catholic schoolgirls, and skulls unearthed from a Colorado mental institution. This book is about her relationship with Italy—she's third generation—and emphasizes the artist's sense for everyday incongruity. Portraits, landscapes, and still lifes show how Modica's use of light, focus, and negative space convey an ambiguous intimacy. Though her subject matter is exactly what it appears to be, there are occasional, if subtle, surrealist flourishes: A head and glass tilt forward in a display of improbable balance; the soft and poetic mirroring of a fern branch and a bare crotch recalls Julia Margaret Cameron and Man Ray.

Modica is a keen manipulator of absence and obfuscation; reading this book sometimes feels like wandering through a haunted villa. In one image, light shines through a dress hanging in the foreground as a person, perhaps its wearer, peeks out in the background, awash in white. In another frame, a nude man lays behind a sheer bed canopy like half of a pietà, his body shrouded by a veil evoking a delicately chiseled block of Carrara marble. **—Quinn Moreland**

Endnote
Andrew Durbin

Andrew Durbin is the editor in chief of *frieze* and the author of the novels *MacArthur Park* (2017) and *Skyland* (2020). His new biography, *The Wonderful World That Almost Was: A Life of Peter Hujar and Paul Thek*, portrays its subjects—creative and romantic partners for two decades—with the same caliber of psychological depth and rare beauty they themselves brought to their art.

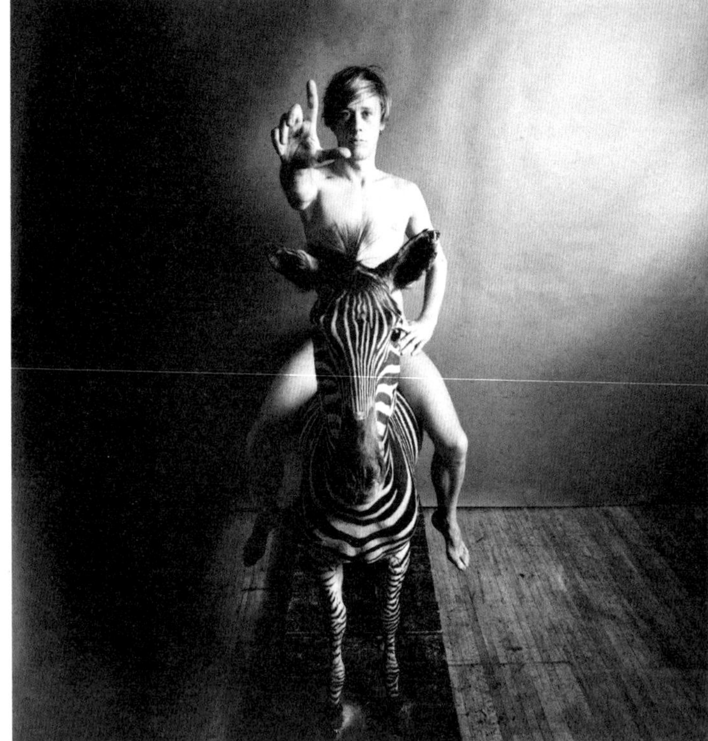

Peter Hujar, *Paul Thek on a Zebra*, 1965

Your new book is about Peter Hujar, the photographer known for his masterful black-and-white portraits, and the peculiar, prescient installation artist Paul Thek—both dark horses of the postwar American art world. What led you to write about the relationship between two artists, rather than approach one of their lives individually?
I began writing a book about Peter Hujar, and almost immediately I realized so much of the book would be about Paul Thek anyway. It was all taking place during this crucial time when the two were lovers and friends. I couldn't understand Peter without understanding Paul, and vice versa. As a writer, I'm drawn to things I don't have a good answer for, and a relationship is the perfect example of that. You can only know so much.

That reminds me of a quote from the dance critic Jill Johnston that's in the book. She suggests that Hujar's photography is about "how we don't know our own secrets."
When I found that I thought, This is the book!

Was there a specific moment when these artists stopped feeling like historical subjects and more like people?
It was when I walked into Paul Thek's old apartment, where his first major lover, Peter Harvey, still lives. It's mostly unchanged since they moved there in 1959. Harvey still has a framed cover of the first edition paperback of *Against Interpretation* on the wall.

An epigraph from Susan Sontag opens one of the chapters: "Some people are their lives." What makes a good epigraph?
I shouldn't admit this, but I don't quite know what she means [*laughs*]. I know exactly what she means, and yet, at the same time, I don't know what she means. I think epigraphs should be a little ambiguous.

There's been a resurgence of interest in Peter Hujar lately. Why do you think that is?
Setting aside the beauty of the pictures themselves for a moment, I believe we're all desperately craving authenticity. And Peter—and Paul—were above all authentic and uncompromising artists.

People project a lot onto Hujar—tragedy, nostalgia, intimacy. Were there key misconceptions you wanted to undo?
I wanted to restore him to the 1960s. I don't think people are very familiar with his relationship to Warhol, to Italian cinema, to the counterculture. I also didn't want this to be a book about AIDS, even though it's a big part of the story. Rather than treat Peter and Paul as these tragic, twilight figures, I wanted to show how all-embracing they were of life.

What would Hujar and Thek think about today's art world?
They would be appalled. In a funny way, they were both always thinking about ways to make a little money but were fundamentally averse to the most obvious ways to do so. They probably wouldn't know what to do if they were parachuted into this moment. It would baffle them.

Was there one photograph that stayed with you during the writing of the book?
Paul Thek on the zebra is a picture I turn over in my mind a lot. It's such an unusual photograph for Peter, almost kooky, and it informed how I thought about their relationship, how they played together, collaborated. It looks like it came out of a dream.